Uncle John's Bathroom Reader®

Puzzle Book #2

Edited by
Stephanie Spadaccini

The Bathroom Readers' Institute
Portable Press
San Diego, CA, and Ashland, OR

For Andrea, the new kid in town

UNCLE JOHN'S
BATHROOM READER
PUZZLE BOOK #2

For information, write
The Bathroom Readers' Institute
5880 Oberlin Drive, San Diego, CA 92121

email: *unclejohn@advmkt.com*

Project Team:
Stephanie Spadaccini: Project Editor
Amanda Wilson: Design and Composition
Nancy Schuster: Project Editor
Allen Orso: Publisher
JoAnn Padgett: Director, Editorial and Production

Cover design by Michael Brunsfeld *(brunsfeldo@attbi.com)*

ISBN: 1-59223-157-8

Printed in the United States of America

04 05 06 07 08   10 9 8 7 6 5 4 3 2 1

CONTENTS

PUZZLES & WORDPLAY

CROSSWORDS

SPECIAL CROSSWORD SECTION

DOUBLE-CROSTICS

MINI-CROSTICS

CRISS-CROSS PUZZLES

Editor

Stephanie Spadaccini is a long-time puzzle constructor, and a project editor for the *Uncle John's Bathroom Reader Plunges into…* series. Her puzzles appear regularly in *People* and *AARP* magazine. A former managing editor of Games magazine and writer on TV's *Jeopardy!*, Stephanie still spends her off-hours dancing the hula. This is the second puzzle book she's edited for Uncle John.

Contributors

Alan Arbesfeld has been constructing crossword puzzles for over 25 years. His puzzles have appeared in the *New York Times*, the *Los Angeles Times*, *Games* magazine, and *Attaché* magazine, as well as numerous crossword puzzle compilations.

Michael Ashley is a veteran contributor of 25 years to *Games* magazine. His puzzles have also appeared in the *New York Times*, the *Washington Post*, the *Wall Street Journal*, and other places too numerous to count. His ninth collection of quotation puzzles, *Random House Crostics by Michael Ashley*, will be published in November 2004.

Patrick Berry is a freelance puzzle constructor whose work has appeared in the *New York Times*, the *Wall Street Journal, Harper's, the New Yorker*, *Games* magazine, and a variety of other publications. He is also the author of *Crossword Puzzle Challenges for Dummies*, a how-to book on crossword construction. And he still doesn't play the guitar very well.

Myles Callum is a former senior editor at *TV Guide* who took up puzzle-making seven years ago. His puzzles have appeared in the *New York Times*, the *Wall Street Journal*, the *Los Angeles Times*, the *Crosswords Club*, *USA Today*, and other publications.

Adam Cohen is a puzzle constructor and editor whose puzzles have appeared in the *New York Times*, *Games* and *World of Puzzles* magazines, and a number of other publications. When he grows up, he wants to be Frank Longo.

Mark Danna is a freelance puzzle maker whose credits include nine word search books, the *Wordy Gurdy* rhyming puzzle syndicated by United Media, and crosswords in the *New York Times* and other publications. His highly unusual career has included stints as an associate editor for *Games* magazine, a staff writer for a TV game show, a sports director on cruise ships, a public relations director on *Wall Street*, and a professional Frisbee player.

Chris DiNapoli is editor of *Dell's Crosswords Crosswords* magazine, but started in puzzles many years ago as *Dell's* word search puzzle editor. These days, when not editing, she spends her time searching for her glasses.

Elizabeth Gorski, a freelance crossword constructor, is a regular contributor to the *New York Times*, the *Washington Post*, the *Crosswords Club* and many other publications. She is a public speaker and delivered her most recent lecture, "The Making of a Crossword Puzzle and Other Unnatural Acts," at Manhattan's Cosmopolitan Club in January 2004.

Francis Heaney's puzzles have appeared in many publications, including *Games* magazine and the *New York Times*. He is the composer and colyricist of the recently produced off-off-Broadway musical, "We're All Dead." His first book of humor is due to be published in fall 2004.

Frank Longo is a full-time puzzle creator and editor who has had close to 3,000 puzzles published in various newspapers, magazines, book series, and Internet sites. He has authored several books, including *Cranium-Crushing Crosswords*, *The New York Times on the Web Crosswords for Teens*, and *Point & Solve Crosswords*. He holds a bachelor's degree in music, and is a former piano teacher and church music director. He is also the diabolical mind behind The World's Hardest Crossword Puzzle.

Nancy Mandl, lapsed librarian, world traveler, aspiring tennis star, and yoga devotee, is back for a second time, having surfed the Web from Abba to ziti in her quest for the best Uncle John's criss-cross puzzle fodder.

Trip Payne is a freelance puzzle constructor from Fort Lauderdale, Florida, whose 5,000 puzzles have appeared everywhere from the *New York Times* to *TV Guide*. He is the author of 11 puzzle books, a contributor to numerous others, and was a two-time winner of the American Crossword Puzzle Tournament.

Merl Reagle is one of the most sought-after crossword puzzle creators in the country. His nationally syndicated crosswords, which have been described as having a "Far Side" sense of humor, appear every Sunday in the *Los Angeles Times*, the *San Francisco Chronicle*, the *Philadelphia Inquirer*, and many other major newspapers. He's written numerous articles about crosswords, most recently for *Readers Digest*, and has appeared on *Nightline with Ted Koppel* in his capacity as a puzzle expert. Merl is the author of ten critically acclaimed crossword books (visit www.sundaycrosswords.com for details) and the constructor of the Entry Puzzle on page 199.

FOREWORD

I've been making crossword puzzles professionally for about 20 years but not until this very moment did I have the opportunity *and* the perfect setting to admit publicly that yes, just like almost everybody else in the world, I get most of my best ideas in the bathroom. (One of the reasons I bought my house was not because of the price or the neighborhood—it was because the black-and-white tiled floor of the bathroom looked like a crossword puzzle.)

But it's also a place where I've gotten a lot of ideas that I *can't* use—like every time I see my bottle of Clean Shower I can't help noticing that it's an anagram of "Clean Whores." Won't be seeing *that* in one of my Sunday puzzles any time soon.

Or the fact that "toilets" is an anagram of "T.S. Eliot." Or that the big management firm of "Deloitte and Touche" is an anagram of "Toilette and Douche." Or that this little "threadbare room" in which I do my best thinking is an anagram of "bathroom reader."

I could go on, but for now, let's just say that I highly recommend the bathroom as a source of great and slightly warped ideas, much like the contents of this book. And on those days when a shower is just a shower and a toilet is just a toilet, you can leave all of your thinking to Uncle John—as long as you have a stack of his books in there with you.

In the meantime, allow me to just shut the door, have a seat, and think. After all, they don't call it "the head" for nothing.

Happy solving.

—Merl Reagle

<u>INTRODUCTION</u>

One of the best things about my job as an editor is that I get to work with my friends, show off their talents a little bit, and get the publisher to pay them for doing the things that they love to do.

Take Merl Reagle, for instance. When I asked him to write the foreword for *Uncle John's Bathroom Reader Puzzle Book #2*, he asked me what the guidelines were. I told him there weren't any. So of course he came up with a delightful little essay on his favorite subject: words.

In fact, our puzzle books are all about words. Words that fit into little boxes, words that spill across the page, words that we've hidden, twisted, and played with until they hardly resemble words anymore. That's where you come in: your job is to uncover, untwist, and whip them back into a recognizable shape. And if you love puzzles as much as we do, there's no "job" to it at all, just the purest enjoyment.

To add to your enjoyment—because that's our mission in life—we're proud to present a Special Crossword Section that begins with three delightful and innovative *New York Times* puzzles that our contributors named as their favorites. After you've polished them off, you'll be ready to tackle the fourth puzzle in that section: the Entry Puzzle to The World's Hardest Crossword Puzzle Contest, constructed by the abovementioned Merl Reagle. It's not an easy puzzle, but we're confident you can do it.

Of course, we're all agog (as we say in Puzzle Land) about the contest and the very generous Grand Prize of $5,000. Even the runners-up win: every contestant who correctly completes The World's Hardest Crossword Puzzle and sends it in by the deadline will win an *Uncle John's Bathroom Reader* T-shirt. If that's not worth it, what is?

Before you get started, just a couple more things: Thanks to Nancy Schuster, all-time puzzle mavenette; Mike Shenk, of http://www.puzzability.com, whom I forgot to thank last time for his fabulous puzzle software; proofreaders Audrey Thompson, Chris DiNapoli, Ellen Ripstein, and Ivan Roth; Amanda Wilson, layout gal and troubleshooter; and the gang at Portable Press: Allen, JoAnn, Bernadette, Jennifer, and Mana. And thanks to our ever-growing covey of contributors without whom I would have to write the whole darn book myself.

—Stephanie Spadaccini

TRUE CONFESSIONS

Confessions so obviously true, they're kind of embarrassing.

ACROSS

1. City transport
4. Actress Lara Flynn ___
9. Not frazzled
13. Razor brand
15. Painter's prop
16. SSS designation
17. He said: "I never wanted to be famous; I only wanted to be great."
19. Duo
20. On cloud nine
21. Casual kind of room
23. Loose
24. Opera's male lead, usually
25. Date
27. TMC alternative
29. He said: "I'm not smart enough to lie."
34. Bilko, for one (abbr.)
37. Astronaut Slayton
38. Prominent
39. Tigger's pal
41. Candlelight watch
43. Membership fees
44. Use sandpaper
46. Billy and Daniel's more famous brother
48. Harden
49. He said: "Sometimes, at the end of the day when I'm smiling and shaking hands, I want to kick them."
52. ___ radio
53. Polished off
54. Reggae fan, perhaps
58. Cooling machines, for short
60. Pick up the tab
62. Island off the coast of China
63. Splotch
65. He said: "I left high school a virgin."
68. Sweater Girl Turner
69. It may cause tears in the kitchen
70. Jib, for one
71. Nervous
72. Had in mind
73. AAA suggestion

DOWN

1. Insertion symbol
2. "And thereby hangs ___"
3. Singer Adams
4. Droplet
5. Boathouse item
6. Fashion monogram
7. Looked lasciviously
8. Otherwise
9. Swipe
10. Comparable
11. *Star Wars* princess
12. Chico or Karl
14. Thespian
18. King of Judea
22. Wolfgang Puck, e.g.
25. H.H. Munro's pen name
26. Adjective for Grace Kelly
28. Brass or rubber follower
30. When pigs fly
31. Pricey timepiece
32. Suit to ___
33. Digs made of twigs
34. Practice punching
35. Desert in Mongolia
36. Chanteuse's offering
40. A couple of laughs
42. Tennis ace Nastase
45. Humid
47. Kind of reef
50. The start of something new
51. Carpenter's mouthful, maybe
55. Say "*%#$&!"
56. Unspoken but understood
57. It's at risk in stiletto heels
58. Competent
59. Dressed (in)
61. Speck
62. It may be pitched at night
64. ___ of Pigs
66. Soon-Yi's mom
67. Junior

ANSWER, PAGE 201

WONTON? NOT NOW!

A palindrome is a word or phrase that's spelled the same backward and forward. Some are sensible enough. Take "Nurses run," for instance. Nice and neat. Then there's "I saw a Santa—at NASA was I." Which is kind of silly, but hey, it works. The phrases below are likewise sensible and silly, but they need one more word or two to make them palindromic. Your job is to complete them by filling in the blanks, each of which stands for one letter.

1. He did, _e_ _h_?

2. Too hot _t_ _o_ _h_ _o_ _o_ _t_.

3. Never odd _o_ _r_ _e_ _v_ _e_ _n_.

4. Sun at noon, _t_ _a_ _h_ _u_ _s_.

5. Todd erases _a_ _r_ _e_ _d_ _d_ _o_ _t_.

6. God saw I _w_ _a_ _s_ _d_ _o_ _g_.

7. Too bad—I hid _a_ _b_ _o_ _o_ _t_.

8. No trace; not _o_ _n_ _e_ _c_ _a_ _r_ _t_ _o_ _n_.

9. Boston ode: _d_ _o_ _n_ _o_ _t_ _s_ _o_ _b_.

10. We panic _i_ _n_ _a_ _p_ _e_ _w_.

11. Panic in a *Titanic*? _i_ _n_ _a_ _p_.

12. Was it Eliot's _t_ _o_ _i_ _l_ _e_ _t_ _i_ _s_ _a_ _w_?

13. Amy, must I jujitsu _m_ _y_ _m_ _a_?

14. Eva, can I stab _b_ _a_ _t_ _s_ _i_ _n_ _a_ _c_ _a_ _v_ _e_?

15. Campus motto: Bottoms _u_ _p_, _m_ _a_ _c_.

16. Live not on evil, madam, _l_ _i_ _v_ _e_ _n_ _o_ _t_ _o_ _n_ _e_ _v_ _i_ _l_.

17. No sir! Away! A papaya _w_ _a_ _r_ _i_ _s_ _o_ _n_.

18. Some men interpret _n_ _i_ _n_ _e_ _m_ _e_ _m_ _o_ _s_.

19. No lava on Avalon; _n_ _o_ _l_ _a_ _v_ _a_, _n_ _o_ _a_ _v_ _a_ _l_ _o_ _n_.

20. Straw? No, too stupid a fad; _i_ _p_ _u_ _t_ _s_ _o_ _o_ _t_ _o_ _n_ _w_ _a_ _r_ _t_ _s_.

21. Anne, I vote more cars _r_ _a_ _c_ _e_ _r_ _o_ _m_ _e_ _t_ _o_ _v_ _i_ _e_ _n_ _n_ _a_.

22. Gateman sees name, garageman _s_ _e_ _e_ _s_ _n_ _a_ _m_ _e_ _t_ _a_ _g_.

completed by Sana Naqvi on thursday july 22nd at 12:23am.

HOW TO WRITE A PERSONALS AD

So you've decided to get a life, huh? About time. But first you need to meet someone special. How about letting us help you write a personals ad? To get you started, look over our list of come-ons and pick a few that you think apply. Then, if you're in the mood, see if you can find them in the heart-shaped grid, reading across, down, and diagonally. You can always write the rest of the ad when hell freezes over.

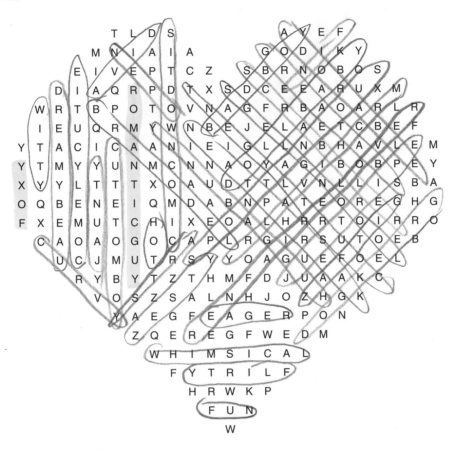

ADORABLE
ARTSY
AVID
BAD BOY
BRA MODEL
COMELY CUTIE
COURTLY GENT
CURVY
CUTE TOMBOY
(Sarah) → DOLLBABY
(Hasan) → DREAMY BEAU
EAGER

FINE
FLIRTY
FOXY
FUN
GREAT ABS
GREEK GOD
HOT
HUGGABUNNY
JAUNTY
JUST RIPE
LOOONG LEGS
MR CHIVALRY

NEAT PHREAK
OPEN
REN FAIRE LOVER
ROMANTIC GUY
SCRABBLER
SITDOWN COMIC
SPONTANEOUS
WHIMSICAL
WITTY
ZAFTIG
ZESTY

Feb 5/05

ANSWER, PAGE 201

IT SLICES! IT DICES!

This puzzle has everything! It has seven products—but wait! There's more! If you order now, you'll also receive seven examples of hype like the world has never seen—at no cost to yourself! All you need to do is match each classic commercial product to the claim it's famous for. If you need the answers, allow 6 to 8 weeks for delivery.

_g_   1. GLH#9 (Hair-in-a-can)

_e_   2. Inside the Eggshell Scrambler

_a_   3. The Miracle Mop

_c_   4. The Pocket Fisherman

_d_   5. The Ronco Bottle and Jar Cutter

_b_   6. The Ronco Rhinestone and Stud Setter

_f_   7. The Veg-O-Matic

Completed on July 22nd (thurs) by Sana F. Noqvi @ 12:29 pm

Sanata Noqvi

a. "It lets you wring out the head without putting your hands into the dirty water!"

b. "It changes everyday clothing into exciting fashions!"

c. "Attaches to your belt, or fits in the glove compartment of your car!"

d. "A hobby for Dad, craft for the kids, a great gift for Mom!"

e. "You'll use it a lot and every time you do, you'll save washing a bowl and fork!"

f. "No one likes dicing onions...the only tears you'll shed will be tears of joy!"

g. "You can use it on your dog!"

ANSWER, PAGE 201

* * * * *

TAKING DEBATE

In 1986, Ann Landers revealed that in the 31 years she'd been writing her advice column, there was one subject that had been the most controversial of them all. What was it?

  a. The in-laws
  b. Abortion rights
  c. The amount of time husbands spend watching sports on TV
  d. The amount of money wives spend shopping
  (e.) Whether toilet paper should come off the top or the bottom of the roll

ANSWER, PAGE 201

PLAY D'OH!

Homer Simpson, America's favorite animated dad, lets fall a few gems. Drop the letters from each vertical column, but not necessarily in the order in which they appear, into the empty squares below them to spell out Homer's homilies, reading from left to right. Words may wrap around from one line to the next; black squares signify the spaces between words.

1.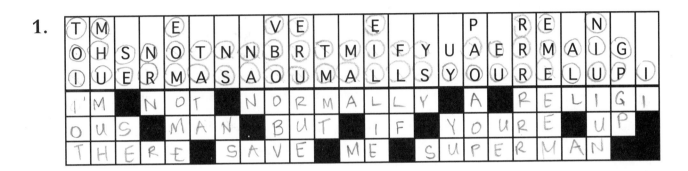

Solution:
```
I'M  NOT  NORMALLY  A  RELIGI
OUS  MAN  BUT  IF  YOURE  UP
THERE  SAVE  ME  SUPERMAN
```

2.

Solution:
```
SON  YOU  TRIED  YOUR  BEST
AND  YOU  FAILED  MISERABLY
THE  LESSON  IS  NEVER  TRY
```

3.

Solution:
```
IF  YOU  REALLY  WANT  SOMET
HING  IN  THIS  LIFE  YOU  HA
VE  TO  WORK  FOR  IT  NOW  QU
IET  THEYRE  ABOUT  TO  ANNO
UNCE  THE  LOTTERY  NUMBERS
```

ANSWER, PAGE 202

CANDY BARS YOU'LL NEVER EAT

Today we've got Snickers, Skittles, and Whoppers. But once upon a time we had Poor Prune, Doctor's Orders, and the Betsy Ross Bar. Yup, there have been some truly strange candy bars over the years...and a few *untruly* strange ones. Which of the following candy bars actually existed, and which are just figments of our sugar-addled imagination?

The Vegetable Sandwich Bar: This 1920s "treat" contained cabbage, celery, peppers, and tomatoes. What were its selling points? According to the makers, it would aid digestion and "will not constipate." Who could resist such a snack? Apparently, everyone, and it died quickly.

The Big-Hearted "Al" Bar: The candy bar named for Al Smith, the Democratic nominee for president in 1928. When Herbert Hoover defeated him in a landslide, the candy bar also became history.

Crumbly Mumblies: Introduced in the 1950s, Crumbly Mumblies were very dry chocolate bars that were supposed to crumble on the tongue. The fact that they tasted like dust wasn't the worst problem: The bars tended to disintegrate in the shipping process. They were yanked soon after the first few shipments.

The Seven Up Candy Bar: No, it wasn't filled with soda. It had seven connected pieces, each with a different filling. But once the 7-Up Bottling Company came on the scene, they bought the bar and retired it.

The Air Mail Bar: In 1930, this snack was introduced to honor the first airmail flight in the United States—in 1918, from Washington, D.C., to New York City. Ironically, the flight being honored never made it because the fuel tank wasn't filled, the pilot got lost, and the plane landed in a cow pasture far from New York. The candy didn't make it either.

The Sal-Le-Dande Bar: This was the first candy bar named after a stripper—famed 1930s fan dancer Sally Rand. Surprisingly, there was later a *second* candy bar named after a stripper: Gypsy, honoring Gypsy Rose Lee. Unsurprisingly, there was never a third.

The Lotsa Matzo Bar: It didn't actually contain matzo meal, but it did have a playful-looking rabbi on the wrapper. One of the few kosher chocolate bars ever developed, it tasted just like any other plain chocolate candy. Eventually, the rabbi and some of the wording ("It's wholly delicious!") were considered offensive, and the bar quietly disappeared.

The Zep Candy Bar: In the 1930s, there were several candy bars that had a dirigible theme. This one had "Sky-High Quality" and featured a Graf Zeppelin on the wrapper. After the Hindenburg exploded in 1937, the bar was quickly taken off the market.

The Chicken Dinner Bar: Introduced in the 1920s, this bar's original wrapper featured a picture of a roasted chicken on a dinner plate, which was supposed to make you think that it was good for you. The company even dispatched trucks disguised as sheet-metal chickens to deliver the bar to stores. But perhaps the weirdest fact about the Chicken Dinner Bar is that it wasn't retired until the 1970s.

The Mood Bar: A true 1970s artifact, man. This groovy fruit candy was supposed to last for hours, and its advertising claimed that its color would change with your mood. It's possible the mood that sucking on the candy inspired was "apathy." It didn't even last a month.

ANSWER, PAGE 202

THE QUOTABLE JOHN

We've taken three little-known but fascinating factoids we found in Uncle John readers and translated them into cryptograms by simple letter substitution code.

For instance, if we encoded UNCLE JOHN, he might end up looking like this: BRJAQ TLPR, where U = B, N = R, and so on. The letter substitutions remain constant throughout any one cryptogram, but they change from one cryptogram to the next. Here are some hints: A lot of words end in E, S, Y, R, and D; a single letter is almost always an A or I; and look for words that begin with the same two-letter combination—those letters might stand for TH, as in THE, THAT, THEY, and so on. (Proper nouns are preceded by an asterisk (*).)

It's All in the Game

VTJFGED   RTSK   LGB   CH   HLGH   G   BGRKBJGE   VGJK
(COMPANY LORE HAS IT THAT A SALESMAN CAME)

YF   MCHL   *S-*C-*B-*I.   ZCUCEK   CEBFCSGHCTE?   ET:
(UP WITH R-I-S-K DIVINE INSPIRATION? NO)

HLK   QCSBH   CECHCGRB   TQ   HLK   *FGSIKS   *ASTHLKSB
(THE FIRST INITIALS OF THE PARKER BROTHERS)

FSKBCZKEH'B   QTYS   PSGEZVLCRZSKE.
(PRESIDENT'S FOUR GRANDCHILDREN)

That Other Babe

*FOFM   *RZRIZNLCQ   CQGM   MQDMIMR   OQ   *OOT
(BABE DIDRIKSON ONCE ENTERED AN AAU)

DIOGN   VMMD   OL   DXM   CQKS   YMILCQ   CQ   XMI
(TRACK MEET AS THE ONLY PERSON ON HER)

DMOV: LXM   HCQ   LZJ   MAMQDL,   FICNM   WCTI   HCIKR
(TEAM: SHE WON SIX EVENTS, BROKE FOUR WORLD)

IMGCIRL   OQR   HCQ   DXM   VMMD   FS   MZPXD   YCZQDL.
(RECORDS AND WON THE MEET BY EIGHT POINTS)

What, Me Worry?

SPXQQ   EVVDQV   UTGBBQN.   ODS   OMLC   SPQJ,   ES
(THREE ISSUES FLOPPED. BUT BACK THEN IT)

SGGC   VG   TGJK   SG   KQS   VMTQV   XQBGXSV   SPMS   M
(TOOK SO LONG TO GET SALES REPORTS THAT A)

UGDXSP   EVVDQ   FMV   MTXQMNZ   EJ   SPQ   FGXCV.   OZ
(FOURTH ISSUE WAS ALREADY IN THE WORKS. BY)

SPQJ,   *WMN   PMN   OQKDJ   SG   VQTT.
(THEN, MAD HAD BEGUN TO SELL.)

Completed by Sana F. Naqvi on July 22nd (Thurs) at 5:29 pm

No wonder you spend so much time ... !

ANSWER, PAGE 202

YE OLDE CRIME AND PUNISHMENT

In *Uncle John's Bathroom Reader Plunges into History* we visited Anytown, Germany, in the Middle Ages, where virtually everything was regulated. For instance, the nobility could invite no more than 48 people to their weddings; servants or day laborers were only allowed 32 guests. Other similarly strange practices follow, but you'll have to select the right answer from among the three given in parentheses.

EVERY DAY IN ANYTOWN

People were only allowed to eat two meals a day. The upper classes were permitted **(two, four, eight)** courses at each meal. The lower classes had to settle for **(one, three, five)** courses, and at the second meal of the day were not allowed to serve **(barnyard animals, pickles, dessert)**. The first meal could last no longer than three hours, which sounds like plenty of time for a meal, except that when the time limit was reached, everyone had to leave his seat immediately or be subject to **(a fine, arrest, execution)**.

In some towns, the **(horses, prostitutes, village idiots)** were required to wear conspicuous clothing, like a kerchief or cape in a particular color.

CRIMES AND MISDEMEANORS

Consider these "crimes" and the creative punishments imposed:
- Men or women who wore overly **(luxurious, revealing, shabby)** clothing could have the forbidden garment stripped off them on the street by the town constables.
- If a husband allowed his wife to rule the home or hit him, his fellow villagers would come to his house and remove **(the roof, the wife, the kids)**.
- The punishment for cursing, swearing, or blaspheming ran the gamut. In some places, the offender would have to run around the church's baptismal font holding a candle. In others, his tongue would be **(slathered with horse droppings, tied to his hat for a week, cut out)**.

A fine was imposed for:
- Going to a **(gambling den, fortune-teller, lady of the evening)**.
- Wearing a dress that was **(too short, more than two colors, purple)**.
- Arriving at a wedding **(late, without a gift, drunk)**.
- Serving wine or meals to guests after a **(baptism, funeral, barn-raising)**.
- Being on the street at night without **(a lighted lantern, permission of the mayor, at least two pfennigs in your pocket)**.

MAKING THE PUNISHMENT FIT THE CRIME?

Public humiliation was a favorite way of teaching those darn miscreants a lesson. For instance, lovers whose lascivious conduct had gone too far were sentenced in this way: The seducer had to push the object of his lust through the streets in a **(shovel, barrel, wheelbarrow)** while onlookers were encouraged to **(blow kisses and laugh, make noises like farm animals, throw garbage)** at them.

So go ahead and invite 49 people to your wedding. And then, when your wife wants to beat you up, let her! Be happy you live in the 21st century!

ANSWER, PAGE 202

HOW FAMOUS CAN YOU GET?

The people listed on this page are so famous that they only need one name for us to recognize them. Can you fit all 39 of them into their proper places in the grid, crossword-style?

(completed crossword grid containing: MICHELANGELO, BACH, IMAN, CHARO, MIDAS, CASTRO, NERO, NEFERTITI, STING, CHER, GALILEO, MEDEA, PICASSO, HANNIBAL, ANASTASIA, BEETHOVEN, OPRAH, EINSTEIN, BLACKBEARD, AESOP, ENYA, and others)

Completed by Sara F. Nogvi on Thurs. July 22/2004 @ 6:27pm.

4-letter words
- ✓ Bach
- ✓ Bono
- ✓ Cato
- ✓ Cher
- ✓ Enya
- ✓ Iman
- ✓ Nero
- ✓ Ovid

5-letter words
- ✓ Aesop
- ✓ Bjork
- ✓ Charo

- ✓ Elvis
- ✓ Evita
- ✓ Medea
- ✓ Midas
- ✓ Nehru
- ✓ Oprah
- ✓ Plato
- ✓ Sting

6-letter words
- ✓ Castro
- ✓ Chanel
- ✓ Merlin

7-letter words
- ✓ Cochise
- ✓ Galileo
- ✓ Picasso
- ✓ Saladin

8-letter words
- ✓ Einstein
- ✓ Hannibal
- ✓ Mohammed

9-letter words
- ✓ Aeschylus
- ✓ Anastasia

- ✓ Aristotle
- ✓ Beethoven
- ✓ Fernandel
- ✓ Nefertiti
- ✓ Sacajawea

10-letter word
- ✓ Blackbeard

11-letter word
- ✓ Charlemagne

12-letter word
- Michelangelo

905 201 0766

ANSWER, PAGE 202

BRAZEN HUSSY!

Mae West wrote most of her own outrageous material. Here are a few of her best lines—can you figure out what was on her mind?

ACROSS

1 Spellbound
5 Cowboy's leggings
10 Archeological sites
14 Morales of *La Bamba*
15 Bowler's button
16 Pasture measure
17 List wrap-up
18 The end of ___
19 *Lawrence of Arabia* director David
20 **"I've always had a weakness for ___"**
23 Hush-hush govt. agency
24 Young newt
25 Social rank
29 Part of a min.
31 Cheryl and Diane
36 ___ *Inferno*
38 Bull's-eye (abbr.)
40 Threesome
41 **"Give a man a free hand and he'll ___"**
44 Like some vaccines
45 ___ double-take
46 Curls the lip
47 Gap locales?
49 Ultimate degree
51 Brief and to the point
52 Flowery bit of verse
54 Swiss river
56 **"Too much of a good thing ___"**
64 It was an Olympic sport till 1936
65 Michael Crichton thriller
66 What's more…
67 "Clumsy me!"
68 Choice in Lucite
69 Turns right
70 Different
71 In flames
72 Mouth off to

DOWN

1 Ray's hangout?
2 Regarding
3 Jack of early TV talk
4 Scrabble piece
5 Obstacles on a climb
6 Dyes that go back to the Egyptians
7 On the Red, perhaps
8 Tapered cigar
9 Boss's backup
10 He painted a surreal "Mae West" in the '30s
11 Bucket for champagne
12 Paté de foie ___
13 Title for Hillary (abbr.)
21 Mini-map
22 NJ shore's ocean
25 Floppy disk upgrade
26 Gene Tierney role
27 One year's official record
28 Moonshine machine
30 Razzle-dazzle
32 ___ *Grows in Brooklyn*
33 Laundromat hot spot
34 Pricey gowns
35 W.C. Fields in *The Bank Dick*
37 In a funk
39 Campers, briefly
42 Mountain man type
43 ___ nous (confidentially)
48 Cry and cry
50 Plane's "garage"
53 Billie Holiday's record label
55 Be crazy about
56 Refrigerate
57 View from Lucerne
58 Victory margin
59 R.E.M.'s "The ___ Love"
60 Car wash supplies
61 Dog bane
62 A Swiss Army knife has lots of them
63 Red ink item
64 "The Raven" writer

NO CAN(ADA) DO

From Uncle John's Canadian collection of Looney Laws…. We've mixed up the letters in a few important words, so we're depending on you to put the letters back in the right place in the blanks above them. Be careful out there.

Ottawa:
Because of an anti-noise ordinance, it's illegal for B E E S to B U Z Z.
ESEB   ZUBZ

Toronto:
It's illegal to P R A G a dead H O R S E along Yonge Street on a Sunday.
ADRG   ERHSO

Nova Scotia:
The law prohibits watering your L A W N if it's R A I N I N G.
WLNA   NAGRIIN

Etobioke, Ontario:
No more than 3.5 I N C H E S of water is allowed in a B A T H T U B.
SHICEN   AUBBHTT

Montreal:
It's a no-no to park your C A R so that it blocks your own D R I V E W A Y.
RCA   VIEWYARD

Halifax, Nova Scotia:
It's illegal to walk a T I G H T R O P E over the main streets.
POTTERHIG

Quebec:
It's a crime to sell A N T I F R E E Z E to Indians.
FIZENEARTE

Completed by Sana F. Naqvi on Thursday July 22 @ 6:35pm.

Vancouver, British Columbia:
It's illegal to ride a T R I C Y C L E over 10 mph.
CITYCELR

Burnaby, British Columbia:
The town has a 10 p.m. C U R F E W for D O G S.
WURCEF   SODG

British Columbia:
It's illegal to kill a S A S Q U A T C H.
HUTSQASCA

Toronto:
There's no riding a S T R E E T C A R on Sunday if you've been eating G A R L I C.
SCATTERER   CRIGAL

ANSWER, PAGE 203

IF THEY MARRIED

completed by Sano F. Nagri on Thurs July 22/04 @ ?? (evening)

Last time we asked you what would happen if Yoko Ono married Sonny Bono, and we told you she'd be Yoko Ono Bono. Remember? Well, since then Yoko's divorced Sonny and married U2's Bono. So now she's Yoko Ono Bono Bono.

In the meantime, we've been carrying marrying to even more ridiculous heights. Fill in the blanks to find out what our new celebrities' married names would be.

1. If country singer Kitty Wells married cartoon shrink Dr. Katz, she'd be K I T T Y K A T Z.
2. If Coco Chanel married Iggy Pop, she'd be C O C O P O P.
3. If Demi Moore married director Jonathan Demme, she'd be D E M I D E M M E.
4. If Cat Stevens married Snoop Dogg, he'd be C A T D O G G.
5. If Boog Powell married Felipe Alou, he'd be B O O G A L O u.
6. If Juan Valdez married Nguyen Van Thieu and Penelope Tree, he'd be J U A N T H I E U T R E E.
7. If G. Gordon Liddy married Boutros-Boutros Ghali, then divorced him to marry Kenny G., he'd be G. G H A L I G.
8. If Jack Handy of *SNL* married Andy Capp, then married Jack Paar, then moved on to Stephen King, he'd be J A C K H A N D Y C A P P P A A R K I N G.
9. If Julie London married Beau Bridges, then married *SNL*'s Jimmy Fallon, followed by Lesley-Anne Down, she'd be J U L I E L O N D O N B R I D G E S F A L L O N D O W N.
10. If Woody Allen married Natalie Wood, divorced her and married Gregory Peck, divorced him and married Ben Hur, he'd be W O O D Y W O O D P E C K H U R.
11. If opera star Kiri Te Kanawa married Jimmy Durante, Martin Mull, Ken Berry, and George Bush, she'd be K I R I D U R A N T E M U L L B E R R Y B U S H.
12. If Dolly Parton married Tommy Smothers, then went even farther back in show business and married Mr. Lucky, then divorced and married Martin Short, then divorced and married football kicker Ray Guy, we could all nod understandingly when we heard, "D O L L Y P A R T O N S M O T H E R S L U C K Y S H O R T G U Y."

ANSWER, PAGE 203

* * * * *

A FEW OF MY FAVORITE THINGS

At the end of 2002, MIT and the Lemelson Foundation polled more than 1,400 Americans to find out what, from among five inventions, they couldn't live without. How did they rank the five choices?

Automobile	Cell phone	Microwave oven	Personal computer	Toothbrush
2	4	5	3	1

ANSWER, PAGE 203

Completed by Sana F. Naqvi on
Thurs July 22 @ ?? (at night)

Sanafatiu Naqvi

THE OBJECT OF MY REFLECTION

Directions: The grid contains a quotation that reads from left to right. The words in it wrap around to the next line; the black squares signify the spaces between the words.

Start by answering as many of the clues as you can. Write your answers on the numbered dashes, then transfer the letters to the correspondingly numbered squares in the puzzle grid.

As an extra-added bonus (or a tool to use if you get stuck), if you read the first letters of the words in the word list in sequence, you'll find an acrostic—a hidden message about the subject of the quotation..

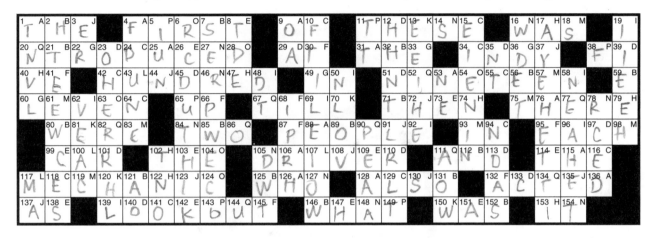

The grid (quotation): THE FIRST OF THESE WAS INTRODUCED AT THE INDY FIVE HUNDRED IN NINETEEN ELEVEN UP TILL THEN THERE WERE TWO PEOPLE IN EACH CAR THE DRIVER AND THE MECHANIC WHO ALSO ACTED AS LOOKOUT WHAT WAS IT

A. John Irving's tenth novel, 2001 (3 wds.)
T H E F O U R T H
31 76 88 4 9 25 106 1 126
H A N D
115 128 53 136

B. All-star epic oater of 1962 (5 wds.)
H O W T H E W E S
2 89 85 71 32 56 146 59 152
T W A S W O N
21 80 121 7 125 131 112

C. The last stop (4 wds.)
E N D O F T H E L I N E
118 64 24 141 10 55 42 15 129 34 94 116

D. Author of *The Manchurian Candidate* (2 wds.)
R I C H A R D C O
101 39 133 12 29 110 45 97 23
N D O N
35 113 140 51

E. Toy for young artists introduced in 1959
E T C H A S K E T C H
73 114 99 103 151 138 142 109 8 26 147

F. Hunger
A P P E T I T E
132 66 87 95 30 68 145 41

G. Got someone all worked up
R I L E D
22 49 60 33 36

H. Kind of window or blind
V E N E T I A N
40 79 122 47 102 153 17 74

I. U.S. Open tennis champ, 1985–87 (2 wds.)
I V A N L E N D L
19 62 96 50 69 92 58 48 139

J. NBA Hall-of-Famer, called The Big E (2 wds.)
E L V I N H A Y E S
135 91 108 123 44 72 137 37 3 130

K. Seminal human invention
W H E E L
150 120 81 13 70

L. Hawaiian island
M A U I
117 100 43 107

M. Arctic phenomenon (2 wds.)
I C E S H E E T
93 119 61 18 98 57 83 75

N. "Do Ya Think I'm Sexy" singer? (2 wds.)
R O D S T E W A R T
46 127 105 14 84 27 16 148 78 154

O. Go back, as the tide
R E C E D E
6 54 124 104 28 63

P. Choice facing someone in the closet?
O U T F I T
143 65 11 38 5 149

Q. Good name
R E P U T A T I O N
82 77 90 144 134 111 67 52 86 20

ANSWER, PAGE 203

STUFF THAT FELL FROM THE SKY

Chicken Little was right! All sorts of strange and mysterious objects have been seen falling out of the sky. You can read about them in *Uncle John's Supremely Satisfying Bathroom Reader*, but in the meantime, see if you can find these 27 items in the grid, reading across, down, and diagonally. The leftover letters will reveal a hidden message about a proverbial saying that you'd think would apply here—but doesn't.

```
M E T E O R I T E A M N D H
A T S T N E M U C O D S I T
B S O P E S V E N R R A I H
N A E O A K L E A V E S A S
S W T D S C Y I T C N S N I
G N N S T G E A A A K A T F
R A I B O Y G J K N E T S Y
E M A O F A E U B S M S L
E U R L C I S H K N A N D L
N H N B D R C D U C K S O E
S D E E S E E R T S A D U J
N G D T C S I V F O S L O T
O H L I E R E S L N A O B R
W E O H C 5 0 0 B I R D S O
R D G W O F F R O G S I S T
```

500 BIRDS	FROGS	METEORITE
ANTS	GOLDEN RAIN	MONEY
BATS	GREEN SNOW	OAK LEAVES
BEANS	HAY	SILVER COINS
BLACK EGGS	HUMAN WASTE	SNAILS
COOTS	ICE CHUNKS	SOOT
DOCUMENTS	JELLYFISH	SPACE JUNK
DUCKS	JUDAS TREE SEEDS	TOADS
FIRE	MEAT	WHITE BLOBS

ANSWER, PAGE 204

Completed by Sana F. Naqvi on
Thursday July 22 @ 11:44 pm

LITTLE THINGS MEAN A LOT

Those little things that we take for granted were once some inventor's bouncing baby brainchild. Well, here's ours: Mark each little story with T for true or F for false.

__T__ **Band-Aid:** Invented by the husband of an accident-prone woman who was constantly cutting and burning herself in the kitchen.

__T__ **Baseball Caps:** Most players wore straw hats until the late 1860s when they started wearing visored caps that were based on the Union and Confederate soldiers' uniform.

__F__ **Can Opener:** Canned food and the can opener were invented by the Campbell Soup Company. Their first soup offering was Chicken Noodle, which is made from the same recipe today.

__T__ **Flyswatter:** The first was a square piece of wire screen attached to a yardstick. The inventor wanted to call it a fly "bat," but "swatter" fans prevailed.

__F__ **Jockey Shorts:** Created by a jockey who was tired of trying to pull up his pants while attempting to control a speeding horse. Pretty soon his fellow jockeys were sporting them, then the fans. The rest is underwear history.

__T__ **Matches:** The first match was a stick that the inventor (who was trying to invent a new kind of explosive) had used to stir his ingredients. When he tried to remove the dried glob on the end of the stick, it ignited.

__F__ **Peanut Butter:** Ground peanuts and peanut oil, it was the brainchild of a doctor whose patient was dying of "protein malnutrition" and, because of a stomach disorder, couldn't eat meat.

__T__ **Running Shoes:** A miler at the University of Oregon heated some rubber in a waffle iron to get the kind of traction he wanted on the soles of his running shoes. He started a shoe business and named the shoes Nikes after the goddess of victory.

__T__ **Stethoscope:** A doctor who was too shy to put his ear to the chest of a pretty patient with a heart condition invented the stethoscope. To his surprise, he could hear her heart much more clearly.

__F__ **Wristwatches:** Only men wore wristwatches for the first 100 years—until French jeweler Jacques Cartier designed a delicate diamond-studded version for the ladies at the end of World War I.

ANSWER, PAGE 204

* * * * *

ASIAN CON-FUSION

All but one of these classic examples of Chinese food were actually invented in America. Which is the authentic Chinese dish?

a. Chop suey
b. Chow mein
(c.) Peking duck
d. Egg foo yung
e. Fortune cookies

ANSWER, PAGE 204

PRIME-TIME PROVERBS

Ever wish you could rattle off the wisecracks like all those TV characters? You could do it, too, if you had your own writer. See if you can match the quotes (1–13) to the speakers (a–m).

_c_ 1. "I've never felt closer to a group of people. Not even in the portable johns of Woodstock."

_g_ 2. "My dad once gave me a few words of wisdom which I have always tried to live by. He said, 'Son, never throw a punch at a redwood.'"

_d_ 3. "You know, if Michelangelo had used me as a model, there's no telling how far he could have gone."

_b_ 4. "A truly wise man never plays leapfrog with a unicorn."

_j_ 5. "As my great aunt Maude always said, 'If you can't win the game, the next best thing is to upset the chessboard.'"

_e_ 6. "Why do they call them tellers? They never tell you anything. They just ask questions. And why do they call it interest? It's boring. And another thing—how come the Trust Department has all their pens chained to the table?"

_h_ 7. "If you've enjoyed this program just half as much as we've enjoyed doing it, then we've enjoyed it twice as much as you."

_m_ 8. "Artists are always ready to sacrifice for art—if the price is right."

_i_ 9. "Never cry over spilt milk. It could've been whiskey."

_a_ 10. "Those little lines around your mouth, those crow's feet around your eyes, the millimeter your derriere has slipped in the last decade—they're just nature's way of telling you that you've got nine holes left to play, so get out there and have a good time"

_k_ 11. "Virgins don't lie."

_l_ 12. "You know somethin'? If you couldn't read, you couldn't look up what's on television."

_f_ 13. "If brains was lard, Jethro couldn't grease a pan."

a. David Addison, *Moonlighting*

b. Banacek, *Banacek*

c. Rev. Jim Ignatowski, *Taxi*

d. Herman Munster, *The Munsters*

e. Coach Ernie Pantusso, *Cheers*

f. Jed Clampett, *The Beverly Hillbillies*

g. Thomas Magnum, *Magnum P.I.*

h. Michael Palin, *Monty Python's Flying Circus*

i. Pappy Maverick, *Maverick*

j. Artemus Gordon, *The Wild, Wild West*

k. Fonzie, *Happy Days*

l. Beaver Cleaver, *Leave It to Beaver*

m. Gomez Addams, *The Addams Family*

ANSWER, PAGE 204

PHRASEOLOGY 201

Even if you didn't complete Phraseology 103 from *Uncle John's Bathroom Reader Puzzle Book #1*, we're still—out of the goodness of our hearts—going to promote you to the next level in Phraseology, in which we answer the age-old question: "Where the heck did *that* come from?"

ACROSS

1 Swindle
5 Metallurgy byproduct
9 Camel's kin
14 Kal Kan rival
15 Letterman rival
16 Joyce Carol ___
17 Term from the 17th-century practice of ranking the largest and most heavily armed warships
19 Cancel a liftoff
20 Ham it up
21 Change the clock
23 ___ soup (London fog)
24 Cartoon Chihauhua
25 Restroom door sign
27 Tummy trouble
29 It originally meant giving up the chance to deal in a card game
34 I beg to ___
38 AFL's partner
39 Scott Turow book
40 He coined "inferiority complex"
41 "Balderdash!"
42 Water park feature
43 Accomplishment
44 Actor DiCaprio
45 Perfectly
46 It's from the act of soldiers violently attacking enemy positions
49 Gossip
50 Women's ___
51 Speedy plane, for short
54 Jungle chest-beater
57 Benjamin Harrison was the last president to have one
59 Make (someone) happy
61 Gem

63 Phrase that's from the traditional place where valuables were kept
65 "Love conquers all" is one
66 Spanish river
67 One in a contest
68 They show a tree's age
69 ___ and gloom
70 Actor Garcia

DOWN

1 Morley of *60 Minutes*
2 Atmosphere, poetically
3 Barbecue wear
4 The vast majority
5 Camera type (abbr.)
6 Finds out
7 Feed the kitty
8 Quarrels with
9 Detest
10 Sci. milieu
11 Over
12 Simple
13 Movie pooch
18 Toughen, as steel
22 Sound rebound
26 Corn serving
28 African virus
30 Hurry
31 Condo apartment
32 Relinquish
33 Swiss painter
34 "Bananas"
35 Brainstorm
36 Antiaircraft fire
37 Held a party for
41 Put into other words

42 Gloomy
44 Handheld harp
45 Three (prefix)
47 Authoritative sources
48 Veteran
51 Greeted at the door
52 Fine mount
53 Football's Bradshaw
54 Slightly open
55 Prefix with "cure"
56 Actor McGregor
58 ___ *Cop*
60 Volcanic flow
62 Breakfast order
64 Joltin' Joe's bro

ANSWER, PAGE 204

THE 7 "OFFICIAL" ATTRIBUTES OF THE PILLSBURY DOUGHBOY

In *Uncle John's Bathroom Reader Puzzle Book #1*, we encrypted such trivial information as crimes punishable by death according to the Code of Hammurabi. But this time, let's get serious—let's talk about little blobs of dough that wear pastry hats and giggle on TV. To that end, we've taken the seven official attributes that make the Pillsbury Doughboy who he is, and we've encrypted them using a simple letter-substitution code.

In this particular puzzle, **the letter substitution remains constant throughout the whole list**. For further instructions and hints on how to solve, see page 7.

1. PVG GXVU SJGI BYYX BVXC LYJOP: "YDD-FPVIC,
   HIS SKIN MUST LOOK LIKE DOUGH OFF WHITE

   GSYYIP, RJI UYI OBYGGM"
   SMOOTH BUT NOT GLOSSY

2. GBVOPIBM BJSVUYJG, RJI UY GPCCU
   SLIGHTLY LUMINOUS BUT NO SHEEN

3. UY XUCCG, CBRYFG, FAVGIG, DVUOCAG, CQAG,
   NO KNEES ELBOWS WRISTS FINGERS EARS

   YA QUXBCG
   OR ANKLES

4. ACQA KVCFG LY UYI VUTBJLC "RJUG"
   REAR VIEWS DO NOT INCLUDE BUNS

5. FQBXG FVIP Q "GFQOOCA"
   WALKS WITH A SWAGGER

6. GIYSQTP VG ZAYZYAIVYUQB IY IPC ACGI YD
   STOMACH IS PROPORTIONAL TO THE REST OF

   PVG RYLM
   HIS BODY

7. PC VG UYI ZYAIBM
   HE IS NOT PORTLY

ANSWER, PAGE 205

* * * * *

LOST IN TRANSLATION

What James Bond film was was originally translated as *We Don't Want a Doctor* in Japan?

Dr. No.

ANSWER, PAGE 204

THE TIME IT TAKES #1

Everything takes time. For instance, it takes .06 seconds for an automobile's airbag to fully inflate, and it took 69 years for the Soviet Union to rise and fall. Here are 10 time-takers; can you put them in order from the least to the most amount of time they take?

_____ The time it takes for a human hair to grow half an inch

_____ The time it takes for a hummingbird's wings to beat 70 times

_____ The time it takes for a newborn baby to wet or soil 80 diapers

_____ The time it takes for a U.S. Marine to go through boot camp

_____ The time it takes for Easter to recur on the same date

_____ The time it takes for Los Angeles to move two inches closer to San Francisco (due to the shifting of tectonic plates)

_____ The time it takes for plutonium-239 to become harmless

_____ The time it takes for the elevator in Toronto's CN Tower to reach the top (1,518 feet)

_____ The time it took for the *Titanic* to sink after it struck the iceberg

_____ The time that the average American spends asleep in a lifetime

ANSWER, PAGE 205

HELLO? DOLLY?

Small crostic puzzles are solved just like the big ones (directions on page 13) but the first letter of the fill-in words **do not** spell out a hidden message.

Completed by Sana Naqvi on ~~Thursday~~ Friday July 23/2004 @ 12:48am

A. Hue
C O L O R
41 10 3 12 28

B. Best Picture of 1986
P L A T O O N
6 24 36 19 2 42 31

C. One of the Teenage Mutant Ninja Turtles
D O N A T E L L O
1 30 43 20 47 15 37 16 33

D. Mall tenant
S T O R E
18 29 22 8 40

E. Jukebox fee, at least when they were invented
N I C K E L
11 38 14 35 45 23

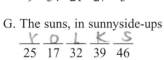

F. NBC morning news stalwart
T O D A Y
9 34 21 27 5

G. The suns, in sunnyside-ups
Y O L K S
25 17 32 39 46

H. Factory
P L A N T
26 4 7 13 44

ANSWER, PAGE 223

THE PRACTICAL YOLK

We visited Uncle John's favorite breakfast hangout, where he and his cronies disucss such philosophical conundrums as "Which came first, the bacon or the egg?" While there, we lifted 38 items straight from the menu. Can you fit all of them in the grid, crossword-style?

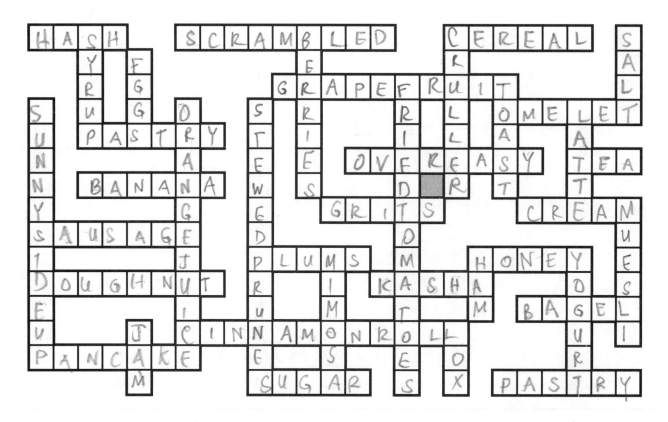

3-letter words	Kasha	7-letter words	11-letter words
Ham	Latte	Berries	Orange juice
Jam	Plums	Cruller	Sunnyside up
Lox	Sugar	Pancake	
Tea	Syrup	Sausage	12-letter words
	Toast		Cinnamon roll
4-letter words		8-letter words	Stewed prunes
Eggs	6-letter words	Doughnut	
Hash	Banana	Over easy	13-letter word
Salt	Butter		Fried tomatoes
	Cereal	9-letter word	
5-letter words	Muesli	Scrambled	
Bagel	Mimosa		
Cream	Omelet	10-letter word	
Grits	Pastry	Grapefruit	
Honey	Yogurt		

ANSWER, PAGE 205

FILL IN THE LIMERICKS

Well, no one reported us for indecency when we published our saucy limericks last time. Of course, one or two old ladies fainted dead away, but once we revived them they wanted to do it again, so we decided to have another go. Fill in the blanks (one for each missing letter) to complete each limerick.

1. There was a young girl from St. Paul
   Wore a newspaper dress to a _b a l l_.
   But her dress caught on fire
   And burned her _a t t i r e_ entire
   Front page, sporting section, and _a l l_.

2. A glutton who came from the Rhine
   Was asked at what hour he'd _d i n e_.
   He replied, "At eleven,
   At three, five, and _s e v e n_,
   And eight, and a quarter to _n i n e_."

3. I'd rather have fingers than toes;
   I'd rather have ears than a _n o s e_;
   And as for my hair,
   I'm glad that it's _t h e r e_.
   I'll be awfully sad when it _g o e s_.

4. There once was an old man of Lyme
   Who married three wives at a _t i m e_;
   When asked "Why a third?"
   He replied, "One's _a b s u r d_!
   And bigamy, sir, is a _c r i m e_."

5. A cute secretary, none cuter,
   Was replaced by a
      clicking _c o m p u t e r_.
   The wife of the boss
   Put the idea _a c r o s s_;
   You see, the computer was _ _ _ _ _ _ _.
      _n e u t e r_

6. There is a young man from Van Nuys
   Who believes he is clever and _w i s e_.
   Now, what do you think?
   He saves gallons of _i n k_
   By simply not dotting his _i's_.

7. A famous bullfighter named Zeke
   Thrilled the crowds with his _ _ _ _ _ _ _ _ _.
      casual _technique_
   Each time he was gored
   He just acted _b o r e d_,
   Pausing only to plug up the _ _ _ _.
      _l e a k_

8. An amorous maiden antique
   Locked a man in her house for a _w e e k_;
   He entered her door
   With a shout and a _r o a r_,
   But his exit was marked by a
      _s q u e a k_.

9. There was a young fellow named Paul
   Who went to a masquerade _b a l l_
   Arrayed like a tree,
   But he failed to _ _ _ _ _ _ _ _ _ _foresee
   His abuse by the dogs in the _ _ _ _ _.
      _h a l l_

10. There was an old gal in a hearse
    Who murmured, "This might have
       been _w o r s e_;
    Of course the expense
    Is simply _ _ _ _ _ _ _ _, _immense_
    But it doesn't come out of *my* _p u r s e_."

TV CATCHPHRASES

Where have you heard them before? On the tube, if you've been listening.

ACROSS

1 Cathedral topper
6 Work well together
10 Beer, slangily
14 ___ marbles (Greek sculptures)
15 Melville novel set in Tahiti
16 Med sch. course
17 *Get Smart* catchphrase
20 Like Stephen King stories
21 Studio sign
22 Weight Watchers' units (abbr.)
24 High style?
26 Chinese statesman Sun ___
27 Bearish?
29 Ranchero helper
31 Snaky shape
32 Soup with sushi
33 Folk singer Pete
35 *Teenage Mutant Ninja Turtles* catchphrase
40 Takes as one's own
41 Flow from Mount Fuji
43 *New Yorker* cartoonist Chast
46 Don ___ Corleone
47 Log-on name
49 Starts the day
51 Therefore
53 Flying Dutchman's choice?
54 Montana or Sanders, once
55 Gentle as ___
57 *Perfect Strangers* catchphrase
63 Mixed bag
64 Aqua ___ (water)
65 Blow, like 41 Across
66 Like Snidely Whiplash
67 But, in Berlin
68 Witherspoon of *Legally Blonde 2*

DOWN

1 Darn
2 Arafat's org.
3 Tentative agreement
4 Tick off
5 Evasive maneuver
6 Hit a low note?
7 Bird from Down Under
8 Blubber
9 Weed whacker
10 Brando's *On the Waterfront* costar
11 Fidgetiness
12 Ray, of the Kinks
13 Actor Daniel and shock jock Howard
18 "Eeks!"
19 Gave for a time
22 Abner's partner on old-time radio
23 ___-a-brac
25 Sandal feature
26 Lotus position discipline
28 Setting of *The Bridges of Madison County*
30 Brain tests, briefly
33 Apartment building mgr.
34 Run the show
36 Word like "badly" or "nicely"
37 ___ de Boulogne (Paris park)
38 Navy or indigo
39 Worse than 66 Across
42 USN bigwig
43 Hit-or-miss
44 Orange bird
45 Colorful annual
47 Unattractive tropical fruit
48 Downpour
50 *Foxfire* author Anya
52 Traffic tracker
56 Stable mom
58 Fed. pollution watchdog
59 Massage
60 Anger
61 Rival of FedEx
62 Sault ___ Marie

ANSWER, PAGE 206

CLOSE ENCOUNTERS
OF THE WAX KIND

If you've ever wanted to get close to your favorite star, now you can. Just head to Las Vegas, to Madame Tussaud's Celebrity Encounter, where you can mingle with Madonna and more than 100 other celebrities. OK, so they're made out of wax. But they're amazingly lifelike.

We've assembled the names of 19 of those celebs, and the city they're displayed in, in the star-shaped grid below. Once you've found them all, reading across, down, and diagonally, the leftover letters will spell out an interesting fact about the way the figures are made.

Each figure is two percent larger than the celebs real size.

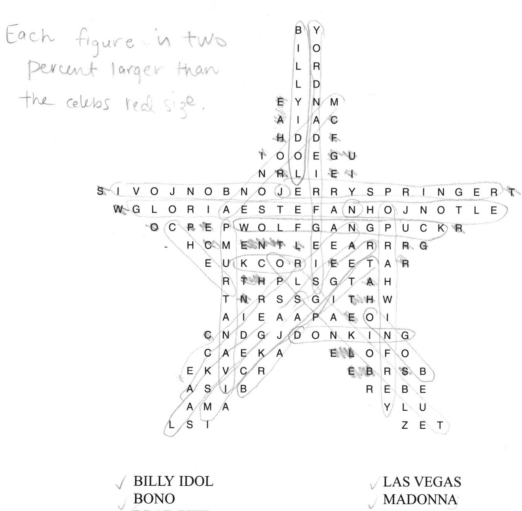

✓ BILLY IDOL
✓ BONO
✓ BRAD PITT
✓ CHER
✓ DON KING
✓ ELTON JOHN
✓ GLORIA ESTEFAN
✓ IVANA TRUMP
✓ JERRY SPRINGER
✓ JON BON JOVI

✓ LAS VEGAS
✓ MADONNA
✓ MICK JAGGER
✓ NEIL SEDAKA
✓ OLGA KORBUT
✓ OPRAH WINFREY
✓ PRINCE
✓ (The) ROCK
✓ SIEGFRIED AND ROY
✓ WOLFGANG PUCK

ANSWER, PAGE 206

DROPPING BOMBECKS

Some choice examples of the wit and wisdom of columnist Erma Bombeck. If you need directions on how to solve, see page 5.

1.

WHEN YOU LOOK LIKE YOUR PASSPORT PHOTO ITS TIME TO GO HOME

2.

A CHILD DEVELOPS INDIVIDUALITY LONG BEFORE HE DEVELOPS TASTE

3.

IF A MAN WATCHES THREE FOOTBALL GAMES IN A ROW HE SHOULD BE DECLARED LEGALLY DEAD

ANSWER, PAGE 205

WAS MURPHY RIGHT?

You know Murphy's Law: "If something can go wrong, it will." They say it's an immutable law of the universe, but you're here to prove them wrong. See if you can complete these other immutable laws of the universe by matching the first half of each (1–10) to its proper ending (a–j). Let's prove them—*and* the anonymous Mr. Murphy—wrong. Yeah!

_b_ 1. Baruch's Observation: "If all you have is a hammer…
_e_ 2. The Golden Rule of Arts and Sciences: "Whoever has the gold…
_d_ 3. Green's Law of Debate: "Anything is possible…
_g_ 4. Hecht's Law: "There is no time like the present…
_a_ 5. Lowe's Law: "Success always occurs in private…
_h_ 6. The Murphy Philosophy: "Smile…
_f_ 7. Thompson's Theorem: "When the going gets weird…
_i_ 8. Todd's Law: "All things being equal…
_j_ 9. Vac's Conundrum: "When you dial a wrong number…
_c_ 10. Zappa's Law: "There are two things on Earth that are universal…

a. …and failure in full public view."
b. …everything looks like a nail."
c. …hydrogen and stupidity."
d. …if you don't know what you're talking about."
e. …makes the rules."
f. …the weird turn pro."
g. …to procrastinate."
h. …tomorrow will be worse."
i. …you lose."
j. …you never get a busy signal."

ANSWER, PAGE 206

* * * * *

THE STUDIOUS ELVIS

Which of the following was NOT among Elvis' favorite reading material?

a. The Bible
b. *The Prophet*, by Kahlil Gibran
c. *Captain Marvel* comics
d. *MAD* magazine
e. *The Inner Elvis: A Psychological Biography of Elvis Aaron Presley*

ANSWER, PAGE 205

Feb 05/05

N | R
~~|||| |||| ~~
|| ||||
||

SaRah WINS!! SaNa Loses.!! 12-7

WHICH HUNT

Life is full of choices—and some are easier to make than others. Pick the right answer to each question.

SaRah
SaNa

1. **Which group tips better?**
   R Democrats ✓
   h Republicans

2. **Which is larger?**
   The world's largest stalactite
   RN The world's largest stalagmite ✓

3. **Which is faster?**
   The average cough ✓
   RN The average sneeze

4. **Which group eats more sugar?**
   R Smokers ✓
   N Nonsmokers

5. **Which weighs more?**
   R Hot water ✓
   N Cold water

6. **Which last longer?**
   N Red blood cells ✓
   R White blood cells

7. **Which group was first given the right to vote?**
   N R Women ✓
   Native Americans

8. **Which has more caffeine?**
   NR A cup of coffee ✓
   A cup of tea

9. **Which does America have more of?**
   Real flamingos
   RN Plastic flamingos ✓

10. **Which lived longer?**
    N R The oldest spider in history
    The oldest cat in history ✓

11. **Which George Washington portrait is more accurate?**
    N The one on the dollar bill
    R The one on the quarter ✓

12. **Which costs the Coca-Cola company more money?**
    N R Buying the can ✓
    Making the cola

13. **Which group comprises more people?**
    N Americans who own pets ✓
    R Americans who don't

14. **Which does the average housecat have more of?**
    Claws
    NR Whiskers ✓

15. **Which is more likely?**
    N Being born an albino
    R Being born with one blue eye and one brown eye ✓

16. **Which is longer?**
    N R The amount of time between a whale's heartbeats ✓
    The memory span of a goldfish

17. **Which does the average American drink more of per year?**
    N Coffee ✓
    R Beer

18. **Which is faster?**
    The average speed of a golf ball in flight on the PGA tour ✓
    NR The top speed of a champagne cork

19. **Which holiday prompts Americans to buy more candy?**

N R Halloween

Easter ✓

20. **Which lasts longer?**

R N The average color TV set

The average American marriage ✓

21. **Which has more calories?**

N Lard ✓

R Butter

22. **Which moves faster?**

N Pain traveling through the human body

R Cracks traveling through glass ✓

23. **Which do more women say they'd rather be?**

"Brilliant but plain" ✓

R N "Sexy but dumb"

24. **Which body of water is saltier?**

The Great Salt Lake

N R The Dead Sea ✓

25. **Which athletes perform better on colder ice?**

N Hockey players ✓

R Figure skaters

26. **Which litter comprised more animals?**

N R The largest recorded litter of dogs ✓

The largest recorded litter of cats

27. **Which group do mosquitoes prefer?**

R Blondes ✓

N Brunettes

28. **Which is faster?**

R The world's fastest mammal ✓

N The world's fastest fish

29. **Which group is more likely to include their pet in their wills?**

R N Dog owners ✓

Cat owners

30. **Which weighs more?**

N The largest pearl ever found ✓

R The largest gallstone ever found

31. **Which age group is more likely to wear seatbelts while driving?**

R N 18-24 ✓

65 and over

32. **Which is heavier?**

R An English ton ✓

N A U.S. ton

33. **Which comprises more miles**

N R The distance that the average American car will drive in a year

The distance that the average person will walk in their entire life ✓

34. **Which had a longer life expectancy?**

R Cro-Magnon man ✓

N Neanderthal man

35. **Which is colder?**

N R The North Pole

The South Pole ✓

36. **Which group buys more kosher foods?**

R N Jews

Non-Jews ✓

37. **Which hand does more of the typing?**

R The left hand ✓

N The right hand

38. **Which are longer?**

N R Chinese chopsticks ✓

Japanese chopsticks

39. **Which do Girl Scouts sell more boxes of?**

R Thin Mints

N All the other cookie types combined ✓

40. **Which do more people do when asked to participate in a public-opinion poll?**

R Participate ✓

N Refuse

ANSWER, PAGE 207

EXCESSIVE LANGUAGE

Study closely the 35 multi-word phrases on the list below. They may be redundant, but each one is hidden in the grid only once. When you've found the sum total of them all to your complete satisfaction, a hidden message will appear right before your very eyes.

```
A F F E E U Q I N U Y R E V W O T H E G R
R R T R U E F A C T R R R E B M U N N I P
E A D U N D Y T I R O I R P T S R I F A N
D N O B N O M M O C T S U J U A H T I W T
P K H R A S E E R S S A T R E C F L O R E
I C G N P P I E S W I V E L A R O U N D H
M A P F E U N O R T H S M O A T M S M A O
C N D R H N G I K N T E P M A X E E R G N
A D I E I P A D S C S L O S S I N R G F E
R O O E Y H W N O S A E R F U A D D J I S
D R V G L O I N T G P B A D O R G N E R T
N T D I S A P P E A R F R O M V I E W S T
U H N F A E T L R R S O Y E F U T V U T R
T R A T N E L E P L P R A F N S I V T U
N N L V D I D G R P I N E W R E C R U I T
E T L E D R D A E T G U P E E S R T H M H
Z O U L U L O D W T I U R B D E F E L E L
O O N B N W D A Y T I M I X O R P R A E N
R C I O E O L D L E A G E U E S A A N V D
F E S U W W I L L I N G V O L U N T E E R
S M T N O T A O P V S R E S A E L P E R L
```

COMMON BOND
DISAPPEAR FROM VIEW
DROPPED DOWN
END RESULT
FIRST PRIORITY
FIRST TIME EVER
FRANK CANDOR
FREE GIFT
FROZEN TUNDRA
GRE EXAM
HIV VIRUS
HONEST TRUTH

ILLEGAL POACHING
INNER CORE
LATER TIME
NEAR PROXIMITY
NEW RECRUIT
NULL AND VOID
OLD ADAGE
PAST HISTORY
PIN NUMBER
PLEASE RSVP
PUG DOG
REASON WHY

RED RUBIES
REFER BACK
SAND DUNE
SPEED RATE
SWIVEL AROUND
TEMPORARY REPRIEVE
TIME PERIOD
TRUE FACT
VERY UNIQUE
WILLING VOLUNTEER
WITH AU JUS

ANSWER, PAGE 208

I FOUND IT ON EBAY

A small sampling of the wacky items that have been auctioned on eBay. We've provided the opening bid; using the list at the bottom of the page, see if you can figure out what each item went for.

ITEM: A date.
DESCRIPTION: "With our coworker Brady!!! He drives a Miata!!!"
OPENING BID: 50¢   **WINNING BID:** _$5.50_ $6.19

ITEM: Frog purse, made from a real frog
DESCRIPTION: "Be the first person on your block to own a coin purse made out of most of a frog. Rest assured, you'll never be asked for spare change again."
OPENING BID: $1   **WINNING BID:** _$2.75 $255.01_ $5.50

ITEM: A picture of my butt.
DESCRIPTION: "I'm a sexy guy from Florida, you know you want this, you pay shipping if out of USA."
OPENING BID: 75¢   **WINNING BID:** _$1_ $1

ITEM: One pound real Arkansas Civil War dirt
DESCRIPTION: "100% guaranteed to be from the Civil War era. Comes with certificate of authenticity if desired."
OPENING BID: $1   **WINNING BID:** _$6.19_ $2.75

ITEM: Bridal wedding gown
DESCRIPTION: "Very soiled and spotted."
OPENING BID: 99¢   **WINNING BID:** _$2.75_ $15.50

ITEM: Francis D. Cornworth's virginity
DESCRIPTION: "I figured with the latest eBay craze, I'd see exactly how much I could get for my virginity. I live in Miami, FL. If you live in Florida, I could probably meet you halfway up to Orlando. Otherwise you'll have to arrange to meet me."
OPENING BID: $10   **WINNING BID:** _$15.50_ $10 million

ITEM: Muhammad Ali's broken-jaw X-ray
DESCRIPTION: "Used to determine the extent of his injuries following his bout with Ken Norton."
OPENING BID: $9.99 **WINNING BID:** _$10 million_ $255.01

ITEM: Set of 50 "antique" eyeballs
DESCRIPTION: "Lifelike detail; the veins in the eyes are stunning!"
OPENING BID: $50   **WINNING BID:** _$613_ $613

ITEM: The raft Elian Gonzales's family used to flee Cuba
DESCRIPTION: "A genuine piece of American history…sure to be a big moneymaker!"
OPENING BID: $20   **WINNING BID:** _$280_ $280

ITEM: Cadaver bag
DESCRIPTION: "This bag is new, never used. I would have to be a sick freak to sell these used." $15
OPENING BID: $15   **WINNING BID:** _$15_

| $1 | $5.50 | $15 | $255.01 | $613 |
| $2.75 | $6.19 | $15.50 | $280 | $10 million |

ANSWER, PAGE 206

STATE YOUR NAME!

Most state names didn't come over on the boat like 41 Across did. (Oh, don't look! She'll know we're talking about her!) Anyway, most U.S. states proudly bear names taken from Indian words that were already here before you-know-who arrived. Here's a sampler of both…

ACROSS

1 ___ d'Azur
5 Letters on a boom box
9 Eye-boggling painting style
14 Jet black
15 Toothpaste container
16 Taqueria appetizer
17 State whose name is from Chippewa for "grassy place"
19 Comedian Kovacs
20 Prefix with friendly or system
21 Louis XIV, *par exemple*
22 Money for some subways
23 Knuckleheaded
25 State whose name means "red" in Spanish
28 Mr. Turkey
30 Hall-of-Fame pitcher Wilhelm
31 Fire fanatic, for short
34 The top
36 Don't recycle
41 State named after a king of England
43 State name derived from Algonquian for "large prairie place"
45 Got up
46 He or she has ESP
48 Turned on by
49 Do detective work
51 Droop
53 State name from the Choctaw word for "red man"
57 Wooden peg
61 *The Last of* _____ (1973 flick)
62 "What? And give up show ___?"
64 Tic-tac-toe crossing
65 With "Wipes," a throwaway towel
66 State name from the Sioux for "muddy water"
69 Erich Fromme's *The ___ Loving*
70 At any time
71 A bunch of buffalo
72 *Steppenwolf* author Hermann
73 Ancient stringed instrument
74 Long stretches of time

DOWN

1 Bullied
2 Skating "Holiday"
3 Heavyweight fighter Mike
4 Title for an amb.
5 ___ extra cost
6 Country or easy listening, e.g.
7 Wiretapping org.
8 Chess pieces
9 A few
10 Arctic wear
11 Spotted with blemishes
12 Safari sight
13 "Piggies"
18 Popular cookie brand
22 Poodle category
24 Baby carrier?
26 Electrical unit
27 Lerner's Broadway collaborator
29 It follows *avril*
31 Tiger Woods' org.
32 Wood for an archer's bow
33 One of Pooh's pals
35 Texas Instruments competitor
37 Pal
38 Envy is a deadly one
39 Explosive letters
40 Donald Trump has a big one
42 "Grow up!"
44 Time pds.
47 Common street name
50 "Gotcha!"
52 Cutting tool
53 Chicago airport
54 Superman's Earthling family
55 Beach resorts
56 Baseball's Doubleday
58 The one doing the chasing
59 Special newspaper edition
60 Laundry batches
61 Former leader of Iran
63 Concerning
66 Director Brooks
67 Clinging vine
68 *Murder, ___ Wrote*

ANSWER, PAGE 208

YOU'RE GETTING MARRIED IN THE MORNING

Congratulations, you're going to make a lovely bride. You've planned everything down to the last detail, and all according to the following wedding superstitions. What? You don't know about them? You'd better give them a quick read-through and figure out which will bring you the good kind of luck and which will ruin your life forever.

R = Sarah   N = Sana

R | N
~~HH~~ | HHt
|||| ← WINS!!

	Good	**Bad**
1. Picking a date when the moon is waxing (increasing in size)	(R)	N
2. Picking a date when the tide is going out		(RN)
3. Timing the wedding so that it ends in the second half of the hour	(R)	N
4. Scheduling the wedding for early in the morning	RN	
5. Wearing a white wedding dress	(RN)	
6. Wearing a black wedding dress		(RN)
7. Wearing a red wedding dress	R	(N)
8. Wearing your grandmother's wedding veil	(RN)	
9. Looking in the mirror after you've finishing dressing		(RN)
10. Being seen in your veil by anyone but your family before the ceremony		(RN)
11. Wearing earrings	(N)	R
12. Wearing pearls	R	(N)
13. On the way to the wedding:		
a. Seeing lambs, doves, wolves, spiders, or toads	(N)	R
b. A bird flying over your car	(R)	N
c. A pig crossing your path	RN	(RN)
14. A bat flying into the church	(RN)	
15. Crossing the threshold of the church right foot first	(RN)	
16. Making your own wedding dress	N	(R)
17. Making your own wedding cake	R	(N)
18. Eating anything while getting dressed		(RN)
19. Crying	(RN)	

ANSWER, PAGE 208

MIX-UP AT THE HONKY-TONK

Country music expresses universal sentiments like "You Stuck My Heart in an Old Tin Can and Shot It Off a Log." Yeah. For this quiz, we've taken 10 actual country song titles and removed two key words from each one. Can you put the 20 removed words back in their proper places? Everybody down at the honky-tonk would be mighty grateful.

1. "He's Been _____ Since His Wife's Gone _____"
2. "I Don't Know Whether to KILL Myself or Go Bowling"
3. "If Fingerprints Showed Up on hands, Wonder Whose I'd Find on You"
4. "I'll marry You Tomorrow but Let's honeymoon Tonite"
5. "I've Been _____ from the touch of Your Heart"
6. "I've Got the hungries for Your Love and I'm Waiting in Your _____ Line"
7. "Mama Get the hammer (There's a Fly on Papa's Head)"
8. "_____ Me with More Than Your _____"
9. "She Made _____ Out of the _____ of My Heart"
10. "When We Get Back to the _____ (That's When We Really Go to _____)"

BATHROOM	BOWLING	DRUNK	FARM
FINGERPRINTS	FLUSHED	FLY	HAMMER
HANDS	HONEYMOON	HUNGRIES	KILL
MARRY	PUNK	SKIN	TIMBER
TOOTHPICKS	TOUCH	TOWN	WELFARE

* * * * *

7 OF PRESIDENT GROVER CLEVELAND'S NICKNAMES

And none of them very nice. We've encrypted them using a simple letter substitution code, where H might equal T, X equal C, and so on. In this particular puzzle, **the letter substitution remains constant throughout the whole list**. For further instructions and hints on how to solve, see page 7.

1. LSQ   LFFJBFPK

2. RBF   LXJJPTC   BPOQWPO

3. RBF   KXWL   IDCIBFR

4. RBF   ARXJJFK   IDCIBFR

5. RBF   IDFRFOKFD

6. BSA   PUUSKFOUZ

7. XOUTF   VXWLC

YOU'VE GOT JUNK MAIL!

Directions for solving are on page 13.

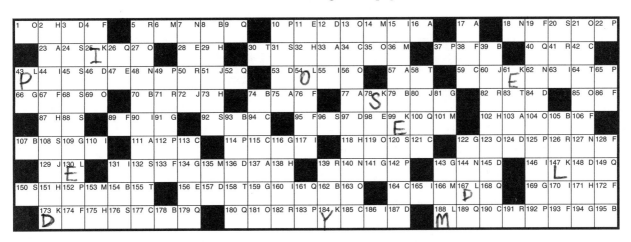

A. Suffering financially or physically (3 wds.)

$\overline{57}\ \overline{75}\ \overline{103}\ \overline{17}\ \overline{16}\ \overline{33}\ \overline{111}\ \overline{77}\ \overline{23}\ \overline{137}$

B. One of the Maritime Provinces (2 wds.)

$\overline{162}\ \overline{178}\ \overline{70}\ \overline{8}\ \overline{39}\ \overline{105}\ \overline{93}\ \overline{195}\ \overline{107}$
$\overline{154}\ \overline{74}\ \overline{79}$

C. Cold soup made with potatoes and leeks

$\overline{177}\ \overline{34}\ \overline{164}\ \overline{121}\ \overline{94}\ \overline{113}\ \overline{190}\ \overline{115}\ \overline{185}\ \overline{42}\ \overline{59}$

D. Nicole Kidman's *Moulin Rouge* flame (2 wds.)

$\overline{148}\ \overline{53}\ \overline{12}\ \overline{46}\ \overline{84}\ \overline{3}\ \overline{187}\ \overline{157}\ \overline{145}\ \overline{97}\ \overline{124}\ \overline{136}$

E. River that flows into the Gulf of Guinea

$\overline{11}\ \overline{28}\ \overline{156}\ \overline{47}\ \overline{98}$

F. John Grisham novel about class-action suits (4 wds.)

$\overline{172}\ \overline{89}\ \overline{174}\ \overline{4}\ \overline{67}\ \overline{76}\ \overline{193}\ \overline{38}\ \overline{86}\ \overline{106}\ \overline{19}$
$\overline{95}\ \overline{128}\ \overline{133}$

G. First photographer to win a Guggenheim Fellowship, 1937 (2 wds.)

$\overline{159}\ \overline{81}\ \overline{134}\ \overline{109}\ \overline{116}\ \overline{91}\ \overline{122}\ \overline{194}\ \overline{141}\ \overline{169}\ \overline{143}\ \overline{66}$

H. Actress who made a splash in *Splash* (2 wds.)

$\overline{138}\ \overline{171}\ \overline{151}\ \overline{32}\ \overline{175}\ \overline{87}\ \overline{2}\ \overline{29}\ \overline{73}\ \overline{102}\ \overline{118}$

I. Duke Ellington's signature song (4 wds.)

$\overline{110}\ \overline{131}\ \overline{117}\ \overline{15}\ \overline{160}\ \overline{170}\ \overline{146}\ \overline{90}\ \overline{63}\ \overline{55}\ \overline{165}$
$\overline{44}\ \overline{186}$

J. They say she had the face that launched a thousand ships

$\overline{129}\ \overline{72}\ \overline{60}\ \overline{80}\ \overline{51}$

K. Where cosmetic shadow goes

$\overline{99}\ \overline{184}\ \overline{61}\ \overline{147}\ \overline{25}\ \overline{173}\ \overline{78}$

L. Sulked about

$\overline{188}\ \overline{54}\ \overline{43}\ \overline{130}\ \overline{167}$

M. Entryway

$\overline{6}\ \overline{153}\ \overline{14}\ \overline{166}\ \overline{135}\ \overline{36}\ \overline{101}$

N. Dover-Calais connector, to travelers

$\overline{62}\ \overline{127}\ \overline{140}\ \overline{144}\ \overline{18}\ \overline{48}\ \overline{7}$

O. Baseball's Mr. October (2 wds.)

$\overline{123}\ \overline{21}\ \overline{163}\ \overline{13}\ \overline{85}\ \overline{27}\ \overline{1}\ \overline{119}\ \overline{35}\ \overline{56}\ \overline{69}$
$\overline{104}\ \overline{181}$

P. Sue Grafton mystery of 1999 (4 wds.)

$\overline{183}\ \overline{112}\ \overline{10}\ \overline{37}\ \overline{152}\ \overline{49}\ \overline{65}\ \overline{125}\ \overline{142}$
$\overline{22}\ \overline{192}\ \overline{114}$

Q. Kids' two-handed card game (2 wds.)

$\overline{149}\ \overline{179}\ \overline{180}\ \overline{26}\ \overline{9}\ \overline{189}\ \overline{161}\ \overline{52}\ \overline{40}\ \overline{100}\ \overline{168}$

R. Boisterous merrymaking; horseplay (2 wds.)

$\overline{82}\ \overline{41}\ \overline{126}\ \overline{71}\ \overline{139}\ \overline{50}\ \overline{182}\ \overline{5}\ \overline{191}$

S. Old-time battle cry (3 wds.)

$\overline{176}\ \overline{132}\ \overline{120}\ \overline{45}\ \overline{150}\ \overline{31}\ \overline{96}\ \overline{20}\ \overline{24}$
$\overline{88}\ \overline{92}\ \overline{68}\ \overline{108}$

T. "Purple Rain" singer/songwriter

$\overline{30}\ \overline{64}\ \overline{83}\ \overline{58}\ \overline{155}\ \overline{158}$

ANSWER, PAGE 209

Sarah R|N ||||
Sana

Shut-out?!
Whaaat;?

WELL, IT'S GOT TO BE *ONE* OF THEM...

Have you ever been asked a question that's so tough, you can't even think of a possible answer? Well, you don't have to worry here, because each of the following questions has a very obvious set of *possible* answers. All you have to do is pick the right one.

1. Which lung is bigger on average?
   NR The left lung
   The right lung ✓

2. Which nostril is more accurate when identifying smells?
   R The left nostril ✓
   N The right nostril

3. Which of Columbus's three ships did he actually sail on?
   N The *Niña*
   The *Pinta*
   R The *Santa Maria* ✓

4. Which blood type did no Native Americans have before Columbus's arrival?
   N O
   A ✓
   B
   R AB

5. Which automobile tire wears out the fastest?
   N The left front tire
   R The right front tire
   The left rear tire ✓
   The right rear tire

6. Which of the Great Lakes is situated entirely within the United States?
   Lake Superior
   Lake Michigan ✓
   RN Lake Huron
   Lake Erie
   Lake Ontario

7. On which finger does the fingernail grow the fastest?
   R The thumb
   The index finger
   The middle finger ✓
   N The ring finger
   The little finger

8. Which sense is the first to go as a person ages?
   Sight ✓
   R Smell ✓
   N Hearing
   Taste
   Touch

9. Which toe only contains two bones, rather than three?
   The big toe ✓
   The second toe
   The middle toe
   The fourth toe
   RN The pinky toe

10. On which night do people watch the most primetime TV?
    Monday
    Tuesday
    Wednesday
    NR Thursday
    Friday
    Saturday
    Sunday

ANSWER, PAGE 209

57 VARIETIES

By the time Henry J. Heinz hit upon that immortal "57 Varieties" ad slogan back in 1892, his company was already selling more than 60 products. But H.J. liked the sound of 57 and so it stuck—right up to the present day when the company, with all its divisions and subsidiaries, now markets more than 1,300 varieties.

We've stuffed the names of 20 Heinz products (some old, some new) into the ketchup bottle below. Words will run horizontally, vertically, or diagonally, but always in a straight line. After you've found all the products in the grid, the leftover letters will reveal a hidden message about an advertising ploy that H.J. Heinz once placed six stories up on a building in a busy section of New York City.

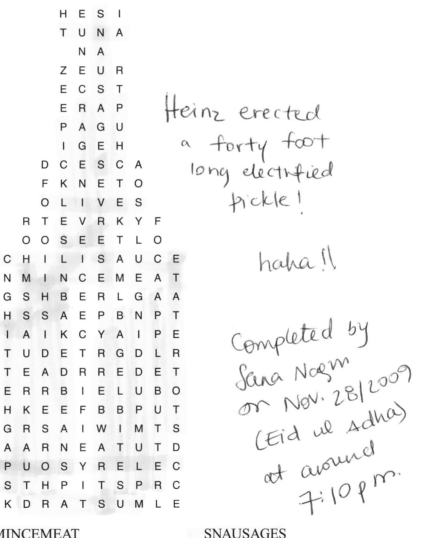

```
                H E S I
                T U N A
                  N A
                Z E U R
                E C S T
                E R A P
                P A G U
                I G E H
            D C E S C A
            F K N E T O
            O L I V E S
          R T E V R K Y F
          O O S E E T L O
        C H I L I S A U C E
        N M I N C E M E A T
        G S H B E R L G A A
        H S S A E P B N P T
        I A I K C Y A I P E
        T U D E T R G D L R
        T E A D R R E D E T
        E R R B I E L U B O
        H K E E F B B P U T
        G R S A I W I M T S
        A A R N E A T U T D
        P U O S Y R E L E C
        S T H P I T S P R C
        K D R A T S U M L E
```

Heinz erected a forty foot long electrified pickle!

haha!!

Completed by Sana Nagm on Nov. 28/2009 (Eid ul Adha) at around 7:10 p.m.

APPLE BUTTER	MINCEMEAT	SNAUSAGES
BAGEL BITES	MUSTARD	SPAGHETTI
BAKED BEANS	OLIVES	STRAWBERRY PRESERVES
CELERY SOUP	PICKLES	TATER TOTS
CHILI SAUCE	PLUM PUDDING	TUNA
HORSERADISH	RELISH	VINEGAR
KETCHUP	SAUERKRAUT	

ANSWER, PAGE 209

LOGO A-GO-GO

The stories behind some very familiar doohickeys.

ACROSS

1 "My word!"
6 Mock
10 Smell horrible
14 *Dog Day Afternoon* director
15 "If ___ a nickel for every..."
16 Target for a grease gun
17 Logo designed as a corporate morale-booster
19 Actor Burns of TV's *Dear John*
20 Early Bloomer?
21 Wrap up
23 Speeder stopper
24 She played Cagney
27 Snap course
29 Start of a magic incantation
33 List ending abbr.
34 NBC premiere of 1975
35 Secluded valleys
37 Ratched's rank in *One Flew Over the Cuckoo's Nest*
42 Ecological logo inspired by a Möbius strip
44 Luyendyk or Unser, e.g.
45 Shaving cut
46 Say "No way!"
47 Avon lady, for short
49 Inquires
50 Churchill Downs libation
53 Helga was his muse
55 Hydrocarbon suffix
56 Seaman
58 Main arteries
63 Milquetoast
65 Logo designed to conjure swiftness
68 Small sewing kit
69 James Bond's alma mater
70 Fields of comedy
71 Apollo's instrument
72 Pulled out the hanky
73 Red sky and black cat

DOWN

1 Joy Adamson's cub
2 Garland's birth name
3 Françoise's friend
4 Big name in computers

5 *New Yorker* cartoonist William
6 Skippy rival
7 Cry of discovery
8 What seconds measure?
9 First family's home
10 Old British rule in India
11 Corporate biggies
12 "Crazy Legs" Hirsch
13 ___ straight face (don't laugh)
18 School founder Elihu
22 Where to get a Grand Slam Breakfast
25 Work ___
26 Broadway backdrop
28 Wellesley graduate
29 Taj Mahal's location
30 "Sacre ___!"
31 Certain quadrilateral (abbr.)
32 "Who'd like to answer?"
34 1960s campus grp.
36 Cursive writing

38 Jibe
39 Sluggers' stats
40 Argyle, e.g.
41 Fraternal group
43 Left Coast baggage tag
48 Sch. auxiliaries
50 Alaska-born pop singer
51 First principle of Kwanzaa
52 Ring-tailed critter of Madagascar
53 Pen pal's request
54 Do-it-yourselfer's bookstore section
57 From square one
59 1/132 of the White House
60 PBS donor's gift
61 Q ___ Quebec
62 Cows and sows
64 Pub "pasty"
66 Sennett policeman
67 Otolaryngologist, briefly

ANSWER, PAGE 210

THE HOPE DIAMOND

Some highlights from the life of the world's most famous cursed jewel. Choose the correct answer from among the selections in parentheses—or else.

Maybe it's just an idol (ahem) rumor, but somewhere in India sits a Hindu idol with a hole in its head, the precise spot where the Hope Diamond rested until **(a British Army officer, a charlatan posing as a guru, an unknown thief)** stole it, thus angering the goddess **(Sita, Minerva, Ishtar)**, who placed a curse on the stone.

In the 1600s jewel merchant Jean Baptiste Tavernier came home from India with a **(45, 76, 112-plus)** carat diamond. The color of the stone was a **(steely gray-blue, pinkish opal, greenish yellow)**. It's long been proposed that it was swiped from the goddess mentioned earlier.

The story goes that Tavernier died a terrible death, **(trampled in a wild horse stampede, eaten by cannibals, torn apart by dogs)**. But before that happened he sold the diamond to France's King Louis **(XII, XIV, XV)** who had it recut to a measly **(28, 45, 67)** carats to show off its flawless brilliance. By the end of his reign, the king had experienced severe military defeats, financial catastrophes, and France was nearly bankrupt.

The king's great-grandson, Louis **(XIV, XV, XVII)** made the diamond a ceremonial jewel. But it's said that his mistress, Madame **(de Pompador, du Barry, Tussaud)** wore it, and you know what happened to her: She eventually **(was squashed by her four-foot-high wig, fell from favor and was executed, was torn apart by dogs)**.

The curse really hit the fan when Louis **(XV, XVI, XVIII)** ascended to the throne. You've probably heard about it—the French Revolution? Anyway, in 1791, the king and his queen, **(Marie Antoinette, Empress Carlotta, Jeanne d'Arc)** went to the guillotine and the diamond went to the national treasury. But not for long. In 1792, it was stolen.

It supposedly made its way into the hands of Wilhelm Fals, a Dutch **(explorer, jeweler, jewel thief)**, who was robbed and murdered by his **(son, butler, eighth wife)**. The killer committed suicide in 1830.

The next recorded owner was wealthy London banker **(Henry Philip, Elizabeth Jane, Bob)** Hope, after whom the diamond was named. When Hope died in 1839—of unrecorded causes—the diamond was passed down to a nephew and eventually to the nephew's grandson, who put it to good use by **(selling it to pay his debts, displaying it at the British Museum, having it set in an engagement ring)**. Years later, an opera singer named May Yohe married into the Hope family. She wore the diamond and died in **(a train wreck, poverty, Hoboken)**.

By 1911, the stone fell into the hands of famous French jeweler Pierre **(Cartier, Tiffany, Cardin)** who sold it to Evalyn Walsh McLean.The jeweler warned Evalyn about the curse, but she never believed in it, even though **(her oldest son was run over and killed, her husband squandered most of her fortune and ran off with another woman, her 19-year-old daughter ran off with a 57-year-old senator who had been Evalyn's own boyfriend, all of the above)**.

One more nonbeliever was the mailman who delivered the Hope Diamond to its final resting place. James Todd told the press he didn't believe in the curse either when they interviewed him after **(his leg was crushed in a traffic accident, his head injured in another, his house burned down, his wife died of a heart attack, his dog strangled to death on his leash, all of the above)**.

Who's the lucky owner of it now? Well, it's housed in the **(Louvre, Smithsonian, British Museum)** so if you're **(French, American, British)**, you are! How's your luck been lately?

HOW DARE YOU, SIR!

Looking for that perfect putdown? Especially one that won't be understood by the ninnyhammer it's intended for because he's bigger than you? You've come to the right place. And don't worry if you're something of a juggins when it comes to words: All it takes in this quiz is a little common sense to match the words (1–12) with their definitions (a–l).

_____ 1. bedswerver

_____ 2. eyeservant

_____ 3. micromaniac

_____ 4. nihilarian

_____ 5. pinchgut

_____ 6. plunderbund

_____ 7. quakebuttock

_____ 8. smellfeast

_____ 9. snivelard

_____ 10. verbigerator

_____ 11. voluptuary

_____ 12. woodpusher

a. A quivering coward
b. One who is so miserly that he or she will not buy food
c. An unfaithful spouse
d. Someone who believes that he or she is very small, or that a part of his or her body has shrunk or is in danger of shrinking
e. A person who deals with things of no importance
f. One who senselessly repeats words
g. A person who sniffs out a meal and shows up uninvited
h. One whose life is given over to luxury and sensual pleasures
i. A person who whines or speaks through his or her nose
j. An inferior chess player
k. One who works only when being watched; a slacker
l. A thieving group of businessmen

ANSWER, PAGE 210

* * * * *

ELVIS' GREATEST HITS

Elvis Presley's first #1 hit was "Heartbreak Hotel" in 1956; his last was "Suspicious Minds" in 1969. Can you build a word ladder, by changing **one letter at a time**, from HOTEL to MINDS in five steps? For example, to build a word ladder from WARM to COLD, the quickest way is: WARM, WORM, WORD, CORD, COLD.

HOTEL
MOTEL
MOTES
MITES
MINES

MINDS

ANSWER, PAGE 209

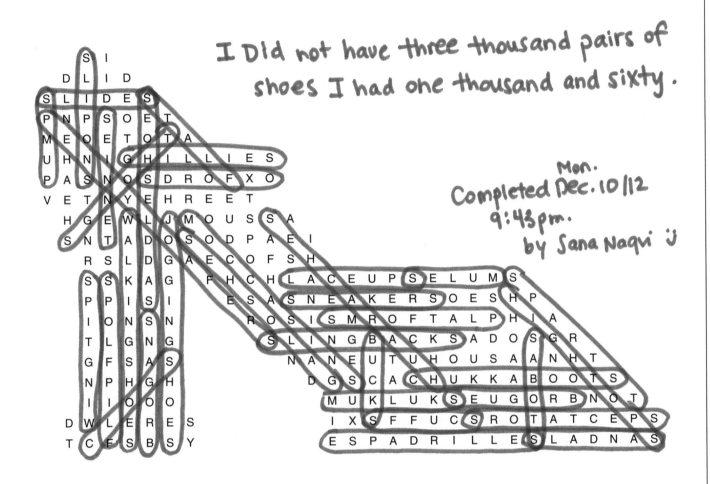

IT'S A SHOE-IN

There's no business like shoe business, especially when you're a collector. We've got 35 pairs of them, hidden in the shoe-shaped grid below, reading across, down, and diagonally. Once you've found them, the leftover letters will reveal a quote by someone who would scoff at our measly 35.

I DId not have three thousand pairs of shoes I had one thousand and sixty.

Mon. Completed Dec. 10/12 9:43pm. by Sana Naqvi

- BROGANS
- BROGUES
- BUCKS
- CHUKKA BOOTS
- CLOGS
- ESPADRILLES
- FLATS
- FLIP-FLOPS
- GALOSHES
- GHILLIES
- HIGHTOPS
- HUARACHES

- JOGGING SHOES
- LACE-UPS
- MOCCASINS
- MUKLUKS
- MULES
- OXFORDS
- PENNY LOAFERS
- PLATFORMS
- PUMPS
- SABOTS
- SADDLE SHOES
- SANDALS

- SCUFFS
- SLIDES
- SLING-BACKS
- SLIP-ONS
- SNEAKERS
- SPECTATORS
- TENNIES
- THONGS
- T-STRAPS
- WALKING SHOES
- WINGTIPS

ANSWER, PAGE 210

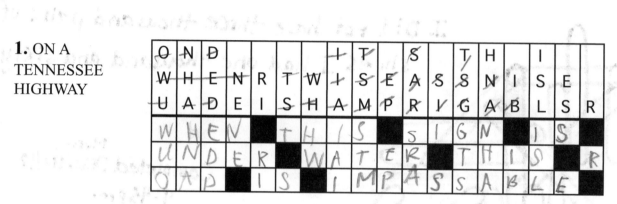

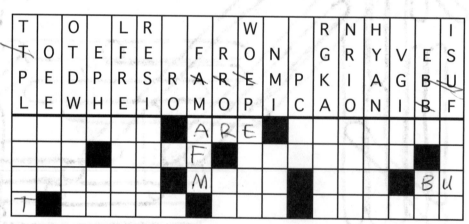

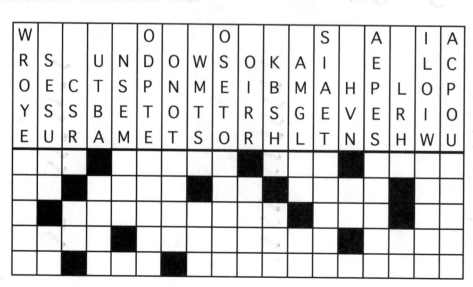

SIGNS O' THE TIMES

Sometimes communication can be difficult…even in your native language. These are actual signs posted across America, but to read them, you have to drop the letters from each vertical column—not necessarily in the order in which they appear—into the empty squares below them to spell out the sign, reading from left to right. Words may wrap around from one line to the next; black squares signify the spaces between words.

1. ON A TENNESSEE HIGHWAY

2. IN A PENNSYLVANIA CEMETARY

3. AT A SHOP IN MAINE

ANSWER, PAGE 209

LOONEY LAWS

There's the law of gravity...the law of the jungle...the law that says you can't ridicule public architecture in Star, Mississippi. If you're a model citizen, you should have no problem with the legal quandaries below.

1. In Austin, Texas, you're breaking the law if you...

   a. go barefoot
   b. ride a tricycle
   c. eat a rattlesnake

   ...without a $5 permit.

2. If you complain about the condition of the street in Baton Rouge, Louisiana, you could be forced to...

   a. walk down the street naked
   b. publicly apologize to the street
   c. fix the street yourself

3. In Lexington, Kentucky, it's illegal to carry...

   a. an ice cream cone
   b. a baby cactus
   c. a dead goldfish

   ...in your pocket.

4. In case you're tempted to do something impossible, you should know that in Santa Ana, California, you're prohibited from...

   a. walking in two directions at once
   b. swimming on dry land
   c. removing your own brain

5. In Massachusetts, goats are not allowed to...

   a. mate with horses
   b. wear trousers
   c. make noise after sundown

6. If you're riding on a train that's passing through North Carolina, you'd be breaking the law by...

   a. joking about the train's speed
   b. illing out federal tax forms
   c. drinking a glass of milk

7. Homemakers in Oregon are legally prohibited from...

   a. wiping their dishes dry
   b. folding their underwear lengthwise
   c. publicly emptying a vacuum cleaner bag

8. In Wilbur, Washington, it's illegal to ride down the street on...

   a. a one-humped camel
   b. a car with no wheels
   c. an ugly horse

9. A resident of Lawrence, Kansas would be breaking the law by...

   a. hiding money
   b. carrying bees
   c. sneezing

   ... in his hat.

I just don't want to do this ↑
Who's making you?

10. In Virginia, you're prohibited from "corrupt practices or bribery by any person...

   a. ...other than candidates."
   b. ...under ten years of age."
   c. ...who should know better."

HOROBOD.

ANSWER, PAGE 210

THE PRICE WAS RIGHT

How do you think you'd do if you were called from the audience to be a contestant on *The Price Is Right*? Not too badly? Well, what if they put you in a time machine first? (In case Bob Barker asks, a good time machine will run you at least $35,000 nowadays.) Try guessing what the following items cost in the given years; count yourself correct if you come within 10 percent of the answer.

1. A bicycle, in 1900
2. A Polaroid camera, in 1960
3. A dozen eggs, in 1920
4. A Cadillac Eldorado, in 1980
5. A pack of cigarettes, in 1910
6. An electric toaster, in 1930
7. A tennis racket, in 1970
8. A coffeemaker, in 1940
9. A grand piano, in 1900
10. A washing machine, in 1930
11. A Mercedes-Benz 220S, in 1960
12. A bottle of Coca-Cola, in 1910
13. A roll of film, in 1950
14. A year's worth of life insurance premiums, in 1920
15. A pound of sirloin steak, in 1970
16. A cordless telephone, in 1980
17. A seven-shot revolver, in 1900
18. A refrigerator, in 1960

ANSWER, PAGE 211

* * * * *

THE 5 MOST-READ U.S. NEWSPAPERS

We've encrypted the top five newspapers in the US using a simple **letter substitution code that remains constant throughout the list**. For hints on how to solve cryptograms, see page 7.

1. LYU DEKK HLNUUL CQFNZEK
   (THE WALL STREET JOURNAL)

2. FHE LQSEP
   (USA TODAY)

3. LYU KQH EZWUKUH LAJUH
   (THE LOS ANGELES TIMES)

4. LYU ZUD PQNV LAJUH
   (THE NEW YORK TIMES)

5. LYU DEHYAZWLQZ TQHL
   (THE WASHINGTON POST)

ANSWER, PAGE 237

THEIR NAMES LIVE ON

The crossword was named for Julius Von Crossword, a 17th-century court servant who was commanded by the king to come up with a new form of entertainment. Okay, not really. But this crossword does feature four people whose names DO continue to live on in just such a fashion.

ACROSS

1 Loses color, like jeans
6 Meat served with mint jelly
10 Slightly open
14 Word on some wanted posters
15 Ending for "switch"
16 Actress Andersson
17 Strikingly original
18 Hourglass material
19 Radar-screen detection
20 British captain who an entire town refused to deal with
23 TV chef Martin
24 Word a toreador adores
25 Sizzling
26 French acrobat who designed his own outfit
32 "Darn it!"
35 Feeble
36 *The Gold-Bug* author
37 Folk wisdom
38 Period of duty
40 Type of page or plate
41 Act like
42 Nonsense author Edward
43 Peachy keen
44 Leader of an 18th-century band of vigilantes
48 Thin swimmer
49 Mr. Potato Head part
50 Dennis Quaid film
53 Texas farmer whose unbranded calves strayed far from the herd
58 Stephen King thriller
59 Go off-course
60 Squander
61 Neighbor of Yemen
62 Author Hunter
63 *Family Matters* nerd
64 Resembling a cube
65 They help preserve preserves
66 Rotini or rotelle, e.g.

DOWN

1 All decked out
2 Wahine's welcome
3 Foyer piece
4 Penultimate word in a fairy tale
5 Popular concert
6 Renter
7 Mideasterner, typically
8 It's simpler than stereo
9 Kathleen Turner drama
10 "Who's on first?" comic
11 Leave at the altar
12 Slightly
13 Forego scissors
21 Annex shape
22 Stick in the oven
26 "Average" guy
27 Spin about
28 Sportscaster Berman
29 Each
30 Apple variety
31 "Home on the Range" animals
32 Common side
33 Kachina doll makers
34 Former pitcher Hershiser
38 Altitude comparison
39 Highlands headwear
40 "What'd ya say?"
42 Stead
43 Make a mess of things
45 Sour, perhaps
46 Pines
47 Part of USNA (abbr.)
50 They may be floppy
51 Small choir
52 Webelos leader
53 Japanese sport
54 Trojan War hero
55 One of the Twelve Tribes of Israel
56 Honey-flavored beverage
57 ___ avis
58 Male swan

ANSWER, PAGE 211

LIFESTYLES OF THE
NOT-YET-RICH-AND-FAMOUS

Sure, they're famous now, but there was a time when these celebs had regular jobs, just like the rest of us. Did we say regular? Some of these occupations border on the bizarro. See if you can guess who did what way back when.

1. Before he hit it big with Black Sabbath—and now his own "family" show on TV—Ozzy Osbourne worked as a:
   a. Dog walker
   b. Slaughterhouse laborer

2. Sean Connery landed his big break as James Bond in 1962's *Dr. No*. But before he was 007, Connery was a:
   a. Coffin maker
   b. Kilt maker

3. If girls just wanna have fun, what the heck was Cyndi Lauper doing as:
   a. A dog kennel cleaner
   b. An obituary writer

4. Before Whoopi Goldberg made her fortune, she made her living as a:
   a. Bricklayer
   b. Funeral home cosmetician

5. Former *Taxi* star Danny DeVito trained to be:
   a. A driving instructor
   b. A hairdresser

6. Ellen DeGeneres has been a standup comic, sit-com star, and talk-show host. But once upon a time she worked as:
   a. An oyster shucker
   b. A tour guide at Graceland

7. Character actor Wilford Brimley, of *Cocoon* and TV's *Our House*, was once employed as:
   a. Bodyguard to eccentric billionaire Howard Hughes
   b. An alligator wrestler

8. Shirley MacLaine probably knows this because she's his sister (and anyway, she's \ psychic), but did you know that Warren Beatty was once employed as:
   a. A rat catcher
   b. A script typist

9. Would you believe that one of Brad Pitt's previous occupations was that of:
   a. Mattress tester
   b. Driver for strippers in a men's club

10. Before he got his big break playing Sonny Corleone in *The Godfather*, James Caan was:
    a. Manager of a pickle factory
    b. A rodeo rider

11. Clark Gable, best known as Rhett Butler in *Gone With the Wind*, once made his living as:
    a. A telephone repairman
    b. A pool hustler

12. British star Jeremy Irons (*Reversal of Fortune, Brideshead Revisited*) was once:
    a. A social worker
    b. An Elvis impersonator

13. As a child, the future general and Secretary of State Colin Powell made 25 cents a week by:
    a. Shining shoes on an Army base
    b. Turning the lights on and off at a synagogue

14. Actor and comedian Denis Leary was once paid to be:
    a. A semi-pro hockey player
    b. A movie usher

15. Sixties sexpot Raquel Welch worked as:
    a. A truck driver
    b. A TV weather girl

16. Before he starred in movie hits like *From Here to Eternity* and *Bird Man of Alcatraz*, Burt Lancaster was employed as:
    a. A lingerie salesman
    b. An auto mechanic

17. Do Ya Think Rod Stewart's Sexy? And would you have thought he was when he worked as:
    a. A circus clown
    b. A gravedigger

18. The Divine Miss M, a.k.a. the divine Bette Midler, was born and raised in Hawaii where she once had a job:
    a. As "chief chunker" in a pineapple factory
    b. Teaching parrots to sing

19. *Cheers* bartender Woody Harrelson says he was a Master of Odd Jobs, which included:
    a. Babysitting and burger flipping
    b. Valet parking and cleaning motel rooms

20. Before he was a movie and TV star (*Menace II Society* and *Cookie's Fortune*), Charles S. Dutton was:
    a. Incarcerated for homicide
    b. A kindergarten teacher

21. *Deliverance* star Burt Reynolds posed nude for *Cosmopolitan* and made millions from *Smokey and the Bandit* et al., but before that he:
    a. Managed a shop that sold sex toys
    b. Was a star running back at Florida State University and was even drafted by the NFL

22. Ronald Reagan is probably the only U.S. president who ever:
    a. Posed nude as an artist's model
    b. Worked as a male nurse in a maternity ward

ANSWER, PAGE 211

* * * * *

NO THANKS, I'M A VEGETARIAN

How did cheese on toast come to be known as Welsh rabbit?

a. "Rabbit" is Welsh slang for ale, which is usually added to the cheese to flavor it.
b. The original name was Welsh rarebit, with "rarebit" translating roughly to "lightly-cooked morsel." Only later did "rarebit" become "rabbit," through phonetic similarity.
c. The name is actually an ethnic slur used by the British—it implies that a Welshman, being both poor and untrustworthy, would be unable to afford meat and would try to pass off cheese as a rabbit.

THE WORST-SELLER LIST

We were halfway through Harold Landy's 1977 book *How to Avoid Intercourse with Your Unfriendly Car Mechanic* (hey, it was either that or James Charles Thomson's *Constipation and Our Civilization*), when it suddenly dawned on us that the title might be, you know, a little *weird*. But it's certainly not the only bizarre title ever published. We've taken 10 of the all-time strangest actual book titles (1–10) and removed some of their key words (a–j). Can you match them back? You'll have to be a little weird yourself to get all of them right.

____ 1. ___: *A New Musical Comedy*
_A_ 2. *Fish Who ___*
____ 3. *___ for Beginners*
____ 4. *The Gentle Art of ___*
____ 5. *Grow Your Own ___*
____ 6. *Harnessing the ___*
____ 7. *The History and Romance of ___ Since the Dawn of Time*
____ 8. *___ of Los Angeles*
____ 9. *Proceedings of the Second International Workshop on ___*
____ 10. *A Toddler's Guide to ___*

a. *Answer the Telephone*
b. *Cooking Wives*
c. *Earthworm*
d. *Elastic Webbing*
e. *Manhole Covers*
f. *Nude Mice*
g. *Swine Judging*
h. *The Baron Kinvervankotsdorsprakingatchdern*
i. *The Rubber Industry*
j. *Hair*

ANSWER, PAGE 212

* * * * *

UNCLE OSCAR'S BIG NIGHT #1

We've taken some Academy Award-winning actors and actresses, and the movies they won Oscars for, which were also Best Picture winners, and mixed them up in two ways. First, we scrambled all the names and titles. Then we mixed up the order in the columns. The numbers that follow each anagram reflect the number of letters in the names; for example, JOHNNY DEPP would be (6 4), can you unscramble the names and titles and match them up again?

The Stars	The Films
1. AIDE TAKEN ON (5 6)	a. A MEDUSA (7)
2. AMERICAN YELLS "HI!" (7 8)	b. HI, LALANNE (5 4)
3. FARRAH MAY RUMBA (1 6 7)	c. MISSING DIVA IS DRY (7 4 5)
4. JEDIS CAN'T SAY (7 5)	d. NOTED MEN FARM TREES (5 2 10)

ANSWER, PAGE 212

TOMB IT MAY CONCERN

In the olden days, families had special symbols carved into gravestones to tell something about their loved ones, or to express their grief, or reflect their belief in eternal life. Here's a list of 30 symbols and what they represent. First find all them in the grid; when you're done the leftover letters will tell you about a few more.

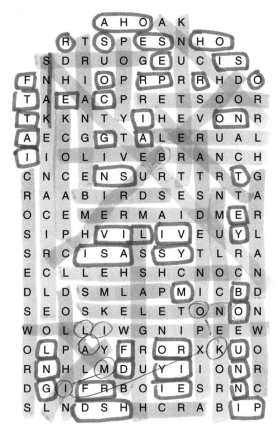

A horseshoe is for protection against evil

Ivy is a symbol for undying friendship.

Completed by Sana Naqvi on Dec. 10/12

ANCHOR: steadfast hope
ARCH: rejoined with partner in heaven
BIRDS: the soul
BROKEN COLUMN: early death
CHERUB: divine wisdom or justice
CONCH SHELL: wisdom
CROSSED SWORDS: life lost in battle
CROWN: reward and glory
DOLPHIN: salvation, bearer of souls across water to heaven
DOVE: purity, love, the Holy Spirit
GARLAND: victory over death
GOURDS: deliverance from grief
HEART: devotion
HOURGLASS: time and its swift flight
LAMB: innocence
LAUREL: victory

LILY: purity and resurrection
MERMAID: the dualism of Christ—half God, half man
OLIVE BRANCH: forgiveness
PALMS: martyrdom
PEACOCK: eternal life
POPPY: eternal sleep
ROOSTER: awakening, courage, vigilance
SHATTERED URN: old age
SIX-POINTED STAR: the Creator
SKELETON: life's brevity
SNAKE IN A CIRCLE: everlasting life in heaven
TREE TRUNK: the brevity of life
TRIANGLE: truth, equality, trinity
WEEPING WILLOW: mourning, grief

ANSWER, PAGE 212

"SPECIAL" EVENTS
FOR TOURISTS

Uncle John is always on the lookout for bizarre tourist attractions, and these events—which attract tens of thousands of people every year—definitely qualify. At least, three of them do. Figure out which one doesn't exist so you'll know which one not to go to this year.

THE BUG BOWL

Location: Purdue University, West Lafayette, Indiana

Background: In 1990, a Purdue professor named Tom Turpin organized a cockroach race on campus to attract students to the field of entomology (the study of insects). Like roach problems, the Bug Bowl grew; today the Bug Bowl draws more than 12,000 people a year. But now there's a new attraction—tourists come not only to look at bugs, but to eat them.

Don't Miss: The exotic menu. Items include: mealworm chow mein; caterpillar crunch (a trail mix made with waxworms); chocolate chirpy chip cookies, which contain crickets; and basic bug quiche, made with sauteed bee larvae "or crickets, depending on your mood." There's also a cricket-spitting contest.

THE REDNECK GAMES

Location: East Dublin, Georgia

Background: The only rule for tourists: If you don't like rednecks, stay home. "Some folks would prefer we didn't have this celebration of being a redneck," says East Dublin mayor George Goruto, "but they don't have to come down here. I mean, man, I wouldn't go to an opera!"

Don't Miss: The Mudpit Belly Flop, the Hubcap Hurl, Bobbing for Pigs' Feet, and the Armpit Serenade—a talent competition in which "pimply-faced prepubescents stick one hand up their T-shirts, flap the other arm and perform flatulent renditions of classics like 'Old MacDonald' and 'Green Acres.'" First prize: "a crumpled can of Bud."

THE WORLD'S LARGEST RATTLESNAKE ROUNDUP

Location: Sweetwater, Texas

Background: Started in 1958 and taking place on the second full weekend of March, the Roundup was inspired by area farmers and ranchers trying to get rid of the rattlers "that were plaguing them and their livestock." About 30,000 people show up each year to hunt and eat rattle-snakes. As of 1996, an astounding 231,636 pounds of western diamondback rattlesnake had been collected.

Don't Miss: The Rattlesnake Review Parade, the Miss Snake Charmer Queen Contest, rattlesnake dances, a snake-handling demonstration, instructions on snake-milking techniques, and, of course, guided snake hunts. After the snakes are gutted and eaten, "the severed heads are adorned with blue wigs and Dallas Cowboys helmets."

THE HAUNTING OF PETTIFOG HOUSE

Location: West Salem, Massachusetts

Background: Pettifog House is a sprawling 103-room mansion on 64 acres that was used as an insane asylum until one night in 1873 when everyone in the place vanished—never to be seen again. Never to be seen alive, that is. According to the legend (and the mansion's spine-tingling press release), every July on the anniversary of that disappearance, the former residents return to haunt the place. And the public is invited.

Don't Miss: The whole event has gotten pretty Disneyfied in the last 20 years or so; if there are any real ghosts still haunting Pettifog House, they're probably drowned out by the special effects. All the same, you can get a good scare in the Carriage House (watch your back), the Haunted Forest (5-plus acres of eyes watching you), and the Deep Dark Dungeon (a maze that some have spent an entire night trying to escape from).

ANSWER, PAGE 212

BRAND X

What's in a brand name? Sometimes more—or less—than you think. See the answer page for further explanations.

ACROSS

1 Lavisher of attention
6 Eschew food
10 "Excuse me..."
14 Overact
15 *A Death in the Family* author
16 Archie Goodwin's boss Wolfe
17 Crowns
18 Milk company named after a brand of cigars
20 27 Across, in Paris
21 ___ spumante
23 Guzzles
24 Appliance company named after its two founders, who designed the first commercial drink mixer
27 Coffee alternative
28 Bobble
29 ___ *Te Ching*
32 Subject of Broadway's *Mamma Mia!*
35 Gladiator's whacker
38 Special occasion
40 An amoeba has one
41 Poet Sylvia
43 Opposed
44 Ness of note
46 In addition
47 Puts to work
48 Famous Bosox outfielder
49 Ending for sex or age
51 Hole-maker
53 Mechanical devices named after a fastener
60 Count ___
61 New Age singer
62 Vardalos of *My Big Fat Greek Wedding*
63 Food storage item named after a tree in India
65 Moved like a 10-month-old
67 Actor Alan
68 Color of unbleached linen
69 Peninsula west of Japan
70 Part of CD
71 Be bombastic
72 Kind of statement

DOWN

1 Swimming pool marking
2 Nick Nolte's hometown
3 Clan emblem
4 Summer in Cannes
5 Kind of purchase
6 Ipso ___
7 Once more
8 Sun. homily
9 More on edge
10 Zany
11 Intensifies
12 Love god
13 "___ *Dieu*!"
19 Cognizant
22 Post office buy
25 Author Calvino
26 Red root veggies
30 Pay to play
31 Singer Redding
32 ___-deucy
33 Actor Lugosi
34 Snowstorms
36 Famous Texas fort
37 Baseball's Ripken
39 Bank's inner sanctum
42 Songwriter Carmichael
45 Follow-up basket
50 Active volcano
52 Hits
54 Sir ___ Newton
55 Hear (of)
56 Data to enter
57 *Año* starter
58 More mature
59 Evil one
60 Indonesian isle
63 Blue
64 Zenith competitor
66 Use your scull

ANSWER, PAGE 213

HOW TO AVOID GETTING HIRED

Three excerpts from real—but hard to believe—job applications. Drop the letters from each vertical column, but not necessarily in the order in which they appear, into the empty squares below them, reading from left to right. Words may wrap around from one line to the next; black squares signify the spaces between words.

1.

M	Y			O	M	T		J	O		S		L	M		E		Y		S	S	
A	E	E	C	O	R	E	A	N	Y	U	T	M	E	E	P	L	E	Y	A	S	S	C
R	P	E	G	P	A	P	V	I	U	S	M	A	D	I	K	M	O	M	E	R	T	H

2.

O		S	S			O		A	Y			D	N			I				V			
S	O	T	E		P	L	E	M	O		F	I	U	R		A		J	M	J	E		
N	N	A	T	R	U	E	B	H	R	F	U	O	G	N	N	E	T	N	O	I	O	C
N	E	V	E	R	J	E	V	E	S	P	Q	I	T	T	O	E	H	A	B	B	S	B

3.

	Y		S			E		K		L	E			I	N	G				A		G
E	E	R	T	V	E	P	R	C	L	B	E	A	I	I	A	D		A	U	U	S	G
E	R	A	T	O	E	O	U	U	B	N	D	T	V	W	G	H	K	U	O	S	O	D
R	T	J	F	B	H	O	S	M	C	O	Y	D	N	I	H	O	N	T	L	F	N	T

ANSWER, PAGE 212

WOULD WE LIE TO YOU?

Who, us? Each question is accompanied by three very likely choices—all having to do with the origins of brand names and identities. Only one is correct, of course.

1. BMW's logo is a circle divided into four sections. What is it supposed to represent?
    a. BMW stands for Bavarian Motor Works, and that's Bavaria's flag. (Or at least, it's Bavaria's flag if viewed through a small round window.)
    b. It represents an airplane propeller. BMW used to manufacture planes as well as cars.
    c. Actually, BMW's original logo was a swastika in a circle. After WWII they discreetly changed it to the current logo, which is vaguely similar but avoids the evil connotation.

2. Where did the brand name Oreo come from?
    a. "Oreo" means *hill* in Greek. The first Oreos were mound-shaped, not flat.
    b. Originally Oreos had orange filling and were named "Orioles," after the black-and-orange birds. After realizing that the color was causing people to assume the cookies were orange-*flavored*, Nabisco switched to white filling and altered the name slightly.
    c. The name doesn't really mean anything. Nabisco execs wanted a name that would appeal to kids, and Oreo was "a fun word to say."

3. Is the guy who founded Kinko's really named Kinko?
    a. Yep. (Hey, there are sillier names.)
    b. No—but he was nicknamed Kinko in college, because of his kinky red hair.
    c. No—the name was meant as an homage to his late father, a carnival performer known as Kinko the Clown.

4. Where did the brand name Sanka come from?
    a. The name is a contraction of *sans caffeine*, which means "without caffeine" in French.
    b. The name is a contraction of *Sri Lanka*, where the beans for Sanka were originally grown.
    c. Sanka is the decaffeinated version of Chase & Sanborn coffee. The original name proposed was "Sancha" (*San*born + *Cha*se), but the founders didn't like the sound of it and suggested "Sanka" as an alternative.

5. Why did the inventor of LifeSavers decide to punch holes in his candies?
    a. He wanted his candies to be visually distinctive from other brands.
    b. He was a notorious tightwad and wanted to save money on materials.
    c. He made his first candies using a defective pill-making machine that left a hole in each one.

ANSWER, PAGE 212

BUMPER STICKERS SEEN AROUND THE UNIVERSE

If you can read these bumper stickers, you're probably following too closely behind a scientist. We've encoded them for your solving pleasure by using a simple letter substitution code; the code is the same for all 10.

1. KOXGMNXGRRVM   FVXXGM   KN   V   PVN
   INTERSTELLAR MATTER IS A GAS

2. PMVTKXJ—KX'N   XBG   RVC
   GRAVITY ITS THE LAW

3. NXIY   AIOXKOGOXVR   QMKZX
   STOP CONTINENTAL DRIFT

4. FIRGAWRVM   UKIRIPKNXN   CGVM   QGNKPOGM   PGOGN
   MOLECULAR BIOLOGISTS WEAR DESIGNER GENES

5. ZMKAXKIO   AVO   UG   V   QMVP
   FRICTION CAN BE A DRAG

6. URVAE   BIRGN   MGVRRJ   NWAE
   BLACK HOLES REALLY SUCK

7. LWVNVMN   VMG   ZVM   IWX
   QUASARS ARE FAR OUT

8. OGWXMKOIN   BVTG   UVQ   UMGVQXB
   NEUTRINOS HAVE BAD BREADTH

9. PMVTKXJ   UMKOPN   FG   QICO
   GRAVITY BRINGS ME DOWN

10. FIRGAWRVM   UKIRIPKNXN   VMG   NFVRR
    MOLECULAR BIOLOGISTS ARE SMALL

ANSWER, PAGE 212

* * * * *

SO YOU THINK YOU'RE A TOUGH GUY?

Who among these actors was NOT considered for the part of Rambo in *First Blood*?

   a. Robert De Niro   c. Paul Newman   e. George C. Scott
   b. Dustin Hoffman   d. Nick Nolte

ANSWER, PAGE 212

PERFECT 10 #1

In this quiz, the 10 statements are *almost* perfect, except that their numbers have been switched around. As a solving aid, we'll tell you that the numbers have been switched in *pairs*—i.e., if the number 1 should replace the 10, the 10 should also replace the 1. (That's just an example, of course.) Can you restore the perfect 10?

It takes **1** minute for a fresh mosquito bite to begin to itch.

The water in one inch of rain is the equivalent of **2** inches of snow.

Baby giraffes can grow as much as **3** inches every two hours.

It takes the average person **4** minutes to fall asleep.

Albert Einstein couldn't read until the age of **5**.

The average female mannequin is **6** feet tall.

Boys are **7** times more likely to stutter than girls are.

The average American home contains **8** pounds of pennies.

Captain Kangaroo won a total of **9** Emmy awards.

A cubic yard of air weighs **10** pounds.

ANSWER, PAGE 213

TALK ABOUT YOUR LIBERAL MEDIA

Small crostic puzzles are solved just like the big ones (directions on page 13) but the first letter of the fill-in words **do not** spell out a hidden message.

1 F	2 E	3 C	4 D		5 E	6 C	7 D	8 B		9 D	10 C	11 F	12 B		13 B	14 A	15 D
16 E	17 F	18 A	19 B	20 D		21 D	22 E	23 F		24 F	25 A	26 B		27 D	28 A	29 E	
30 F	31 D	32 A	33 E		34 B	35 A	36 C	37 E	38 D		39 A	40 B	41 F	42 C	43 D	44 E	45 F

A. Movie or play venue
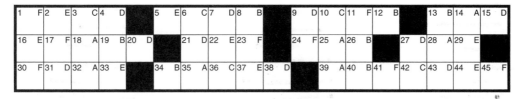
THEATRE
18 25 14 35 39 28 32

B. Critic who had a cameo in *Superman* (2 wds.)
___ ___ ___ ___ ___ ___ ___
40 12 8 13 19 26 34

C. Really smart person
___ ___ ___ ___ ___
42 3 6 36 10

D. Deeply or meaningfully
___ ___ ___ ___ ___ ___ ___ ___ ___ ___
15 7 9 21 31 43 27 20 4 38

E. Smooth Michael Jackson move
___ ___ ___ ___ ___ ___ ___ ___
5 16 22 44 29 2 37 33

F. What con men and magicians practice
___ ___ ___ ___ ___ ___ ___ ___
24 23 41 11 1 45 17 30

ANSWER, PAGE 213

THE FUR SIDE

The innocent-looking kitty below has eaten all 52 of the furry friends listed below. Can you find them in the grid, reading across, down, and diagonally? When you're done, the leftover letters will reveal a fascinating fact about a fiercer furry friend.

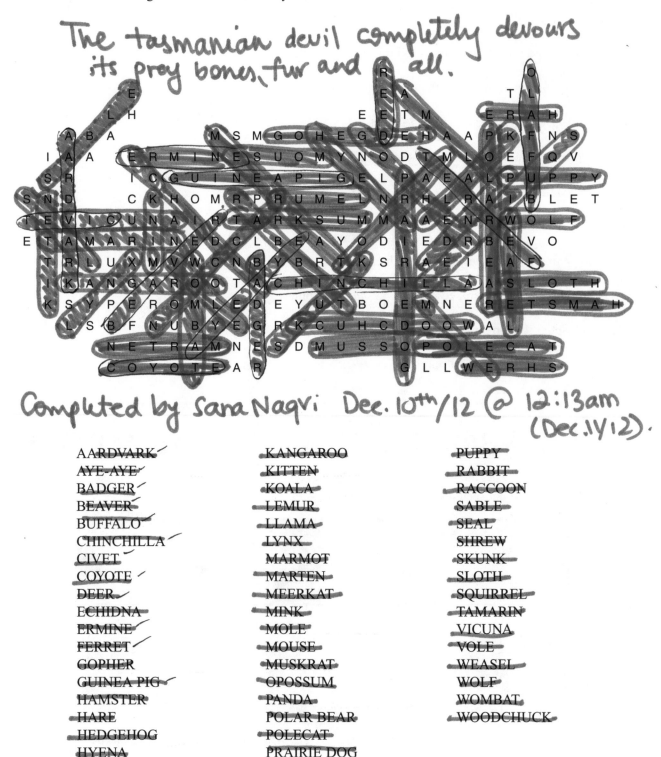

The tasmanian devil completely devours its prey bones, fur and all.

Completed by Sara Naqvi Dec. 10th/12 @ 12:13am (Dec. 11/12).

AARDVARK	KANGAROO	PUPPY
AYE-AYE	KITTEN	RABBIT
BADGER	KOALA	RACCOON
BEAVER	LEMUR	SABLE
BUFFALO	LLAMA	SEAL
CHINCHILLA	LYNX	SHREW
CIVET	MARMOT	SKUNK
COYOTE	MARTEN	SLOTH
DEER	MEERKAT	SQUIRREL
ECHIDNA	MINK	TAMARIN
ERMINE	MOLE	VICUNA
FERRET	MOUSE	VOLE
GOPHER	MUSKRAT	WEASEL
GUINEA PIG	OPOSSUM	WOLF
HAMSTER	PANDA	WOMBAT
HARE	POLAR BEAR	WOODCHUCK
HEDGEHOG	POLECAT	
HYENA	PRAIRIE DOG	

ANSWER, PAGE 213

MR. & MS. QUIZ

The Battle of the Sexes rages on; here's the latest report from the front. Check the appropriate blank to the left of each question when you've figured out which gender is more likely to…

MEN	WOMEN		
_____	✓	1.	…have larger brains?
_____	✓	2.	…have better hearing?
_____	✓	3.	…cry?
✓	_____	4.	…make jokes
_____	✓	5.	…laugh at jokes?
✓	_____	6.	…start a flirtation?
✓	_____	7.	…be nervous on a first date?
_____	✓	8.	…think that they're attractive to the opposite sex?
✓	✓	9.	…believe that "the way to a partner's heart is through their stomach?"
_____	✓	10.	…sleep on the right side of the bed, if married?
_____	✓	11.	…say that sex gets better after marriage?
_____	✓	12.	…blame themselves if sex goes badly?
✓	_____	13.	…commit suicide after an unhappy love affair?
✓	_____	14.	…blame their divorce on the kids?
✓	_____	15.	…spend more time in their car?
✓	_____	16.	…be involved in an auto accident?
_____	✓	17.	…use more shampoo as a teenager?
✓	_____	18.	…use more deodorant as a teenager?
✓	_____	19.	…nap on the job?
_____	✓	20.	…go on a diet?
_____	✓	21.	…feel warmer at a given room temperature?
✓	_____	22.	…rid their bodies of caffeine quicker?
✓	_____	23.	…buy Father's Day cards?
✓	_____	24.	…smile when delivering bad news?

ANSWER, PAGE 214

* * * * *

A CAPONE BY ANY OTHER NAME

Al Capone's older brother Vince Capone…

a. Was a policeman in Nebraska
b. Died in the St. Valentine's Day Massacre
c. Was an opera star at La Scala in Milan

ANSWER, PAGE 212

DONE BY SANA FATIMA NAQVI ON *THURSDAY.* FEBRUARY 04/2010 at 9:53 P.M.

TV OR NOT TV...

…that is the question. Even Shakespeare knew that a one-word title could spell success—even for just one season. See if you can fit all 45 TV shows on the list into the grid, crossword-style.

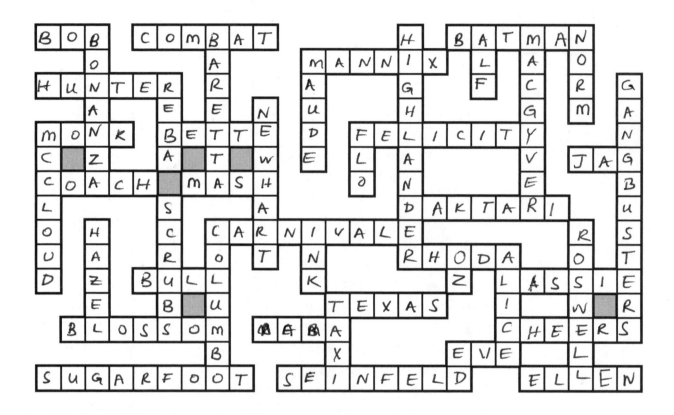

2-letter words	Norm	Combat	8-letter words
Ed	Reba	Hunter	Felicity
Oz	Taxi	Lassie	MacGyver
		Mannix	Seinfeld
		Scrubs	
3-letter words	5-letter words		9-letter words
ALF	Alice		Carnivale
Bob	Bette	7-letter words	Sugarfoot
Eve	Coach	Baretta	
Flo	Ellen	Blossom	10-letter word
Ink	Hazel	Bonanza	Highlander
JAG	Maude	Columbo	
	Rhoda	Daktari	11-letter word
4-letter words	Texas	McCloud	Gangbusters
Bull		Newhart	
Mama	6-letter words	Roswell	
MASH	Batman		
Monk	Cheers		

ANSWER, PAGE 214

EVERYBODY'S A CRITIC!

Uncle John's mother used to say, "If you can't say anything nice…" You know the rest. Obviously, these critics weren't as well brought up as our relatives.

ACROSS

1 Lint collector
5 Crack in the cold
9 His name was from "baby" in Italian
14 Therapist's 55 minutes
15 "Fatha" Hines's real first name
16 Constellation that contains Betelgeuse
17 Gillette razor
18 "Stoney End" songwriter Laura
19 Sign on the treble staff
20 Bette Midler, on Princess Anne: "She loves nature in spite of ___"
23 Drift of popular opinion
24 MapQuest recommendation (abbr.)
25 Cottonwood, e.g.
28 Macadam, e.g.
32 She came out on TV in '97
33 Freebie on long flights
35 Late dictator Amin
36 *Time* critic Richard Schickel, on Betty Grable: "She was… a sort of great ___"
40 Mauna ___
41 Enthusiasm
42 Butler from Charleston
43 Manor settings
46 Belief systems
47 Attack, to a dog
48 John Hersey's *A Bell for* ___
50 Robert Redford, on Paul Newman: "He has the attention span of ___"
56 Where you live
57 Diana, host of *Mystery!*
58 Off-Broadway award

59 Report this to an M.D.
60 Female friend, in Grenoble
61 Calls the game
62 "Ladder" for Rapunzel's swain
63 Fix up
64 Russian rejection

DOWN

1 Warm up
2 Type of IRA
3 Glow of a sort
4 One who gabs too much
5 Gridiron snapper
6 Composer Joseph, called "Papa"
7 Rival of Sure
8 Trudge after a hard day's work
9 Colombia's capital
10 Built like McDonald's sign
11 The ___-High City (Denver)
12 Dutch settler in old South Africa
13 Gershwin's *Concerto* ___
21 Man of Tehran
22 Homely little doll with spiky hair
25 Positive thinker Norman Vincent ___
26 *Stand and Deliver* star
27 Kilt feature
28 Huck Finn's floater
29 *Carmen* composer
30 Archie's missus
31 Reduces the fare?
33 Federal lenders Sallie and Ginnie
34 U.S.N.A. grad's rank

37 It's spoken in Brno
38 Borneo primate
39 From Dayton, originally
44 Comments to the audience
45 Bengal felines
46 Like 45 Down
48 Japanese cartoons
49 "Eat! Eat!"
50 But (Ger.)
51 They say it makes the world go round
52 Streetcar to Soho
53 Do as you're told
54 Long term?
55 Try out
56 Back on board?

ANSWER, PAGE 215

RAW MATERIALS

We now think of mercury mainly as a filler for thermometers, but it was once also ingested as a cure for syphilis. (Gee, we wonder why *that* practice died out.) See if you can match these interesting uses for various materials (1–12) to the materials themselves (a–l).

____ 1. Until 1850, golf balls were filled with…

____ 2. Some hummingbirds hold their nests together with…

____ 3. Among other ingredients, dynamite contains…

____ 4. At weddings during the Middle Ages, you were supposed to pelt the bride and groom with…

____ 5. The filaments for the first electric lamp were made out of…

____ 6. George Washington used to whiten his teeth with…

____ 7. During World War II, the Oscar statues were made of…

____ 8. Sufferers of venereal disease in 16th-century France were advised to eat…

____ 9. In old England, a common hangover cure was to rub one's hands and legs with…

____ 10. Most types of lipstick contain…

____ 11. Goodyear once made a tire entirely out of…

____ 12. Ancient Romans dyed their hair with…

a. bamboo

b. bird droppings

c. chalk

d. chocolate

e. corn

f. eggs

g. feathers

h. fish scales

i. peanuts

j. plaster

k. urine

l. spiderwebs

ANSWER, PAGE 215

* * * * *

STRANGE TOURIST ATTRACTIONS…

…followed by the names of the states they call home (in parentheses). We've encrypted said tourist attractions using a simple **letter substitution code that remains constant throughout the list**. For further instructions and hints on how to solve, see page 7.

1. XDR DBNN SE OSWWRW (KBWDMLCXSL)

2. UDMNMU OSIIMW ZMCBIRXXR XSFIW (HMICMLMB)

3. XDR WSBU XFIRRL OFWRFO (LRK ARIWRT)

4. XDR XRWXMZNR ERWXMHBN (OSLXBLB)

ANSWER, PAGE 215

IT'S IN THE GARAGE SOMEWHERE...

Anyone who owns a garage knows it's not just a place to keep your car. It's a place to store every other darn thing you own that won't fit in your house. And, if you're not careful, a great place to lose things in. See if you can find the 49 items strewn around the garage-shaped grid below. Once you've found them all, the leftover letters will reveal some good advice to remember the next time you pass the hardware store and see that must-have chainsaw in the window.

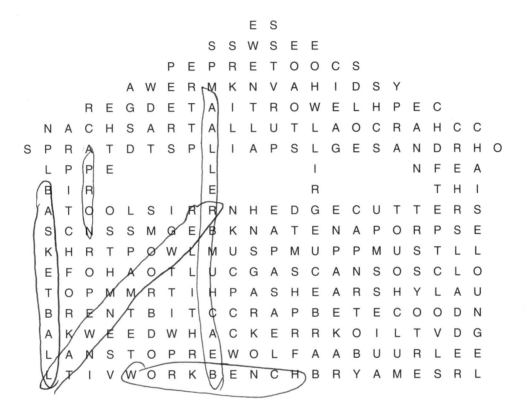

APRON	LADDER	SLED
AUTO	LAWNMOWER	SPADE
BARBECUE GRILL	LIME	SPREADER
BASKETBALL	MULCH	STAKES
BEACH UMBRELLA	OILCAN	SUMP PUMP
BICYCLE	PAIL	TARPS
BOOTS	PAINT	TENT
BROOMS	PITCHFORK	TILLER
BUG SPRAY	PROPANE TANK	TOOLS
CHAISE LOUNGE	RAGS	TOPSOIL
CHARCOAL	RAKE	TOYS
EDGER	ROPE	TRASH CAN
FLOWERPOTS	SAND	TROWEL
GAS CAN	SCOOTER	WEED WHACKER
GLOVES	SEEDS	WORKBENCH
HEDGE CUTTERS	SHEARS	
HOSE	SHOVEL	

ANSWER, PAGE 215

LAWYERS ON LAWYERS

Everyone likes to make fun of lawyers. Even other lawyers. Just choose a letter from each column and drop it into its correct place in the grid.

1.

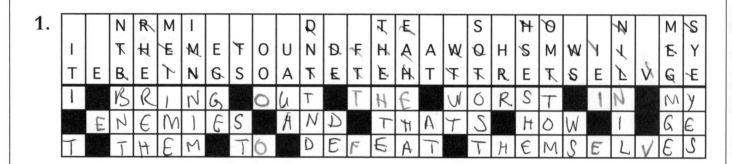

I BRING OUT THE WORST IN MY
ENEMIES AND THATS HOW I GE
T THEM TO DEFEAT THEMSELVES

2.

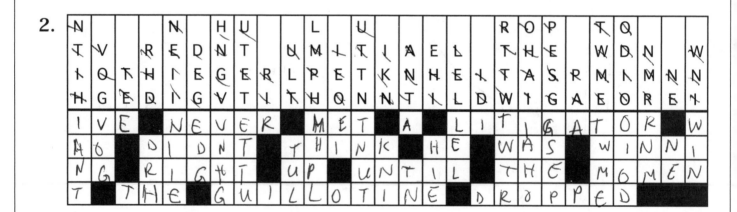

IVE NEVER MET A LITIGATOR W
HO DIDNT THINK HE WAS WINNI
NG RIGHT UP UNTIL THE MOMEN
T THE GUILLOTINE DROPPED

3.

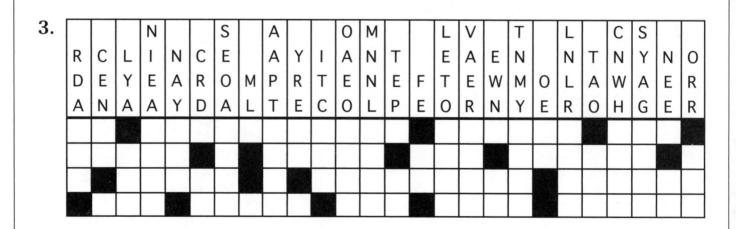

MISFITS

Most of the answers in this quiz are so outrageous, you might have trouble believing that any of them fit their categories—but most of them do. What you're looking for is the **one answer** in each group that **doesn't** fit the category.

1. Additional murder weapons in the original edition of Clue:
   a. Bomb
   b. Axe
   c. Hypodermic syringe
   d. Scissors

2. Celebrity assets covered by insurance policies:
   a. Bruce Springsteen's voice
   b. Jamie Lee Curtis's legs
   c. Julia Roberts's lips
   d. Dolly Parton's chest

3. Landmarks that P.T. Barnum tried to buy:
   a. The Grand Canyon
   b. Pompeii
   c. Niagara Falls
   d. Shakespeare's birthplace

4. Reasons why J. Edgar Hoover might fire FBI agents:
   a. Because their heads were pointy
   b. Because their eyes were shifty
   c. Because their palms were sweaty
   d. Because they looked like truck drivers

5. Side effects of spending time in zero-G:
   a. High risk of kidney stones
   b. Overproduction of blood
   c. Atrophied muscles
   d. Atrophied bones

6. Letters not used by the World Meteorological Institute when naming hurricanes:
   a. Q
   b. U
   c. V
   d. Y

7. Monster movies among the AFI's Top 100 American Films of the 20th Century:
   a. *Dracula* (1931)
   b. *Frankenstein* (1931)
   c. *King Kong* (1933)
   d. *Jaws* (1975)

8. Little-known months to celebrate:
   a. National Sauce Month (March)
   b. National Try a New Hairstyle Month (June)
   c. National Hypnosis Awareness Month (August)
   d. National Toilet Tank Repair Month (October)

9. Alternate suit symbols in standard foreign card decks:
   a. Hearts, leaves, acorns, and bells (Germany)
   b. Roses, shields, acorns, and bells (Switzerland)
   c. Swords, batons, cups, and coins (Italy)
   d. Castles, flowers, coins, and daggers (France)

10. Odd life choices by famous people's sons:
    a. Benjamin Franklin's son became an opponent of American independence
    b. Mahatma Gandhi's son converted to Islam
    c. Jane Fonda's daughter is a registered Republican
    d. R.J. Reynolds's son became an antismoking activist

ANSWER, PAGE 215

HETERONYMS AND PROUD OF IT

Heteronyms are words that are spelled the same but have a different meaning and sound. Take for instance, "The **Polish** maid was just about to **polish** the furniture" or "It's my birthday, so when are you going to **present** me with my **present**?" The blanks equal the number of letters in each missing entry.

1. Hey, King Lazybones, how are you going to _LEAD_ the people if you can't get the _LEAD_ out?

2. A soldier like Rommel, a.k.a. "The _POLISH_ Fox," would never __ __ __ __ __ __ his post.

3. Her arm was turning blue because the bandage was _WOUND_ too tightly around the _WOUND_.

4. Move away from the door: you're standing too _CLOSE_ to it to _CLOSE_ it.

5. After a _NUMBER_ of injections of Novocain, my mouth finally got _NUMBER_.

6. He used to zoom happily all over town, but he _MOPED_ for weeks afters someone stole his _MOPED_.

7. I feel so sorry for that poor _INVALID_; he just found out that his insurance policy is _INVALID_.

8. You big fat _SOW_! You'll reap what you _SOW_!

9. What did you expect, for goodness _SAKE_? You drank way too much _SAKE_ at the sushi bar last night.

10. The town dump was so full it had to __ __ __ __ __ __ __ __ __ __ __.

ANSWER, PAGE 216

PHRASEOLOGY 202

More of those familiar phrases you hear every day...

The completed grid (handwritten answers):

¹L	²E	³N	⁴A		⁵C	⁶A	⁷M	⁸P	⁹Y	¹⁰J	¹¹A	¹²V	¹³A

ACROSS

1 Musical Horne
5 Like gay humor
10 Coffee order in a diner
14 Legal eagle Dershowitz
15 Chicago's airport
16 Eager
17 Spray can output
18 Hotfoots it
19 Welfare payment
20 Phrase from Elizabethan theater describing actions or events that took place offstage
23 White House nick-name in the '20s
24 Eligible to be drafted
25 Get around like Bugs
28 Toothpaste type
30 Muzzle
34 "Do I have to draw you ___?"
36 Fly like an eagle
39 Up, at Shea
41 Phrase from the early textile industry, when primitive machines had a habit of breaking down
44 In the lead
45 Science magazine
46 Gobbles up
47 Two-time loser to Dwight
49 "And so on..."
51 Vietnamese holiday
52 Haughty one
55 Rush
57 Phrase from the stealing and butchering of livestock, when the thief was discovered, literally, with blood on his hands
65 Pulitzer-winning journalist Quindlen
66 Path starter?
67 Phony talk
68 What to do after a bon voyage party
69 Completely wreck the car
70 Radio transmission word
71 James of jazz
72 In an upright position
73 Supply for sweater-making

DOWN

1 Mary had a little one
2 Nobelist author Wiesel
3 Old car that had the first reclining seats
4 Playful prank
5 Like some phones
6 At the drop of ___
7 "___ Man" (Village People hit)
8 Spend time at the mirror
9 Green lights
10 Green gem
11 Company that rings a bell?
12 Loathsome
13 Summer pick-me-ups
21 Long shot at the track
22 Panama, for one
25 "That's a good one!"
26 Where Boys Town was founded
27 Did road work
29 Crazy
31 Oklahoma tribe
32 Vessel in *Das Boot*
33 With 40-Down, the Pepsi challenge
35 Ring out
37 Branch
38 Actress Russo
40 See 33-Down
42 Make ___ for (try to catch)
43 Refuse to reveal
48 Completely
50 KGB adversary
53 Actor/director Welles
54 Ms. Midler
56 Take pleasure in
57 Perry Mason work
58 Med. school subject
59 Apartment in a condo
60 Oscar night party, perhaps
61 College official
62 Aria singer
63 Eternally
64 Bruce or Laura

ANSWER, PAGE 216

THIS LITTLE PIGGIE & PALS

Sure, some animals are smart, but did you know they're multilingual, too? That's right. Pigs in America go, "Oink oink!" but in Germany they go, "Grunz!" and in Russia, they say "Kroo!" Which prompted us to put together a list of 30 international animal sounds and hide them in this little piggie. After you've found them all, reading across, down, and diagonally, the leftover letters will reveal the sounds that chickens make in two different languages.

```
                                            K   K
      T                                   O   U
  H       E           U  U  H  U  H  U  H  U  H  G  K  U  F  R
  E       K       K  V  A  C  K  K  V  A  C  K  R  A  R  N  H  C  G
      H       N  O  K  I  K  I  R  I  K  O  O  R  H  O        C  R
  S       O  W  O  N  W  O  N  A  K  H  I  Z  Y  C  O        O  U
      T  H  B  H  R  E  T  T  A  N  H  C  S  R  E  T  T  A  N  H  C  S
      C  O  O  A  K  O  T  O  G  I  I  R  V  A  H  V  A  H  Z  A  C  C
      O  W  O  U  T  N  H  R  K  C  K  O  K  I  K  O  K  O  V  B
      K  H  B  Q  A  O  O  U  D  C  O  A  K  E  K  F  T  K  O  I  N
      A  O  R  N  A  I  B  H  A  K  I  C  C  N  W  F  A  W  I  T
          O  U  H  N  S  M  W  H  K  A  K  K  A  I  V  W  K  A
              K  A  A  K  K  Q  U  A  K  Q  U  A  K  O
              U  C  C       A  K  A  K  A       G  W  F
              G  A  K                           A  I  F
              W  K  A                           G  K  A
```

Pigs
English: OINK OINK!
French: GROIN GROIN!
Russian: KROO!
German: GRUNZ!

Dogs
English: BOW-WOW!
Swedish: VOFF VOFF!
Hebrew: HAV HAV!
Japanese: WON-WON!
Swahili: HU HU HU HUUU!

Roosters
Russian: KU-KA-RZHI-KU!
Japanese: KO-KI-KOKO!
Greek: KI-KI-RI-KOO!

Frogs
Spanish: CROACK!
German: QUAK-QUAK!
Swedish: KOUACK!
Russian: KVA-KVA!

Ducks
Swedish: KVACK KVACK!
Chinese: GA-GA!
French: GUAHN QUAHN!

Geese
English: HONK HONK!
Arabic: WACK WACK!
German: SCHNATTER-
        SCHNATTER!
Japanese: BOO BOO!

Owls
English: WHO-WHOO!
Japanese: HO-HO!
German: KOH-KOH-A-OH!
Russian: OOKH!

Tweety-birds
French: KWI-KWI!
Chinese: CHU-CHU!

Cats
Spanish, Portuguese, and
German: MIAU!

ANSWER, PAGE 216

BASEBALL NAMES

In *Uncle John's Bathroom Reader Puzzle Book #1*, we ran a quiz called "Basketball Names"—AND THE FANS WENT WILD!!! Well, maybe not wild, but at least sort of enthusiastic. That's why we decided to replay it, this time with baseball team names. Once again, we've thrown you a few curve balls: not all the stories are true. Can you figure out which ones should be pitched?

Los Angeles Dodgers: The streets of 19th-century Brooklyn were full of trolleys—and pedestrians constantly scurrying out of their way. Hence the name of its baseball team: the Brooklyn Trolley Dodgers, later shortened to just "Dodgers." The team moved to L.A. in 1958, to Brooklyn's great chagrin.

Pittsburgh Pirates: Originally known as the Alleghenies (after the nearby Allegheny River), they earned the "Pirates" nickname in the 1890s after stealing a few players from a rival Philadelphia team.

San Francisco Giants: Logging was a big industry in New York back in the late 1800s, and the owner of the New York Gothams wanted to honor the men who provided the wood for their bats. The team almost became the New York Lumberjacks, but instead became the Giants—with Paul Bunyan as their mascot. Paul Bunyan didn't catch on, but the name did, and the team moved to San Francisco in 1958.

Cleveland Indians: The Indians were another team that tore through nicknames early in their career. The Forest Citys, the Spiders, the Blues, the Broncos, the Naps…whew. Player-manager Nap Lajoie loved cigars, and was almost never seen in the dugout without a cigar in his hand. When a lot of Nat's teammates abandoned chewing tobacco for cigars, rival teams joked that they looked like a bunch of cigar-store Indians. Cleveland decided they liked that name and kept it.

Montreal Expos: Given that the reason Montreal was awarded a baseball franchise in the first place was that the 1967 Montreal World's Fair (otherwise known as Expo '67) was such a success, it seemed only fair to name the team in honor of the event.

Cincinnati Reds: When the team was originally formed in 1869, they were the Red Stockings. (What is the obsession baseball teams have with their socks?) That got shortened to the Reds—until the early '50s, when McCarthyism was rampant. No one wanted to be called a "Red" in those days, so the team actually made an official name change, to the Redlegs. When the patriotic panic died down, they quietly switched back to being the Reds.

New York Yankees: Originally called the Highlanders and the Hilltoppers (because their park was located at the highest point in the city), sportswriters grumped about the difficulty of squeezing the long name of the team into headlines. In 1909, a newsman arbitrarily called them Yankees—patriotic slang for "Americans." Around World War I, when jingoistic fervor was at its peak ("The Yanks are coming!"), the team officially became the Yankees.

San Diego Padres: Although they became a major league team in 1969, the Padres had been a minor league team since 1936. Their religious-sounding name was inspired by the original manager's strict rules against drinking, smoking, chewing tobacco, and entertaining ladies in hotel rooms. He quit in a huff after he discovered that every single player was breaking his rules, but there was no corresponding name change to the San Diego Sinners.

ANSWER, PAGE 214

THE SIXTH ELEMENT

Uncle John's sixth sense tells him you're going to like this. Can you complete each list by figuring out what the missing sixth element is?

The 6 Nobel Prize Categories
Peace
Chemistry
Physics
Physiology & Medicine
Literature

Economics

The 6 Layers of the Earth
Crust
Upper mantle
Lower mantle
Outer core
Transition region

inner core

The 6 Wives of Henry VIII
Katherine of Aragon
Anne Boleyn
Jane Seymour
Catherine Howard
Catherine Parr

Anne of Cleves

The 6 Branches of the U.S. Armed Forces
Army
Navy
Air Force
Marines
Coast Guard

National Guard

The 6 Parts of the Circulatory System
Arteries
Arterioles
Capillaries
Venules
Veins

Heart

The 6 Elements in Buddhism
Earth
Water
Fire
Space
Consciousness

Wind

The 6 Categories of Dog Breeds
Working
Sporting
Terriers
Nonsporting
Toy

Hounds

The 6 Hockey Positions
Left wing
Right wing
Left defense
Right defense
Goalie

Centre

ANSWER, PAGE 216

* * * * *

JUKE JOINT

What song is the most popular jukebox song of all time? Here are some hints:

It came out in 1962.
It's a country song, but crossed the barriers into pop.
The singer is a woman.

Crazy — it's a song! by Patsy Cline (a singer) umm who?

ANSWER, PAGE 215

THAT BITES!

Directions for solving are on page 13.

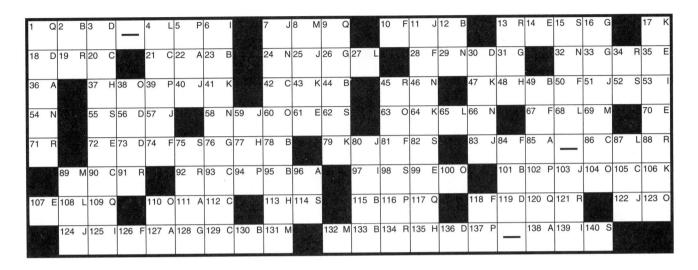

A. Came up with a scheme

$\overline{36}$ $\overline{111}$ $\overline{138}$ $\overline{85}$ $\overline{22}$ $\overline{127}$ $\overline{96}$

B. New York's nickname (2 wds.)

$\overline{130}$ $\overline{101}$ $\overline{49}$ $\overline{133}$ $\overline{78}$ $\overline{23}$ $\overline{12}$ $\overline{115}$ $\overline{2}$ $\overline{44}$ $\overline{95}$

C. Bowled-over kind of feeling

$\overline{93}$ $\overline{20}$ $\overline{90}$ $\overline{105}$ $\overline{129}$ $\overline{86}$ $\overline{42}$ $\overline{112}$ $\overline{21}$

D. Moviedom's *Scorpion King* (2 wds.)

$\overline{136}$ $\overline{56}$ $\overline{119}$ $\overline{18}$ $\overline{73}$ $\overline{3}$ $\overline{30}$

E. Pitches the tent, lights the fire, etc.

$\overline{61}$ $\overline{107}$ $\overline{35}$ $\overline{14}$ $\overline{99}$ $\overline{72}$ $\overline{70}$

F. Ancient Rome's most famous two-lane road (2 wds.)

$\overline{50}$ $\overline{28}$ $\overline{74}$ $\overline{10}$ $\overline{84}$ $\overline{126}$ $\overline{67}$ $\overline{81}$ $\overline{118}$

G. Botanist Burbank

$\overline{76}$ $\overline{31}$ $\overline{128}$ $\overline{33}$ $\overline{16}$ $\overline{26}$

H. One of the D-Day beaches

$\overline{113}$ $\overline{37}$ $\overline{48}$ $\overline{135}$ $\overline{77}$

I. World Series champs in 1987 and 1991

$\overline{97}$ $\overline{139}$ $\overline{125}$ $\overline{6}$ $\overline{53}$

J. Biggest test of a thespian's nerves (2 wds.)

$\overline{25}$ $\overline{83}$ $\overline{57}$ $\overline{51}$ $\overline{59}$ $\overline{40}$ $\overline{7}$ $\overline{124}$ $\overline{122}$ $\overline{103}$ $\overline{80}$ $\overline{11}$

K. Dishes of meat and peppers wrapped in tortillas

$\overline{17}$ $\overline{43}$ $\overline{47}$ $\overline{106}$ $\overline{79}$ $\overline{64}$ $\overline{41}$

L. Title for Bovary or Curie, e.g.

$\overline{4}$ $\overline{87}$ $\overline{27}$ $\overline{68}$ $\overline{65}$ $\overline{108}$

M. Jesse of the 1936 Olympics

$\overline{8}$ $\overline{89}$ $\overline{132}$ $\overline{131}$ $\overline{69}$

N. Cinema style of Malle, Truffaut, Godard et al. (2 wds.)

$\overline{46}$ $\overline{54}$ $\overline{24}$ $\overline{32}$ $\overline{29}$ $\overline{58}$ $\overline{66}$

O. Final stage of a chess match (2 wds.)

$\overline{38}$ $\overline{123}$ $\overline{60}$ $\overline{63}$ $\overline{104}$ $\overline{110}$ $\overline{100}$

P. Big name in keyboards and guitars

$\overline{137}$ $\overline{102}$ $\overline{94}$ $\overline{39}$ $\overline{116}$ $\overline{5}$

Q. Uses a VCR

$\overline{9}$ $\overline{120}$ $\overline{1}$ $\overline{117}$ $\overline{109}$

R. Fast-food side order (2 wds.)

$\overline{19}$ $\overline{88}$ $\overline{45}$ $\overline{71}$ $\overline{92}$ $\overline{121}$ $\overline{34}$ $\overline{13}$ $\overline{134}$ $\overline{91}$

S. Denzel Washington whodunit of 2003 (3 wds.)

$\overline{62}$ $\overline{75}$ $\overline{55}$ $\overline{140}$ $\overline{114}$ $\overline{82}$ $\overline{98}$ $\overline{15}$ $\overline{52}$

ANSWER, PAGE 216

YOU'RE (NOT) THE TOPS

A number of top-three lists are presented below, but there's a hitch: They all contain four items. Can you figure out which item in each list doesn't belong among the tops?

1. The top three condiments in America:
   a. Ketchup
   b. Mustard
   c. Mayonnaise
   d. Salsa

2. The top three products for coupon redemption in supermarkets:
   a. Deodorant
   b. Crackers
   c. Cold cereal
   d. Soap

3. The three most common arrests in America:
   a. Assault
   b. Drugs
   c. Theft
   d. Drunk driving

4. The three most common American town names:
   a. Midway
   b. Oak Grove
   c. Fairview
   d. Hillsdale

5. The three most landed-on spaces in Monopoly:
   a. Go
   b. Community Chest
   c. Illinois Ave.
   d. B&O Railroad

6. The three largest Native American tribes in America:
   a. Navaho
   b. Cherokee
   c. Seminole
   d. Chippewa

7. The three most hated foods in America:
   a. Liver
   b. Yogurt
   c. Tofu
   d. Prunes

8. The top three biting dogs:
   a. German shepherds
   b. Pit bull terriers
   c. Chows
   d. Poodles

9. The top three reasons for being late to work:
   a. Oversleeping
   b. Traffic
   c. Car trouble
   d. Procrastination

10. The top three "problem" employees, according to *The Wall Street Journal*:
   a. "The Know-It-All"
   b. "The Non-Stop Talker"
   c. "The Screamer"
   d. "The Practical Joker"

ANSWER, PAGE 216

* * * * *

WHAT'LL YOU HAVE?

Which beverage does the average American drink more of per year, coffee or beer?

ANSWER, PAGE 217

EXPECT THE UNEXPECTED

Someone's been fooling around with some of our favorite proverbs....

ACROSS

1 Danielle's "darling"
6 More than a tee-hee
10 Wood file
14 Rocker Eddie Van ___
15 "Nope"
16 Actress Falco
17 Marriage acquisition
18 Brussels-based grp.
19 Big co.
20 "Happiness..."
23 Prefix meaning "joint"
26 Gray and Moran
27 "The Devil finds work..."
32 Wide schoolboy collars
33 Randy in Hollywood
34 Designer Vera
35 Sentry
36 Be a nag
40 Nashville sound?
41 Iranian faith
42 "A friend in need..."
45 Ask, as for a loan
47 "Permit me"
48 "Laugh, and the world thinks..."
53 Raison d'___
54 Rover's reward
55 Sinking-ship getaway vessels
59 Makes a collar
60 Novel ending?
61 Disagree
62 ___ were (so to speak)
63 New Mexico art colony
64 Cosmetician Lauder

DOWN

1 ___-Town, a.k.a. the Windy City
2 Solo of *Star Wars*
3 Pipe bend
4 Getting to
5 Toward the center
6 Bonnie of *Jerry Maguire*
7 *Pequod* skipper
8 Rwandan people
9 Sailor's call
10 Guinness Book item
11 Handsome young man
12 Lorelei, for one
13 Notable English diarist
21 Cambodia's Lon ___
22 On the ___ (recuperating)
23 ___ *Good Men*
24 *The Godfather* composer Nino
25 Disney film and video game
28 Sugar substitute brand
29 Avian fertilizer
30 One of the Keys
31 Be of service
35 Presidential inits.
36 Augusta and Olympia, e.g.
37 "Excuse me..."
38 Tabula ___ (blank slate)
39 Feel sorry for
40 Make a video
41 How brutes take things
42 MGM musicals pianist José
43 Least dubious
44 502, to Caesar
45 Laughing ___
46 Wee bits
49 Help in a heist
50 Part of N.B.
51 Keen on
52 Kiki and Sandra
56 Dieter's no-no
57 Half a bad fly
58 Thar-blows link

ANSWER, PAGE 217

PARLEZ-VOUS EUPHEMISMS?

Here's a whole new batch of doublespeak words and phrases used by businesses, educators, advertisers, and even the government (imagine that!). All are 100% guaranteed real. Can you figure out exactly what subjects these euphemisms are tiptoeing around and unscramble the real English translations to their right?

1. "Preventative detention"   J A I L
              AJLI

2. "Creative altruism"   L O V E
             VEOL

3. "Gifts"   M O N E Y
        EOYMN

4. "Weed"   C E N S O R
       ONRCES

5. "Producer cooperative"   C A R T E L
              TALCER

6. "Data transport system"   B R I E F C A S E
               FEEBISCAR

7. "Variance"   M I S T A K E
        KITMESA

8. "Implement a lean concept of synchronous organizational structures"

    F I R E   S O M E O N E
     EIRF   MOOSEEN

9. "Wet deposition"   A C I D   R A I N
           CDIA   NIRA

10. "Personal manual database"   C A L E N D A R
                 DANRECLA

11. "Negative gain in test scores"   D R O P   I N   T E S T   S C O R E S
                   ODPR   NI   ETTS   CESOSR

12. "Uncontained engine failure"   E X P L O S I O N
                 PINLOXSEO

13. "Grief therapist"   U N D E R T A K E R
           DEKRUTNERA

14. "Human kinetics"   P H Y S I C A L   E D U C A T I O N
           SYCLHIPA   CUTEINODA

COMPLETED BY SANA NAQVI ON THURSDAY FEBRUARY 04, 2010 AT 9:58 P.M.

ANSWER, PAGE 217

IT'S FOR YOU, MR. PRESIDENT

In which we take you behind the scenes at 1600 Pennsylvania Avenue.

ACROSS

1 Jets org.
4 Nag, nag, nag
8 Lab containers
14 Wrath
15 Water, to Juan
16 Computer whiz
17 "___ whiz!"
18 Get it off your chest
19 Loretta Young movie of 1936
20 First president to have a 25 Across in his office
23 "___ is human..."
24 Trouble
25 Desktop ringer, briefly
28 President arrested for running down an elderly woman in his carriage
33 Char, as a steak
34 Prefix with surgeon
35 Big dogs, for short
39 Commotion
42 African antelopes
43 Spoken exams
45 Actress Elisabeth
47 President who exercised by playing ping-pong
53 Recede
54 Neither's partner
55 Russian range
57 President who taught his parrot to curse
62 Unanchored
64 That certain something
65 ___-Magnon
66 Civil War battle
67 Space between louvers
68 Balloon filler
69 Stomach problem
70 London's ___ Park
71 Charlotte of *Diff'rent Strokes*

DOWN

1 Dusk to dawn
2 Unencumbered by
3 Ogler
4 Carlsbad ___
5 Teen follower?
6 Little guy
7 Route
8 TV series that starred 29 Down
9 Do not delete
10 Company in Road Runner cartoons
11 Brief, like a Broadway bomb
12 Relatives
13 Bering, for one
21 Victoria's Secret item
22 Possess
26 L'Eggs shade
27 They're born toward the end of 60 Down
29 Actor Berry
30 Taoism founder ___-Tzu
31 St. Pat's people
32 Hosp. readout
35 Actor Rob
36 Man of Oman
37 Uncivilized
38 Camera type, briefly
40 ___ Na Na
41 Switz.'s continent
44 Summon
46 Teach
48 Bridge positions
49 Test for college srs.
50 Annoy
51 Daytona 500 org.
52 Steinem or Estefan
56 Make zzzzzz's
58 African flower?
59 Scrub clean
60 Month named for Caesar
61 Like Death Valley
62 Tempe sch.
63 UPS rival

ANSWER, PAGE 217

IT'S IN THE BAG

Ready for anything: Our carry-all is crammed with 57 very important travel items. See if you can find all of them in the grid, reading across, down, and diagonally. When you're done, the leftover letters will reveal a bit of trivia about another bag you may have heard about.

```
            A  S  P  I  R  I  N
         S  E  U  S  S  I  T  L  E  B
         P  A  N  I  G  H  T  G  O  W  N
   R  A  I  N  H  A  T         P  A  E  A
S  S  P  U  E  K  A  M  A      G  L  W  O
E  T  M  A  G  A  Z  I  N  E   A  L  S  B  R
S  B  A  P  O  T  P  A  L  M  Y   N  E  P  G  D  N  E
S  P  O  R  D  H  G  U  O  C  W  E  B  E  A  T  A  L  O  Z  E  N  G  E  S
A  E  S  R  U  P  G  U  T  C  L  E  N  N  C  S  P  O  R  D  E  Y  E  M  H
L  E  F  I  R  S  T  A  I  D  K  I  T  O  O  R  E  V  N  T  E  D  S  D  A
G  S  T  R  I  H  S  T  O  O  B  J  P  H  M  A  R  E  M  A  C  P  A  A  V
N  M  L  E  W  R  A  I  N  C  O  A  T  P  B  E  T  S  S  B  A  O  R  T  I
U  O  C  A  R  K  E  Y  S  E  T  T  E  L  E  W  O  T  W  M  N  C  I  E  N
S  S  S  C  A  R  F  T  R  A  V  E  L  E  R  S  C  H  E  C  K  S  B  G
S  H  H  O  L  K  E  G  Y  R  L  E  W  E  J  E  S  A  C  Y  G  E  A  O  K
P  A  J  A  M  A  S  S  T  P  H  E  Z  C  Q  D  S  G  O  N  D  T  F  O  I
      A  P  M  I  N  T  S  T  I  E  F  T  H  N  H  E  I  R  O  P  F  K  T
      S  L  I  P  P  E  R  S  R  L  I  S  O  U  O  W  T  E  K  C  A  J
         T  R  O  P  S  S  A  P  L  U  C  H  E  W  I  N  G  G  U  M
         S  O  C  K  S  L  M  S  E  S  S  A  L  G  E  Y  E
```

ASPIRIN	LOTION	ROBE
BELT	LOZENGES	SCARF
BOOTS	MAGAZINE	SEWING KIT
CAMERA	MAKEUP	SHAMPOO
CAR KEYS	MAPS	SHAVING KIT
CELL PHONE	MINTS	SHIRTS
CHEWING GUM	MONEY	SHOES
COMB	MOUTHWASH	SLACKS
COUGH DROPS	NAIL CLIPPERS	SLIPPERS
DATEBOOK	NEWSPAPER	SOAP
EYE DROPS	NIGHTGOWN	SOCKS
EYEGLASSES	PAJAMAS	SUNGLASSES
FILM	PASSPORT	TISSUES
FIRST-AID KIT	PILLS	TOWELETTES
GLOVES	POCKET PC	TRAVELERS CHECKS
JACKET	PURSE	TWEEZERS
JEWELRY	Q-TIPS	UNDERWEAR
KEYS	RAIN HAT	VEST
LAPTOP	RAINCOAT	WALLET

ANSWER, PAGE 217

PLITZ-PLATZ, I WAS TAKING A BATH

When you were a kid, your parents probably told you that trains go "choo-choo" and cars go "beep beep." Well, that's not necessarily true—especially in other countries of the world, where parents tell *their* children something completely different. First, look at the list—from "aah-choo!" to "upsy-daisy"—then check out the way that some other cultures interpret them and fill in the blanks with what Mom and Dad taught you.

AAH-CHOO!   **CHOO-CHOO!**   **KITCHY-KITCHY-KOO!**   **UH-OH!**

BEEP BEEP!   **CHUGALUG!**   **UPSY-DAISY!**   **SPLASH!**

1. _aah-choo_
Portuguese: Ah-chim!
German: Hat-chee!
Greek: Ap tsou!
Japanese: Hakshon!
Italian: Ekchee!

2. _Splash_
Hindi: Dham!
Russian: Plukh!
Danish: Plump!
Spanish: Chof!

3. _choo choo_
Chinese: Hong-lung, hong-lung
Danish: Fut fut!
Japanese: Shuppo-shuppo!
Swahili: Chuku-chuku!
Greek: Tsaf-tsouf!

4. _upsy daisy_
Arabic: Hop-pa!
Italian: Opp-la!
Japanese: Yoisho!
Russian: Nu davai!
Danish: Opse-dasse!

5. _Kitchy kitchy koo_
Chinese: Gujee!
French: Gheely-gheely!
Greek: Ticki-ticki-ticki!
Swedish: Kille kille kille!

6. _Uh oh_
Chinese: Zao le!
Italian: Ay-may!
Japanese: Ah-ah!
Swahili: Wee!
Swedish: Oy-oy!

7. _beep beep_
Chinese: Dooo dooo!
Hindi: Pon-pon!
Spanish: Mock mock!
French: Puet puet!
Japanese: Boo boo!

8. _chug a lug_
Arabic: Gur-gur-gur!
Hindi: Gat-gat!
Hebrew: Gloog gloog!
Russian: Bool-bool!
Chinese: Goo-doo, goo-doo!

ANSWER, PAGE 218

AND IF YOU BELIEVE THAT ONE...

Each group of answers on this page consists of three odd-yet-true facts and one outright lie. Can you spot the lies?

1. **Great moments in marketing**
   a. Diet Pepsi was originally called "Patio Diet Cola."
   b. The frisbee was first called a "Pluto Platter."
   c. The first potato chips were called "Murphy Crackers."
   d. The first TV remote control was called "Lazy Bones."

2. **Mis-stated**
   a. Wyoming Valley is located in Pennsylvania.
   b. The Alabama swamps can be found in New York.
   c. The Colorado Desert is located in south eastern California.
   d. Oregon City is a town in the state of Washington.

3. **How appropriate!**
   a. The first Charmin commercial was filmed in Flushing, New York.
   b. The first man to translate Dante's *The Divine Comedy* into English was named Christian Paradise.
   c. The legendary racehorse Man O' War was only beaten once—by a horse named Upset.
   d. Astronaut Buzz Aldrin's mother's maiden name was Moon.

4. **Explanatory letters**
   a. The Q in Q-tip stands for "quality."
   b. The G in G-string stands for "groin."
   c. The D in D-day stands for "decision." → *stands for Day!*
   d. The V in V-chip stands for "violence."

5. **Animal not-rights**
   a. The koala bear is not a bear. *koala is marsupial*
   b. The Angora goat is not a goat.
   c. The firefly is not a fly. *firefly is a beetle*
   d. The glass snake is not a snake. → *a lizard!!*

6. **The Weirdo of Menlo Park**
   a. Thomas Edison spent his later years working on a machine that would talk to the dead.
   b. Thomas Edison preferred reading in Braille, though he wasn't blind.
   c. Thomas Edison proposed to his second wife in Morse code.
   d. Thomas Edison was afraid of the dark.

7. **What's in a name?**
   a. The "black box" that records cockpit conversations is actually yellow.
   b. Camel's hair brushes use squirrel hair.
   c. There's no actual glass in safety glass.
   d. Crab-eating seals don't eat crabs.

ANSWER, PAGE 218

TOM SWIFTIES

Even if you didn't read Tom Swift books when you were a kid—heck, even if you've never *heard* of him—you still might get a kick out of the punny wordplay based on the overly adverbed style of his books. Here's a typical example: "I love playing hockey," Tom said puckishly.

Now see if you can match each Tom Swifty (1–10) with the adverb (a–j) that goes best with it.

F__ 1. "Hey, these pants are getting too small for me," Tom said...

H__ 2. "I never use that Parmesan cheese that comes in a can," Tom said...

B__ 3. "I took her picture when she wasn't looking," Tom said...

C__ 4. "I've got a great anagram for 'Santa,'" Tom said...

A__ 5. "I've got to buy some new sunglasses," Tom said...

D__ 6. "It's not nice to pull your sister's Barbie doll apart," Tom said...

E__ 7. "Look! I filled in that big crack in the ground," Tom said...

I__ 8. "My office is on this floor," Tom said...

G__ 9. "She's got an apartment in London," Tom said...

J__ 10. "Wow, honey, that's a really big cup you won," Tom said...

a. brightly   c. devilishly   e. faultlessly   g. flatly   i. levelly
b. candidly   d. disarmingly   f. fitfully   h. gratingly j. lovingly

ANSWER, PAGE 218

I CAME, I SEWED, I CONQUERED

Small crostic puzzles are solved just like the big ones (directions on page 13) but the first letter of the fill-in words **do not** spell out a hidden message.

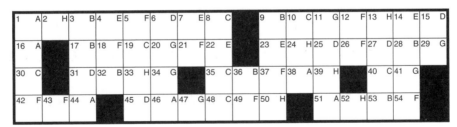

A. Maker of Stratocaster and Telecaster guitars

‾51‾ ‾38‾ ‾1‾ ‾16‾ ‾44‾ ‾46‾

B. Richard Boone's *Have Gun Will Travel* role

‾3‾ ‾36‾ ‾32‾ ‾53‾ ‾9‾ ‾17‾ ‾28‾

C. Center point of the Levant

‾30‾ ‾10‾ ‾35‾ ‾19‾ ‾8‾ ‾40‾ ‾48‾

D. Chewy caramel candy

‾25‾ ‾27‾ ‾31‾ ‾45‾ ‾6‾ ‾15‾

E. Taboos (hyph.)

‾14‾ ‾7‾ ‾23‾ ‾4‾ ‾22‾

F. Chaplin's 1931 final silent film masterpiece (2 wds.)

‾49‾ ‾26‾ ‾42‾ ‾21‾ ‾5‾ ‾12‾ ‾54‾ ‾43‾ ‾18‾ ‾37‾

G. World Series champs of 2002

‾29‾ ‾41‾ ‾34‾ ‾47‾ ‾20‾ ‾11‾

H. Noblest knight of the Round Table

‾13‾ ‾24‾ ‾52‾ ‾33‾ ‾50‾ ‾2‾ ‾39‾

ANSWER, PAGE 218

OUCH!

If you worship at the altar of the lowly pun, you've come to the rite place. (Sorry.) Here are some of Uncle John's favorite groaners, which we've translated into cryptograms by simple letter substitution, where A might equal X, F might equal M, and so on. The code changes from one pun to the next. For further instructions and hints on how to solve, see page 7.

Two Eskimos sitting... JS K PKDKP FNXN MIJAAD, TGQ FINS QIND
IN A KAYAK WERE CHILLY BUT WHEN THEY

AJQ K BJXN JS QIN MXKBQ, JQ CKSP, VXUYJSH USMN
LIT A FIRE IN THE CRAFT, IT SANK, PROVING ONCE

KSW BUX KAA QIKQ DUG MKS'Q IKYN DUGX PKDKP KSW
AND FOR ALL THAT YOU CAN'T HAVE YOUR KAYAK AND

INKQ JQ, QUU.
HEAT IT TOO. hehehe ☺

This guy goes to a costume party... JQNS I RQWH XV SQK EILU. "JSIN
WITH A GIRL ON HIS BACK. WHAT

NSB SBLU IWB AXG?" IKUK NSB SXKN. "Q'O I KVIQH,"
THE HECK ARE YOU? ASKS THE HOST. I'M A SNAIL,

KIAK NSB RGA. "EGN AXG SIFB I RQWH XV AXGW EILU,"
SAYS THE GUY. BUT YOU HAVE A GIRL ON YOUR BACK,

WBYHQBK NSB SXKN. "ABIS," SB KIAK, "NSIN'K *OQLSBHHB."
REPLIES THE HOST. YEAH, HE SAYS THATS MICHELLE

There's a nudist colony... UIA PIYYLZFCBC. BDI IXT YOZ SAO CFBBFZW
FOR COMMUNISTS. TWO OLD MEN ARE SITTING

IZ BJO UAIZB GIAPJ. IZO BLAZC BI BJO IBJOA SZT CSNC,
ON THE FRONT PORCH. ONE TURNS TO THE OTHER AND SAYS,

"F CSN, IXT EIN, JSKO NIL AOST *YSAV?" SZT BJO IBJOA
'I SAY, OLD BOY, HAVE YOU READ MARX?' AND THE OTHER

CSNC, "NOC...F EOXFOKO FB'C BJOCO DFPROA PJSFAC."
SAYS "YES I BELIEVE IT'S THESE WICKER CHAIRS."

Sarah Naqvi →

 WTF

TALKING DIRTY

The king of the schmoozers reveals a dirty little secret. (So *that's* what was going on during all those commercials…)

ACROSS

1 Cable channel for old movie fans
4 Website for bargain hunters
8 Rock trophy?
14 Ripken of baseball
15 Ward who played Helen Kimble in *The Fugitive*
16 Villain of *Uncle Tom's Cabin*
17 Boxing match inits.
18 Use the phone
19 Egg shapes
20 Start of a quip by a late-night host
23 "___ Billie Joe"
24 Possesses
25 Actor Mineo
28 Part 2 of the quip
33 H.H. Munro's pen name
34 Nonsense
35 Hopeful band's tape
39 LBJ was one
42 Cupid, to the Greeks
43 Adjust to change
45 Opinion page, for short
47 End of the quip
54 Golfer's gadget
55 Old Oldsmobile
56 Football legend Bart
57 Author of the quip
61 Daddy Bush aide John
64 ___ *Your Enthusiasm* (HBO comedy series)
65 Health retreat
66 De-creased?
67 Evangelist Roberts
68 Ending for a follower
69 Dracula portrayer
70 Spot
71 Spot

DOWN

1 Exhortation in an ad
2 Manage somehow
3 Four-leafed anomaly
4 Third-party accounts
5 Actor Bridges
6 ___ fair in love…
7 Jodie Foster's alma mater
8 Worldwide
9 Go back to
10 Wide-eyed
11 Hosp. scan
12 Club ___
13 "Roundabout" rock group
21 Travel schedule abbr.
22 "Now I get it!"
25 Use a swizzle stick
26 Gravy Train competitor
27 Levis alternative
29 Sombrero, e.g.
30 Just get by, with "out"
31 President after Johnson
32 *Uno, due, ___…*
35 Bonkers
36 *The Sopranos* actress Falco
37 Designation on a driver's license
38 Select, with "for"
40 Gibbon or gorilla
41 First word in four state names ___
44 Royal seating
46 Render inoperative
48 Musician Menuhin
49 Ending with bass or ball
50 A or B or C, e.g.
51 Timmy's collie
52 Edema, in the old days
53 Overly decorated
57 Mrs. Jupiter
58 Sgts., e.g.
59 Cosmonaut Gagarin
60 Ending with bureau or auto
61 ___ *vous plait*
62 Country next to Braz.
63 Holiday drink

ANSWER, PAGE 218

I DON'T GET IT...

You're not supposed to. That's because we've mixed up the answers to these perfectly awful jokes. It's your job to match each joke (1–10) to its punch line.

1. **Q:** What is the difference between ignorance, apathy, and ambivalence?
   2 **A:** The National Dyslexics Association.

2. **Q:** What do the letters DNA stand for?
   7 **A:** They're making headlines.

3. **Q:** Did you hear about the two antennas that got married?
   8 **A:** Because he was on a roll.

4. **Q:** What's the difference between mashed potatoes and pea soup?
   6 **A:** "Does this taste funny to you?"

5. **Q:** How many narcissists does it take to change a light bulb?
   1 **A:** I don't know and I don't care one way or the other.

6. **Q:** What did one cannibal say to another while they were eating a clown?
   9 **A:** "Migratious."

7. **Q:** Did you hear about the corduroy pillows?
   10 **A:** Repossessed.

8. **Q:** Why couldn't the sesame seed leave the gambling casino?
   3 **A:** The wedding was terrible, but the reception was great.

9. **Q:** What did the bird watcher exclaim when she saw a flock of geese flying south for the winter?
   4 **A:** Anyone can mash potatoes.

10. **Q:** What do you get if you don't pay your exorcist promptly?
    5 **A:** One. He holds the bulb while the world revolves around him.

ANSWER, PAGE 219

* * * * *

HE LOOKS MUCH TALLER IN PERSON

What, if anything, is the significance of the number of steps at the Lincoln Memorial?

   a. There are 16 steps, because Lincoln was the 16th president.
   b. There are 36 steps, because there were 36 states in the reunited Union in 1865.
   c. There are 56 steps, because Lincoln was 56 years old when he died.
   d. There are 72 steps, for no reason except aesthetics.

ANSWER, PAGE 218

STAMP OF APPROVAL

Here's our 37-cents' worth—or whatever the cost of first-class postage is by the time you're reading this. We've listed the names of 25 fabulous women who've been honored with appearances on US postage stamps. Even if you don't recognize what each woman is famous for, we hope you'll recognize them in the grid, reading horizontally, vertically, or diagonally. After you've found them all, the leftover letters will deliver some interesting info about a certain African-American who not only appears on a stamp but who also left her stamp on society.

Madame C.J. Walker became one of America's

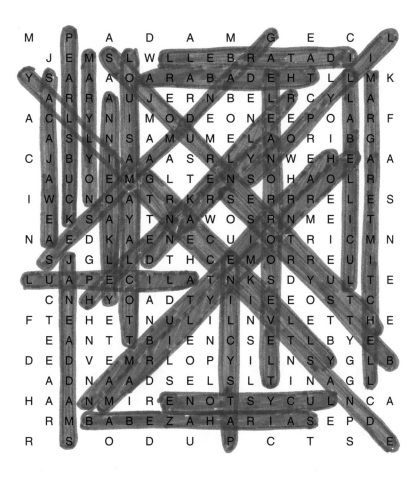

ALICE PAUL
ANNIE OAKLEY
AYN RAND
BABE ZAHARIAS
BETSY ROSS
EDNA ST. VINCENT MILLAY
ELEANOR ROOSEVELT
GRACE KELLY
GRANDMA MOSES
HARRIET TUBMAN
HELEN KELLER
IDA TARBELL
JANE ADDAMS

LILY PONS
LOUISA MAY ALCOTT
LUCILLE BALL
LUCY STONE
MARGARET MITCHELL
MARILYN MONROE
MARY LYON
PATSY CLINE
PEARL S. BUCK
SACAJAWEA
SOJOURNER TRUTH
THEDA BARA

ANSWER, PAGE 220

THE TIME IT TAKES #2

More time-takers. See if you can put them in the correct order, from the least amount to the most amount of time they take.

____ The length of Nolan Ryan's pitching career

____ The time it takes for 3,000,000 gallons of water to flow over Niagara Falls

____ The time it takes for a human muscle to respond to stimulus

____ The time it takes for a mouse to reach sexual maturity

____ The time it takes for a newborn baby's brain to grow 1.5 mg

____ The time it takes for winter to come and go

____ The time it takes to cook a 20-pound turkey at 325 degrees F

____ The time it takes to receive your FBI file after making the appropriate request

____ The time it took for Handel to compose "The Messiah"

____ The time it took to complete the Great Wall of China

ANSWER, PAGE 219

SUDDENLY IT ALL COMES CLEAR

Small crostic puzzles are solved just like the big ones (directions on page 13) but the first letter of the fill-in words **do not** spell out a hidden message.

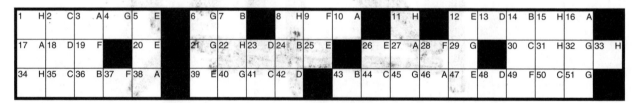

A. Tartness

3 46 27 16 17 10 38

B. The King

36 14 43 24 7

C. Vodka with lime juice and soda

41 44 35 2 30 50

D. Hit song for Joey Dee and Tears for Fears

48 42 13 23 18

E. Follows surreptitiously

5 39 20 25 47 26 12

F. Labors

28 9 49 37 19

G. Relative of a snit (2 wds.)

29 6 45 4 51 21 40 32

H. Taking five, e.g.

33 34 22 11 31 15 8 1

ANSWER, PAGE 219

TOILET TECH

How did we ever get along without these advancements in bathroom technology? Well…just fine, actually. And we'll continue to get along without a few of them, since some of them are made up. See if you can get a handle on which ones.

PLEASE RISE
Of course you're familiar with public toilets that use sensors to determine when to automatically flush for you (and usually fail dramatically). Well, Seth Otway of Leeds, England, has developed a similar device to solve the problem of men who don't lift the toilet seat when, um…when it would be the polite thing to do. Otway's toilet uses a modified face-recognition program to determine when someone is standing still while facing the toilet; when the sensor is triggered, the seat rises automatically (and lowers after flushing, of course).

FAKE

YOU'RE CLEARED TO LAND
You know how, when you wake up in the middle of the night needing to use the bathroom, you always blind yourself when you turn on the light? Brooke Pattee of Lake Forest, California, found a solution: "landing lights" that illuminate the inside of your toilet bowl so you can see it in the dark. The lights are triggered by a sensor in the lid of the toilet, and turned off by an automatic timer.

✓

FLUSHED WITH COLOR
Patricia Lyman, a physical therapist from Orono, Maine, has invented a toilet outfitted with an armrest that monitors your stress level. (The toilet seat contains monitors for your heart rate, body temperature, and amount of perspiration.) If the light in the armrest turns red, you need to relax. But if it stays a soothing blue, you're, um, good to go.

FAKE

IT'S A GAS
The Flatulence Filter Seat Cushion, developed by UltraTech Products of Houston, Texas, contains a hidden carbon filter to absorb any and all unfortunate odors. The company also makes a smaller version of the filter that can be worn inside one's underpants, originally called the "TooT TrappeR."

✓

TIME FOR A CHANGE
Karel Dvorak of Toronto, Ontario, has devised a disposable diaper that contains a moisture sensor, which sets off a flashing LED light when wetness is detected. The sensor touches the baby's skin and can detect the change in electrical conductivity when the diaper becomes wet, which sets off the blinking light in a way that we're sure makes perfect sense to scientists.

✓

BLOWIN' IN THE WIND
The Japanese love their high-tech toilets; this one is just your standard combination toilet/bidet with a heated seat and a remote control. Oh, that's not enough? It also includes a hot-air dryer that will gently dry you while you remain seated. Robot dancing girls not included.

✓

ANSWER, PAGE 219

MURPHY, JR.

More of those predictable situations brought to you by 10 anonymous but brilliant observers of the laws of nature. You know the score: Take the first part of each truism (1–10) and match it with its proper ending (a–j).

_____ 1. Harrison's Postulate: "For every action…

_____ 2. Hutchin's Law: "You can't out-talk a man who…

_____ 3. Issawi's Law of Progress: "A shortcut…

_____ 4. Johnson and Laird's Law: "A toothache tends to start…

_____ 5. Johnson's Law: "If you miss one issue of any magazine…

_____ 6. Kirby's Comment on Committees: "A committee is…

_____ 7. Murphy's Paradox: "Doing it the hard way…

_____ 8. Perkins' Postulate: "The bigger they are…

_____ 9. The Queue Principle: "The longer you wait in line…

_____ 10. The Salary Axiom: "A pay raise is just large enough to increase your taxes and…

a. …it will be the issue that contained the article, story, or installment you were most anxious to read."

b. …on Saturday night."

c. …knows what he's talking about."

d. …the greater the likelihood that you are standing in the wrong line."

e. …is the longest distance between two points."

f. …the harder they hit."

g. …just small enough to have no effect on your take-home pay."

h. …the only life form with 12 stomachs and no brain."

i. …there is an equal and opposite criticism."

j. …is always easier."

ANSWER, PAGE 219

* * * * *

WHERE'D YOU GET THOSE DUDS?

There's no telling what you'll find in the back of the closet. Answer T for true or F for false.

____ The TUXEDO is named for Tuxedo Park, New York, where it made its debut at a country club in 1886.

____ STETSON is a variation on "State Son," honoring Texans who died at the Alamo.

____ PAJAMAS were named for the Central American town they originated in: Pajama, Costa Rica.

____ NEGLIGEE is from the Latin "neglegere," meaning "to neglect," referring to housework.

____ SHOES were named for, and first popularized by, Japanese leather merchant Shu' Ze.

ANSWER, PAGE 221

PAGE ONE

Not all stories begin "Once upon a time…"

The completed crossword grid (filled-in answers):

M	I	R	A		D	A	Y	O		M	E	D	I	C
E	T	A	L		O	V	U	M		O	R	A	T	E
A	C	T	I		T	I	R	E		R	O	U	S	E
T	H	E	G	R	E	A	T	G	A	T	S	B	Y	
			N	I	L			A	M	A				
E	M	S		F	L	O	G		O	L	D	H	A	T
N	A	T	A	L		G	L	E	N		A	I	D	E
T	H	E	S	E	C	R	E	T	G	A	R	D	E	N
R	E	E	K		H	E	A	T		D	E	E	P	S
E	R	R	A	T	A		M	A	U	I		R	T	E
			A	R	C			M	E	D				
T	H	E	C	O	L	O	R	P	U	R	P	L	E	
T	R	I	C	K		A	L	A	I		A	L	U	M
N	A	C	H	O		M	E	I	R		C	A	L	M
T	Y	S	O	N		P	O	L	E		O	N	L	Y

ACROSS

1 Actress Sorvino
5 Harry Belafonte hit
9 Doc
14 Inclusive list ender
15 Egg cell
16 Speak to a crowd
17 Start of a play
18 Michelin, e.g.
19 Give a morning nudge
20 Novel that begins: "In my younger and more vulnerable years, my father gave me some advice that I've been turning over in my mind ever since."
23 Zilch
24 Org. for 9 Across
25 Long dashes, to a typesetter
28 Whip
31 Outdated
36 Relating to birth
38 ___ plaid
40 Assistant
41 Novel that begins: "When Mary Lennox was sent to Misselthwaite Manor to live with her uncle, everybody said she was the most disagreeable-looking child ever seen."
44 Smell to high heaven
45 Miami team
46 Oceans, to Longfellow
47 Printing goofs
49 Hawaiian island
51 U.S. 1, for one
52 Circle part
54 Sea that fronts the Fr. Riviera
56 Novel that begins: "You better not even tell nobody but God."
64 Halloween option
65 Jai _____
66 Grad
67 First bite of a Mexican meal
68 One-time Israeli premier Golda
69 At peace
70 Mike or Cicely
71 Peary's destination
72 "If ___ I had known…"

DOWN

1 Spam, e.g.
2 Poison ivy symptom
3 Size up
4 Set straight
5 "No kidding!"
6 Sneaker brand
7 Mongolian tent
8 The ___ Man (Charlton Heston movie)
9 Human, to Shakespeare
10 Cupid
11 Slap on the paint
12 ___-bitsy
13 So-so grade
21 Marksman's weapon
22 In the midst of
25 Between, in Blois
26 Politically Incorrect host Bill
27 Take the wheel
29 Fairy tale monster
30 Shine
32 Have the guts
33 One who's not "It"
34 Skillful
35 Jittery
37 "___ silly question..."
39 Butch and Sundance's girlfriend Place
42 One of Xavier Cugat's exes
43 "Ta-ta!"
48 Add
50 Call the strikes
53 C-shaped tool
55 Harry Potter's nemesis Malfoy
56 Cafeteria item
57 Guzzler's sounds
58 Repeat
59 Fake butter
60 Racetrack fence
61 Think ahead
62 Quiet interlude
63 Will & Grace won one in 2003
64 Explosive stuff

completed by Seema Rizvi
S. Rizvi
Sana Naqvi

ANSWER, PAGE 221

at 2:27 am on Friday Feb. 05th/2005.

FICTIONARY

In *Uncle John's Ahh-Inspiring Bathroom Reader*, we presented the winners of the annual *Washington Post* contest that asks readers to come up with alternate meanings for various words. We've taken 20 of the best and hidden them in the gargoyle (see the list for "gargoyle"'s punny definition). After you've found all the capitalized words in the grid, the leftover letters will reveal one more word and its brand-new meaning.

```
            L       K
            Y       C
            M       O                       R
        E P I E T N                         C
        A T H E I S M A             R E
        N A F S T G I O N       H I D
        S F T H C N E B E       L S X A
        O I   F I E F T         H A O N
    C A T   L H T A F       F T D D A
  E L Y O G R A G E N L     R Y R A L
O U R E C T I T U D E A X I F E R P
    A R E N U A D E B M A Y D A S
  D   A B N S L L D G B O E N L P E
  E Y O U L D T E L C O E D M S A E
    B C A R C I N O M A R B E Z B
        A G C C K O G A S
        A A E A P L A A
        P T E P T L S
        F O E L O E T
      M O R T A R W E
    E R I N N U E N D O
```

ABDICATE (v.) to give up all hope of ever having a flat stomach

ATHEISM (n.) a non-prophet organization

BALDERDASH (n.) a rapidly receding hairline

CARCINOMA (n.) a valley in California, notable for its heavy smog

COFFEE (n.) one who is coughed on

ESPLANADE (v.) to attempt an explanation while drunk

EYEDROPPER (n.) a clumsy optometrist

FLABBERGASTED (adj.) appalled over how much weight you've gained

FLATULENCE (n.) emergency vehicle that transports the victims of steamroller accidents

GARGOYLE (n.) an olive-flavored mouthwash

INNUENDO (n.) an Italian suppository

INSTIGATOR (n.) do-it-yourself reptile kit. Just add water.

LAUGHINGSTOCK (n.) an amused head of cattle

LYMPH (v.) to walk with a lisp

MORTAR (n.) what tobacco companies add to cigarettes

PARADOX (n.) two physicians

PREFIX (n.) the act of completely breaking a partially broken object before calling a professional

RECTITUDE (n.) the dignified demeanor assumed by a proctologist immediately before he examines you

SEMANTICS (n.) pranks conducted by young men studying for the priesthood

ZEBRA (n.) ze garment which covers ze bosom

ANSWER, PAGE 221

PROVERBIAL WISDOM

Funny proverbs from far, far away.

ACROSS

1 Soothing botanical
5 Swedish car
9 Exit huffily, with "out"
14 Titanic sinker
15 Church alcove
16 Voice for most opera heroes
17 Do a number
18 Santa checks it twice
19 Like a hair shirt
20 Proverb from Madagascar: "If it is not a boy it will be a girl," says the...
23 Feed bag morsel
24 Plain dwelling
25 Surgical knife
29 Fashions
33 Bridge fee
34 Inspiring poet for *Cats*
37 Actress Gardner
38 Proverb from Morocco: Every beetle is a gazelle in the...
42 Zugspitze, for one
43 Pentagon VIP.s
44 Other, in Oaxaca
45 Damsel's grateful cry
47 Oxford university
50 Yoga position
53 The ones with the power
54 Proverb from the Fijis: Listen to the wisdom of the...
59 Richie Cunningham's pal ___ Malph
60 French state
61 Gabor and Marie Saint
63 Fibber or Travis
64 Where icicles start
65 MasterCard alternative
66 Outlaw Belle
67 British gun
68 What's more

DOWN

1 Six-pack, to gym rats
2 Norse mariner Ericson
3 "Yes ___?"
4 Chinese appetizers
5 Military gesture of respect
6 You could hear ___ drop
7 Goodwill, perhaps
8 Entertainer Midler
9 Concealed weapon in Renaissance Italy
10 Big name in tea
11 Fairy tale opener
12 Jay of *Jerry Maguire*
13 Get too personal
21 Spigot
22 Kind of bath salts
25 Word with iron or engine
26 With a coquettish look
27 First Hebrew letter
28 *Star Wars* princess
30 Actress Christine
31 Tinker-Chance link
32 Teasdale and Gilbert
35 West Point grads
36 "This ___ sudden!"
39 Start of a 2000 George Clooney film title
40 Cappuccino topping
41 1983 Indy 500 winner
46 Runaway bride?
48 Lend an ear
49 Brian of rock
51 Fonda flick ___ *Gold*
52 Attack
54 Diplomat's skill
55 Gymnast Korbut
56 Sock away
57 Bad to the bone
58 Back talk
59 Realtor's ad abbr.
62 ___ Paulo

THAT'S WHY THEY CALL IT TRIVIA

Because it doesn't get any more trivial than this.

1. Singer-songwriter Luther Vandross started playing the piano at age 3. Then there's this:
    a. He originally wanted a career in synchronized swimming.
    b. His middle name is Ronzoni, after the spaghetti.
    c. He used to make his living reading tarot cards.

2. Little-known fact about best-selling author Danielle Steel:
    a. She invented the Wonderbra.
    b. She is a ouija board fanatic.
    c. Two of her ex-husbands were convicts.

3. "Wanted to be a veterinarian" and "middle name is Fiona" are both true of:
    a. Queen Latifah
    b. Julia Roberts
    c. Rosie O'Donnell

4. Rapper Eminem:
    a. Failed ninth grade three times.
    b. Dropped out of Harvard just before graduation.
    c. Has a doctorate in political science.

5. Comedian/actor Chris Rock:
    a. Was discovered by Eddie Murphy during open-mike night at a New York comedy club.
    b. Once worked as a tattoo artist at Coney Island.
    c. Won $53,000 on *Celebrity Jeopardy!* at the age of 28.

6. Tom Cruise got his big start by dancing in his briefs in *Risky Business*, but he also:
    a. Once purchased 129 cows for his ranch in Australia.
    b. Enrolled in a seminary at age 14 to become a priest.
    c. Studied ballet with Cindy Crawford.

7. Quote from pop singer Tori Amos:
    a. "I had amnesia once or twice."
    b. "Why are our days numbered and not, say, lettered?"
    c. "I have vivid memories of being a prostitute in another life."

8. Something you may not have known about Alicia (*Clueless*) Silverstone:
    a. Her mother was a Russian gymnast who defected during the 1972 Olympic Games.
    b. She won MTV's Villain of the Year award in 1993.
    c. She was once engaged to an Elvis impersonator.

9. Which of these fascinating facts about Demi Moore is true:
    a. She was born Demetria Guynes.
    b. She was engaged to Emilio Estevez.
    c. She and Bruce Willis were married by singer Little Richard.

10. Lisa Kudrow, Phoebe on *Friends*, is something of a pool shark. She also:
    a. Graduated from Vassar with a degree in sociobiology.
    b. Sang with the Mormon Tabernacle Choir.
    c. Plays blindfold chess.

11. Regis Philbin's co-host and former *All My Children* actress Kelly Ripa has:
    a. A five-year supply of lip gloss.
    b. A 4-inch-long tattoo of a flower on the inside of her left ankle.
    c. Two separate rooms in her house for her collections of Barbie and Ken dolls.

12. Find the true statement about famed shock-jock Howard Stern:
    a. He knitted baby booties for each of his three daughters.
    b. He established a college scholarship "for left-handed women broadcast majors with nice…you know."
    c. He was once fired for referring to his station management as "scumbags" while on the air.

13. At age 10, Leonardo DiCaprio was turned down by a talent agent for having a bad haircut, but he survived the snub. Later in life, he won a suit against:
    a. His parents for mismanaging his money.
    b. A stalker who stole his car, kidnapped his dog, and tried to enter his house by disguising herself as a pizza delivery girl.
    c. *Playgirl* magazine to block publication of unauthorized nude photos.

14. Quote from actress Kate (*Almost Famous*) Hudson:
    a. "I like to look nice and dress nice. I'm very Betty Crocker."
    b. "I like to cook. I'm really interested in killing things and eating them."
    c. "I wanted to be Barbie and I was as opposite to Barbie as you could get."

15. Actress Mira (*Mighty Aphrodite*) Sorvino is fluent in:
    a. Italian
    b. Swahili
    c. Mandarin Chinese

16. Before she married Matthew Broderick, Sarah Jessica Parker lived with one of these three men for seven years:
    a. Robert Downey Jr.
    b. Harry Connick Jr.
    c. Buddy Hackett Jr.

ANSWER, PAGE 222

HOOPING IT UP

Whether you're a diehard basketball fan or someone who can't tell a free throw from a finger roll, you can still take a shot! Match the basketball lingo (1–20) with its meaning (a–t).

___ 1. Aircraft carrier

___ 2. Belly up

___ 3. Brick

___ 4. Curtain time

___ 5. East Cupcake

___ 6. Fire the rock

___ 7. French pastry

___ 8. Garbage man

___ 9. Garbage time

___ 10. Hatchet man

___ 11. Ice

___ 12. Kangaroo

___ 13. Leather breath

___ 14. Nose bleeders

___ 15. Shake and bake

___ 16. Submarine

___ 17. Suburban jump shot

___ 18. Three-sixty

___ 19. Wheel and deal

___ 20. Wilson sandwich

a. Showy move where the player dunks the ball while spinning in a full circle

b. The point in the game where there is no way in the world that one of the teams can come back and win

c. A player who's such an incredible jumper that everyone figures he can't be entirely human

d. Get underneath a player who's just gone up for a jump, in an attempt to knock him off balance

e. Shoot very well

f. A player who targets the star players on the other team and tries to foul them out of the game

g. Terrible shot that's tossed without any aim and often hits the backboard with a "thunk"

h. Make amazing offensive moves, then pass the ball to a teammate

i. The "big gun" on a team, a powerful player who's brought in to win the battle

j. Players who jump so high that you almost expect the altitude to affect their sinuses

k. The end of the game, when players toss the ball up without any grace or skill

l. A player who never gets fazed on the court, always staying "cool"

m. Where the easiest-to-beat opposing team hails from

n. What a player "eats" when a shot is blocked right back in his face; also known as a "Spalding sandwich," "Rawlings sandwich," etc.

o. Sign that a player has just had a shot blocked right back in his face

p. Get chest-to-chest with your opponent while playing defense

q. A player who can only seem to make shots when there's no one guarding him

r. A classic shot using perfect form, used by players who grew up playing a less physical game

s. Use every move and fake imaginable to get the ball to the hoop

t. The act of making an easy shot look tough, and a tough shot look even tougher than it is

ANSWER, PAGE 223

IT'S A DOG'S LIFE

A few canine quotes for dog lovers. If you need directions on how to solve this puzzle, see page 5.

1.

WOMEN AND CATS WILL DO
AS THEY PLEASE AND MEN
AND DOGS SHOULD RELAX A
ND GET USED TO THE IDEA

2.

TO A MAN THE GREATEST B
LESSING IS INDIVIDUAL L
IBERTY TO A DOG IT IS T
HE LAST WORD IN DESPAIR

3.

I'VE SEEN A
A QUICKLY

AM

ANSWER, PAGE 246

LITTLE THINGS MEAN A LOT MORE

More of those itty-bitty items we can't live without. Are these the real stories? Put your T's and your F's where they belong.

_____ **Ballpoint Pen:** Invented by a Hungarian who manufactured them in a factory in France that was eventually taken over by the famous British pen-making company, Parker, Ltd.

_____ **Cellophane:** The inventor was trying to make a stainproof tablecloth and came up with the first clear food wrap instead.

_____ **Electric Blanket:** Based on the electric heating pad, the prototype was made of 18 heating pads sewn together.

_____ **Miniature Golf:** Invented by an unusual man who loved his family as much as he loved playing golf. This way he could get his golfing fix and be with the wife and kiddies, too.

_____ **Paper Towels:** When a defective roll of toilet paper—too heavy and very wrinkled—arrived at the Scott company's mill, somebody had the bright idea to sell it as paper towels.

_____ **Scotch Tape:** 3M invented it especially for Detroit automakers to use for painting their two-tone models. The automakers thought 3M had skimped on the tape, so they called it "Scotch" tape ("Scotch" being synonymous with "cheap" at the time). The name stuck, even if the tape didn't.

_____ **Shopping Carts:** The idea didn't catch on right away—shoppers were used to carrying their own baskets around a store—so the inventor (who was also the market owner) hired some phonies to push the carts around and pretend they were shopping. That did the trick.

_____ **Vending Machine:** It dispensed one stick of chewing gum for a penny, and was such a success when it made its debut in 1902 at a New York City subway stop that the police had to be called in to tame the unruly mob.

_____ **Wire Coat Hanger:** When a worker at the Timberlake Wire and Novelty Company arrived at work and found that all the coat hooks were taken, he twisted some wire into what looked pretty much like the ones we use now—and proceeded to hang up his coat.

_____ **Yo-yo:** The word "yo-yo" means "come-come" in Tagalog. It was invented in the Philippines where it was used as a hunting weapon.

ANSWER, PAGE 223

* * * * *

HERE'S THE DEAL...

Which of the following is NOT a variation on the game of poker?

a. Change the Diaper
b. Screwy Louie
c. Linoleum
d. Mexican Sweat
e. Lady in a Closet

ANSWER, PAGE 222

ROOM FOR RENT UPSTAIRS

And four other ways to say someone's stupid.

ACROSS

1 Hound sound
4 Defoe's lost hero
10 Give a hoot
14 "Do Ya" band, for short
15 Inheritance
16 ___-Day vitamins
17 Greek cross
18 His belt doesn't go through ___
20 Moral no-no
21 Spanish "kings"
22 Nettle
23 Happy expression
25 Monopoly quartet (abbr.)
26 Her sewing machine's ___
31 Balky beast
34 Reading room
35 A pop
36 Italian wine region
37 Poop out
38 Montreal nine
39 Goblet feature
40 Nevada town that hosts the annual National Cowboy Poetry Gathering
41 Bridal wear
42 Seat belt feature
43 Scale notes
44 He has an intellect rivaled only by ___
46 Chess pieces
47 Scruggs or Hines
48 On the briny
51 Bikini is one
54 Dr. Seuss's *You're Only ___ Once!*
57 She's proof that evolution can ___
59 Long-jawed fish
60 "Holy smokes!"
61 They may be grand
62 Brian of rock
63 Raimi and Rayburn
64 Give the thumbs-up
65 Part of a gym count

DOWN

1 They're laid with a bookie
2 Jai ___
3 Zealous reformers
4 Spell out carefully
5 Give in
6 Like Lena the Hyena
7 Fill full
8 Folk singer Phil
9 CBS logo
10 Ring-tailed critters, for short
11 Auth. of much verse
12 Auctioned car, often
13 ___ Rawlins of *Devil in a Blue Dress*
19 Best shortening for pie crusts
24 Ritzy Beverly Hills drive
25 Sideline cries
26 Blender maker
27 Helping handily
28 Caster of spells
29 Part of R.E.M.
30 School for little Parisians
31 Important adviser, to some
32 Great bargain
33 Ninnies
36 Mary of *The Maltese Falcon*
38 Author Hunter
42 Least fresh
44 Paraphernalia
45 Mandela of South Africa
46 Puts a patch on
48 Many moons
49 Forum wrap
50 *The King and I* setting
51 Rara ___
52 Faculty socials
53 Novelist Sarah ___ Jewett
55 Between the dotted lines?
56 Smith Brothers bit
58 Fed. pollution watch-dog

ANSWER, PAGE 223

WOODSTOCK III

We've signed up 46 rock acts with only one thing in common: their names consist of one word. See if you can fit them into the grid, crossword-style.

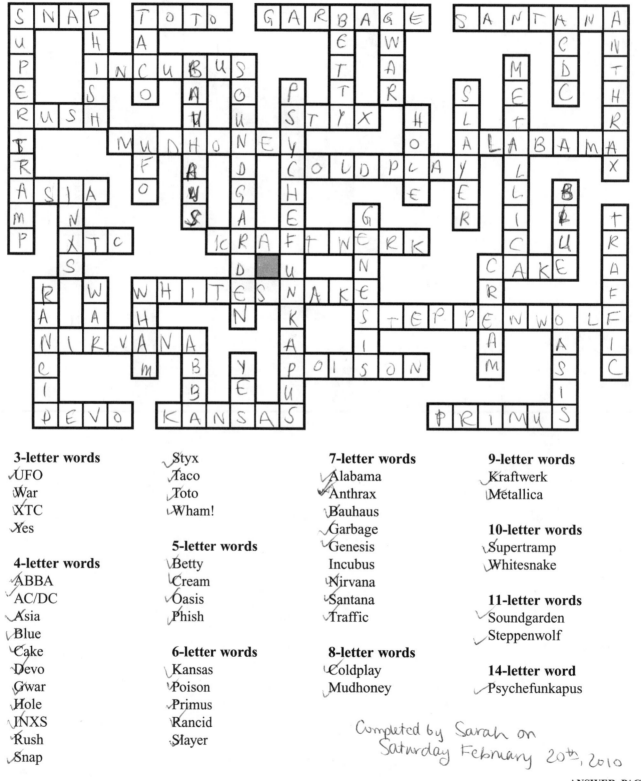

3-letter words
UFO
War
XTC
Yes

4-letter words
ABBA
AC/DC
Asia
Blue
Cake
Devo
Gwar
Hole
INXS
Rush
Snap

Styx
Taco
Toto
Wham!

5-letter words
Betty
Cream
Oasis
Phish

6-letter words
Kansas
Poison
Primus
Rancid
Slayer

7-letter words
Alabama
Anthrax
Bauhaus
Garbage
Genesis
Incubus
Nirvana
Santana
Traffic

8-letter words
Coldplay
Mudhoney

9-letter words
Kraftwerk
Metallica

10-letter words
Supertramp
Whitesnake

11-letter words
Soundgarden
Steppenwolf

14-letter word
Psychefunkapus

Completed by Sarah on Saturday February 20th, 2010

ANSWER, PAGE 223

WHAT'S THE WORD?

We use them, and understand them, but where do they come from?

ACROSS

1 Shape formed by a garden arbor
5 Title for the leader of Qatar
9 Type of joint
14 Hotel reservation
15 Haile Selassie, the ___ of Judah
16 "Get ___!"
17 Word meaning "we do not know" in Latin, and used as the name of a stupid lawyer in a popular 1615 play
19 Money in Iran
20 Hosp. readout
21 Wallach of *The Magnificent Seven*
22 Noah's landfall
23 Lifted, in a way
25 Word derived from Latin meaning "a person clothed in white"
28 Golfer Ernie
30 Final musical passage
31 Therefore
34 Panthers of the Big East Conf.
36 Croc's kin
41 Word derived from Greek for "snare, trap, or stumbling block"
43 Word meaning "little jumping flea" in Hawaiian
45 Small role for a big star
46 Move along easily
48 Canned
49 Worker for J. Edgar Hoover
51 Neighbor of Swe.
53 Word from a Malay phrase meaning "man of the forest"
58 Shadow
62 Popular Van Gogh picture
63 Morsel in a feed bag
65 *Arabian Nights* bird
66 More standoffish
67 Word from ancient Greece meaning "to train naked"
70 *The Status Seekers* author Packard
71 Castle ditch
72 *Bus Stop* playwright
73 Broadway show backer
74 Quite positive
75 Tiger's pocket items

DOWN

1 Sign of spring?
2 Thesaurus man
3 Michael Crichton novel set in Africa
4 Health ins. option
5 Carrier to Tel Aviv
6 Do an impression of
7 Gambling chit
8 Hosp. employees
9 Event for Figaro
10 Epic of the Trojan War
11 Miss America's crown
12 Note equivalent to D-sharp
13 Remainder, in Rouen
18 A movie may be on it
22 Recipe direction
24 Sierra ___
26 Pretend to be
27 Still in the sack
29 Place for sweaters?
31 Computer key
32 Panasonic rival
33 Bit of cheesecake, c. 1945
35 ___ ease (twitchy)
37 Dream interrupter
38 Dallas cowboy?
39 Cheer for flamenco dancing
40 Embarrassed
42 Crude poetry
44 Barbie's boyfriend
47 "...___ sesame seed bun"
50 Greek consonants
52 "I'm ___ here!"
53 Three-time AL batting champ Tony
54 Puerto or Costa follower
55 Ding-___
56 Caroline, to Ted
57 Garciaparra of the Red Sox
59 Pickling liquid
60 Makeup item
61 Pinnacles
64 A penny, e.g., in a piker's game
67 Baseball VIPs
68 Last word of the golden rule
69 Command to Fido

ANSWER, PAGE 222

HOBO LINGO

The grid below is based on one of the secret signs that—back in the good old days of the Depression—hobos would chalk on posts, barns, and railroad buildings to give their fellow knights of the road a warning. This particular triangle with hands sticking out and upraised warned that, "This homeowner has a gun—run!"

Hobos had their own language, too, some of which is listed below. Find all 17 capitalized words or phrases in the grid, and when you're done, the leftover letters will reveal another bit of hobo slang.

```
                          T
                        H E O
      C               K A J B O                       O
    S E   O           F N C A T             R     L A
      D             I A H O M N W             L
    A   O         S B U T H W U S E         U     A
          G C K C I T S E L D N I B
          G K R A M Y S A E M I
        C A I O R O A D K I D U P
      M D C A N N O N B A L L G R E
    M U O D S T I U C S I B R A E P S
    M C O W C R A T E S U O H G I B A
  M T I N O O M E H T H T I W R E V O C
  Y E G G N I P P I D Y E N O H O N C A X R
```

BANJO: a small portable frying pan

BIG HOUSE: prison

BINDLE STICK: a small bundle of belongings tied up with a scarf, handkerchief, or blanket hanging from a walking stick

BULL: a railroad cop

CANNONBALL: a fast train

CHUCK A DUMMY: pretend to faint

COVER WITH THE MOON: sleep out in the open

COW CRATE: a railroad stock car

DOGGIN' IT: traveling by bus

EASY MARK: a hobo sign, or "mark," that identifies a person or place where one can get food and a place to stay overnight

HONEY DIPPING: working with a shovel in a sewer

KNOWLEDGE BOX: a schoolhouse, where hobos sometimes sleep

ROAD KID: a young hobo who apprentices himself to an older hobo in order to learn the ways of the road

RUM DUM: a drunkard

SNIPES: other people's cigarette butts; "snipe hunting" is to go looking for butts

SPEAR BISCUITS: to look for food in garbage cans

YEGG: the lowest form of hobo—one who steals from other hobos

ANSWER, PAGE 224

THE CLASSIFIEDS

Uncle John loves the classified ads. Why, just last week he picked up a Toyota hunchback for only $2,000, and a four–poster bed that's "perfect for an antique lover." Here are a few more unintentionally funny ads we just couldn't resist mentioning. Each has been encrypted into a different letter-substitution code. And look! Uncle John's already getting a head start on you. Better hurry!

For further instructions and hints on how to solve, see page 7.

1. *GIRL WANTED TO ASSIST MAGICIAN IN CUTTING*
   NQBX CPSEFK EJ PIIQIE RPNQAQPS QS AWEEQSN-

   OFF HEAD ILLUSION. BLUE CROSS AND SALARY
   JYY-DFPK QXXWIQJS. *VXWF *ABJII PSK IPXPBH.

2. *MIXING BOWL SET DESIGNED TO PLEASE A COOK*
   ULDLBO TVXF CPY NPCLOBPN YV GFPMCP M EVVW

   WITH ROUND BOTTOM FOR EFFICIENT BEATING
   XLYJ HVQBN TVYYVU SVH PSSLELPBY TPMYLBO.

3. *OPEN HOUSE: OD SHAPERS TON N SA ON FREE*
   EVHM YEPNH: *IEWC NYDVHKN, AEMTML NDJEM. XKHH

   COFFEE AND DONUTS
   SEXXHH DMW WEMPAN.

4. *NORDIC TRACK: THREE HUNDRED DOLLARS*
   *HMVUEO *FVDOW: *FPVYY PGHUVYU UMCCDVN.

   HARDLY USED CALL CHU Y
   PDVUCZ GNYU. ODCC *OPGXXZ.

5. *FREE PUPPIES: HALF COCKER SPANIEL HALF*
   THBB FQFFJBU: AGVT NZNOBH UFGDJBV, AGVT

   SNEAKY NEIGHBOR S DOG
   UDBGOR DBJKAMZH'U EZK.

Completed by Sana Naqvi on Feb. 19/2010 at 1:43am! (So really its Sat Feb. 20)

ANSWER, PAGE 222

* * * * *

SOME DAY...

What's the only day of the week whose name has an anagram? And what is it?

MONDAY (DYNAMO!)

ANSWER, PAGE 215

BIG SPENDERS

Directions for solving are on page 13.

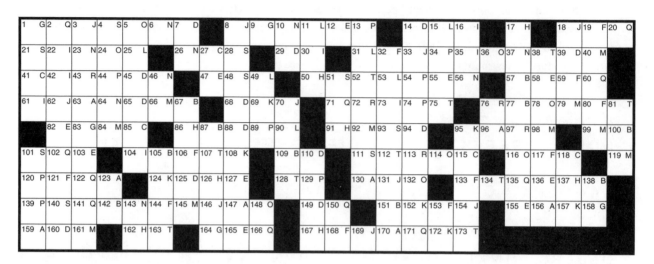

A. *ER* star born in Hollywood (2 wds.)

$\overline{170}\ \overline{159}\ \overline{96}\ \overline{156}\ \overline{130}\ \overline{123}\ \overline{147}\ \overline{63}$

B. Lopez-Clooney film adapted from an Elmore Leonard novel (3 wds.)

$\overline{105}\ \overline{77}\ \overline{151}\ \overline{142}\ \overline{57}\ \overline{109}\ \overline{87}\ \overline{67}\ \overline{100}\ \overline{138}$

C. Ventured into the kiddie pool

$\overline{41}\ \overline{27}\ \overline{85}\ \overline{115}\ \overline{118}$

D. Recent TV portrayer of Rex Stout's Archie Goodwin (2 wds.)

$\overline{45}\ \overline{65}\ \overline{88}\ \overline{110}\ \overline{68}\ \overline{14}\ \overline{94}\ \overline{125}\ \overline{160}\ \overline{7}\ \overline{149}$
$\overline{29}\ \overline{39}$

E. Husband-and-wife sleuth show of the 1980s (3 wds.)

$\overline{165}\ \overline{55}\ \overline{58}\ \overline{155}\ \overline{127}\ \overline{136}\ \overline{82}\ \overline{47}\ \overline{103}\ \overline{12}$

F. Creator of *The West Wing* (2 wds.)

$\overline{121}\ \overline{133}\ \overline{32}\ \overline{168}\ \overline{117}\ \overline{144}\ \overline{59}\ \overline{19}\ \overline{153}\ \overline{106}\ \overline{80}$

G. Place you might find many Buccaneers

$\overline{164}\ \overline{1}\ \overline{158}\ \overline{9}\ \overline{83}$

H. Lively, with abruptly disconnected notes

$\overline{137}\ \overline{91}\ \overline{17}\ \overline{50}\ \overline{167}\ \overline{126}\ \overline{86}\ \overline{162}$

I. Hoity-toity; putting on airs

$\overline{73}\ \overline{61}\ \overline{30}\ \overline{35}\ \overline{104}\ \overline{22}\ \overline{42}\ \overline{16}$

J. Helen Fielding's 2001 novel (2 wds.)

$\overline{18}\ \overline{131}\ \overline{169}\ \overline{8}\ \overline{33}\ \overline{3}\ \overline{70}\ \overline{62}\ \overline{154}\ \overline{146}$

K. Massachusetts college; home of Emily Dickinson

$\overline{152}\ \overline{95}\ \overline{69}\ \overline{157}\ \overline{172}\ \overline{108}\ \overline{124}$

L. Awarded kudos to

$\overline{31}\ \overline{11}\ \overline{15}\ \overline{53}\ \overline{90}\ \overline{25}\ \overline{49}$

M. Judgmentally correct (3 wds.)

$\overline{145}\ \overline{66}\ \overline{99}\ \overline{92}\ \overline{98}\ \overline{84}\ \overline{79}\ \overline{40}\ \overline{119}\ \overline{161}$

N. Peter Falk-Alan Arkin comedy classic (2 wds.)

$\overline{37}\ \overline{46}\ \overline{64}\ \overline{23}\ \overline{6}\ \overline{56}\ \overline{10}\ \overline{26}\ \overline{143}$

O. John Steed and Emma Peel

$\overline{116}\ \overline{24}\ \overline{5}\ \overline{36}\ \overline{114}\ \overline{148}\ \overline{78}\ \overline{132}$

P. Singer of the 1962 #1 hit "The Loco-Motion" (2 wds.)

$\overline{44}\ \overline{139}\ \overline{54}\ \overline{129}\ \overline{74}\ \overline{120}\ \overline{89}\ \overline{34}\ \overline{13}$

Q. Value added to real property

$\overline{102}\ \overline{60}\ \overline{141}\ \overline{71}\ \overline{150}\ \overline{122}\ \overline{166}\ \overline{135}\ \overline{20}\ \overline{2}\ \overline{171}$

R. Reluctance to the point of fear

$\overline{76}\ \overline{113}\ \overline{72}\ \overline{43}\ \overline{97}$

S. Oscar screenplay nominee for *Primary Colors* (2 wds.)

$\overline{101}\ \overline{111}\ \overline{21}\ \overline{4}\ \overline{48}\ \overline{93}\ \overline{140}\ \overline{51}\ \overline{28}$

T. Pumping up the volume

$\overline{112}\ \overline{75}\ \overline{52}\ \overline{134}\ \overline{38}\ \overline{163}\ \overline{173}\ \overline{128}\ \overline{107}\ \overline{81}$

ANSWER, PAGE 224

BATTER UP!

This baseball diamond is crammed with 51 slang words and phrases that players and fans have been chattering and shouting to each other since the game began. Once you've found them all, the leftover letters will spell out three classic Yogi Berra quotes. (You'll find the answer grid, Yogi's golden words, and a list of definitions on the answer page.)

```
                        I  T  C  A
                     B  S  E  U  G  T
                  K  A  C  E  T  A  N  N
               G  E  N  A  T  T  W  R  I  A
            A  O  A  D  H  E  E  U  H  O  K  I
         P  C  R  O  B  R  U  R  R  P  O  U  O  L
      N  I  O  T  U  O  H  C  N  U  P  M  T  N  O  D
   C  R  N  U  A  P  X        F  R  A  C  D  L  O
   H  C  G  O  N  M  T        O  N  N  O  T  T  W
O  U  I  E  O  T  S           E  P  O  R  H  H  N
   K  S  F  Y  C  L  A        O  C  K  N  E  G  T
E  C  O  I  A  O  L           F  O  U  E  H  U  R
U  A  S  I  N  K  B           M  A  L  R  O  A  S
P  T  L  R  T  T  K     E  D  A  S     A  S  S  H  R  C  E
T  C  O  E  T  O  H  E  E  L  K  C  I  P  C  T  F  S  T  N  P  E
H  O  P  E  P  P  E  R  M  E  A  T  B  A  L  L  Y  V  N  F  R  A  E  M
T  O  U  C  Q  S  H  U  C  E  E  E  B  R  N  L  C  O  I  U  I  O  K  R
S  A  M  C  G  T  O  O  L  O  X  A  U  D  L  R  I  N  B  H  E  N
   T  B  E  H  E  L  H  O  A  T  B        E  I  T  G  B  D  W
      S  L  R  E  E  M  O  V  S  T  B     M  I  I  S  O  I  H
      G  E  W  M  E  H  D  U  L  E  E     A  N  N  W  E  L  E
         O  S  M  A  I  U  Y  N  E  R  R  N  A  G  E  C  S  E
         P  E  S  L  S  E  T  C  A  Y  G     H  I  T  R  E  R  L
            H  T  A  L  L  S  V  L  G  C  A  E  H  H  C  L  O  H
               E  T  M  L  A  E  D  E  U  A  M  E  T  E  S  L  O  O
                  R  E  A  I  T  E  C  E  N  E  U  B  E  A  D  U
                  B  R  A  B  U  H  R  O  R  L  H  R  K  S
                  A  E  B  E  A  C  F  A  T  E  C  E
                  L  G  F  R  O  C  N  R  A  E
                  L  N  L  K  O  H  B  T
                  E  I  D  R  I  E
                  E  D  N  D
```

ALLEY
AROUND THE HORN
BACKDOOR SLIDER
BANDBOX
BATTERY
BLAST
BUNT
CAN OF CORN
CAUGHT LOOKING
CELLAR
CHEESE
CHOKE-UP
CIRCUS CATCH
CLOSER

COUNT
CUTTER
CYCLE
DINGER
DISH
FIREMAN
FUNGO
GAP
GOPHER BALL
HEAT
HOMER
HOT CORNER
IN THE HOLE
MEATBALL

NAIL DOWN
ON THE SCREWS
PAINTING THE
   BLACK
PEPPER
PICKLE
PUNCHOUT
RHUBARB
RIBBIE
ROPE
RUBBER GAME
RUTHIAN
SETUP MAN
SWEET SPOT

TABLE SETTER
TATER
TEXAS LEAGUER
TOOLS OF
   IGNORANCE
TOUCH 'EM ALL
UNCLE CHARLIE
WHEELHOUSE
WHEELS
WHIFF
YAKKER

ANSWER, PAGE 225

PHRASEOLOGY 203

Finish this one and you can pick up your diploma at the office. You've earned your Ph.D.—Doctor of Phraseology, that is.

ACROSS

1 French farewell
6 Farm machine
10 Shreds
14 Sheets, napkins, etc.
15 Ready to pluck
16 By mouth
17 Phrase from the days when English farmers paid their rent by using a farm implement to surrender their crops
19 Shot of medicine
20 "___ you kidding?"
21 Part of a semi
22 Thawing of hostilities
24 It's before jr. high
26 Little picture in a map
27 Phrase from the days before mannequins were used in clothing shop displays
33 Hoopster Monroe
34 Bullring injury
35 Qty.
38 Skinny
42 Street salesman
44 T-shirt size (abbr.)
45 Lightbulb, in comics
47 Mayberry kid
48 Phrase from the days when slave galley rest periods were announced by banging a block of wood
52 In the lead
55 Blue dye
56 *In the Cut* star
59 Not .com or .org
60 Feather wrap
63 Swenson of *Benson*

64 Phrase from the days when knights wore garments decorated with the family crest to protect their mail from the weather
67 Glasgow resident
68 A Barrymore
69 Fast food item
70 Coop residents
71 Corn syrup brand
72 Paid out

DOWN

1 ___ Romeo
2 Fashion VIP
3 As to, in memos
4 Mock-scared cry
5 Health agcy.
6 Investigated
7 Actress Tyler
8 Page in the news
9 Existed
10 Squirrel, say
11 Actor Jeremy
12 Phony jewels
13 Winter weather
18 Folk story
23 Sick's partner
25 Food additive
27 Navy diver
28 Piquancy
29 Sudden impulse
30 Achy ailment
31 One-footed jump
32 Anger
35 Purina competitor
36 Golda of Israel
37 Hard journey
39 Jitterbug dance

40 Fuss
41 ___ room
43 Jones' partner
46 Alias
48 Gold measures
49 Fancy punch
50 Generic pooch
51 Plumps up
52 People in *Witness*
53 Consequently
54 Prod
57 Aussie rock band
58 Director Ephron
60 French cheese
61 Warning sign
62 Aide (abbr.)
65 ___ Lingus (Irish airline)
66 Dadaist Jean

ANSWER, PAGE 224

INSIDE HOLLYWOOD

Let's see if you've got what it takes to make it big in Hollywood; all you have to do is identify the movies we're talking about. This is how it works: the first clue, in column A, is a telling detail or memorable plot element; the second (column B) is a quote from the film; and the third (column C) is a bit of information about an actor, writer, or director. Give yourself three points if you recognize the movie in question from just the first clue, two points if it takes two clues, and one if you need all three. Then add up your points and see where you fall amidst the Hollywood hierarchy.

COLUMN A	COLUMN B	COLUMN C
1. Sean Penn has pizza delivered to his history class, taught by Ray Walston.	"This guy's been stoned since third grade."	Nicolas Cage (credited as Nicolas Coppola) and Anthony Edwards have small roles.
2. A $3,000,000 inheritance.	"I'm an excellent driver."	Dustin Hoffman originally wanted Bill Murray to play Charlie.
3. The new sheriff rides in. His saddlebags are marked "Gucci."	"Excuse me while I whip this out."	Richard Pryor was one of five writers of the screenplay.
4. A ring from a Crackerjack box is engraved at a jewelry store.	"Doc, stop calling me that! I'm not Lula Mae anymore!"	Mickey Rooney plays Mr. Yunioshi.
5. It turns out The Chief can talk after all.	"Which one of you nuts has got any guts?"	Christopher Lloyd and Brad Dourif make their screen debuts.
6. Scott Joplin's ragtime music set the mood.	"Glad to meet ya, kid, you're a real horse's ass."	Technical advisor John Scarne doubled for Paul Newman in close-ups of card-sharping.
7. Rufus T. Firefly becomes leader of Fredonia.	"I'll give you my personal note for 90 days. If it's not paid you can keep the note."	Margaret Dumont attempts to sing Fredonia's anthem while ducking oranges.
8. Other customers applaud as Melvin is kicked out of his favorite restaurant.	Melvin makes introductions: "Carol the waitress—Simon the fag."	Harold Ramis, Lawrence Kasdan, Shane Black, and Todd Solondz all have small roles.
9. Three Americans are stranded in Mexico.	"Nobody ever put anything over on Fred C. Dobbs."	Robert Blake plays a young Mexican boy selling lottery tickets.
10. Looking through a phone book for Sarah Connor.	"Your clothes, give them to me now."	Linda Hamilton broke her ankle, and had to have her leg wrapped every day so she could do her chase scenes.

ANSWER, PAGE 224

ELVIS LIVES!

And if he *is* alive, it's all brought to you by the magic of anagrams. Rearrange the letters in each word or phrase so that the result is something that's closely related to it. For example, CASH LOST IN 'EM anagrams to SLOT MACHINES and DIRTY ROOM becomes DORMITORY. The blanks next to each signify the number of letters and the way the words in a phrase break.

1. CONTAMINATED   __ __   __ __ __ __ __ __ __ __ __

2. PUBS MOTTO   B O T T O M S U P

3. SOME SKI   __ __ __ __ __ __ __

4. HAD NO SOLE   __ __   __ __ __ __   __ __ __ __

5. ALIEN FORMS   __ __ __ __ __   __ __   __ __ __ __

6. BENEATH CHOPIN   __ __ __   __ __ __ __ __ __   __ __ __ __

7. SWEN OR INGA   __ __ __ __ __ __ __ __ __ __

8. MOON STARER   A S T R O N O M E R

9. NO CITY DUST HERE   __ __ __ __   __ __ __ __ __ __ __ __ __

10. SIT, CHAT, PAY, SIR   A P S Y C H I A T R I S T

11. HE'S GOT A HOT RELIC   __ __ __ __   __ __ __ __ __ __ __ __ __ __ __

12. FIERCE HITTER HELP   __ __ __ __   __ __ __ __ __ __ __   __ __ __ __ __ __

ANSWER, PAGE 226

* * * * *

UNCLE OSCAR'S BIG NIGHT #2

More scrambled Oscar-winning stars and the Oscar-winning films they won for. For complete directions on how to solve, see page 46.

The Stars	The Films
1. JOT OF DESIRE (5 6)	a. KELPIES HAVE NO EARS (11 2 4)
2. MAINLY LARD (3 7)	b. CELESTE HOLM NABS THIEF (3 7 2 3 5)
3. MONK'S HAT (3 5)	c. SKEWED TELETHON (3 4 7)
4. NEWLY THWART GOP (7 7)	d. FORGET RUMPS (7 4)

ANSWER, PAGE 222

GOOD SPORTS

In *Uncle John's Bathroom Reader Plunges into Great Lives*, we told the story of the 1973 Battle of the Sexes between Billie Jean King and Bobby Riggs. This puzzle is dedicated to the two plucky combatants—and to winners and losers everywhere. Fit all 42 tennis terms into their proper place in the grid, crossword-style.

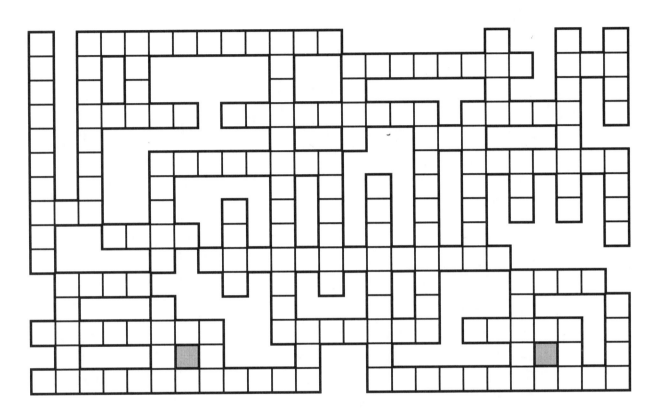

3-letter words
Ace
ATP
Let
Lob
Net
Out!
Set

4-letter words
Chip
Draw
Game
Grip
Love
Pace

Seed
Shot
Spin
Team
USTA

5-letter words
Chair
Deuce
Drill
Poach
Serve
Slice

6-letter word
Player

7-letter words
Racquet
Ranking
Strings

8-letter words
Baseline
Davis Cup
Drop shot
Partners
Tie-break

9-letter words
Foot fault
Hard court

10-letter words
Can of balls
Tournament

11-letter words
Double fault
Tennis elbow

12-letter word
Ground stroke

13-letter words
Overhead smash
Unforced error

ANSWER, PAGE 226

DEEP THOUGHTS

You may be surprised to learn that Jack Handey, the creator of *Deep Thoughts*, is a real person. I mean, honestly, how can one person be so wise? If you need directions on how to solve this puzzle, see page 5.

1.

2.

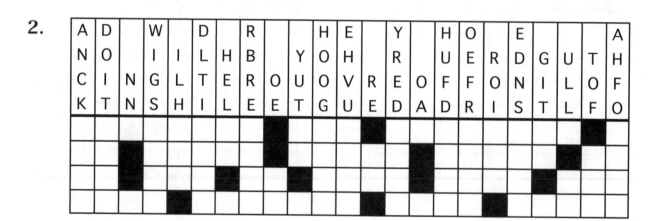

3.

ANSWER, PAGE 224

HEY, LADY!

That's *First* Lady to you, bub. Our Mrs. Presidents have been a quirky bunch. How much do you know about them?

1. Dolley Madison did a few things you might not expect from the most prominent woman in the country, one of them being:
   a. she cursed like a sailor
   b. she was addicted to snuff
   c. she occasionally ran down Pennsylvania Avenue in her underwear

2. At the advice of her doctor, Eleanor Roosevelt ate three of these every day in an attempt to improve her memory:
   a. dove eggs
   b. extra-large jalapeno peppers
   c. chocolate-covered garlic balls

3. Elizabeth Monroe liked to have the White House staff refer to her as:
   a. "Your Majesty"
   b. "Mrs. America"
   c. "Poopsie"

4. Lady Bird Johnson would sometimes leave official functions early so that she could do this instead:
   a. help the White House chefs prepare dinner
   b. watch *Gunsmoke* on TV
   c. take karate lessons

5. One of the things that Harry Truman liked about Bess when he first met her was her ability to:
   a. whistle through her teeth
   b. recite entire books of the Bible from memory
   c. hang in there for days at dance marathons

6. George Washington often wrote Martha's correspondence for her because:
   a. she'd lost a few fingers fighting the Redcoats
   b. she was allergic to ink
   c. she wasn't quite illiterate, but she was the world's worst speller

7. Louisa Adams (Mrs. John Quincy Adams) indulged in the following hobby involving White House animals:
   a. spinning silk from the silkworms that lived in the White House mulberry trees
   b. caring for all 150 fish in the White House aquarium, going so far as to give each fish an individual name
   c. maintaining a beehive near the White House Rose Garden

8. During World War I, Edith Wilson decided that rather than waste manpower mowing the White House lawn, a better solution was to:
   a. paint the lawn red, white, and blue
   b. mow it herself
   c. import some sheep to graze there

ANSWER, PAGE 226

DON'T KEEP YOUR DAY JOB!

Some famous writers and how they kept themselves afloat until that big break.

ACROSS

1 School group
6 Pampering places
10 Detective Charlie
14 Actress Midler
15 RPM gauge, briefly
16 Ruff stuff
17 Smirnoff rival, familiarly
18 It may be found to the left of China
19 "¿Cómo ___ usted?"
20 Vladimir Nabokov's day job
23 English Romantic poet John
24 Piano technicians
25 Okay for the family
28 Snobs put them on
29 G.I. hangout
30 "Woe is me!"
33 Go one better
37 Washington Irving's day job
41 Old hat
42 Per item
43 Comic Costello
44 Gung-ho
46 They're told "You've got mail!"
49 Pueblo homes
52 Winter jacket
54 Daniel Defoe's day job
57 Voiced
58 Change color seasonally
59 Rewrite for the movies
62 Flounder's filter
63 "The joke's ___!"
64 "I'm not kidding!"
65 Peak in Thessaly
66 Lips service?
67 Jerry Maguire, for one

DOWN

1 Dan Rather's network
2 "___ It Be" (#1 Beatles hit)
3 At the peak of
4 Name in a lot of hospital names
5 Took by force
6 House support in swampland
7 Window parts
8 "Dirty Deeds Done Cheap" band
9 It describes the vowel sound in "bit"
10 Makes a pile
11 Don't marry in this, it's said
12 Person in a cast
13 Draws nigh
21 Major name in restaurant guides
22 New coins of 2002
25 Sitter?
26 Where Nepal is
27 Oodles
28 Concerning
31 Go ahead
32 Jean of Dada
34 Tall story
35 Designer Christian
36 Burden
38 Columbus's patron
39 Cut off
40 Eyeball benders
45 Feels not so hot
47 Figure skater Baiul
48 Maltese, for example
49 Whiskey-___ (first U.S. disco)
50 Day at the movies?
51 Track shapes
52 Salon jobs
53 Queen ___ lace
55 Paul of *The Good Earth*
56 Bulldogs' bailiwick
60 Bowling alley target
61 New Year holiday in Hanoi

ANSWER, PAGE 226

THE FACE IS FAMILIAR...

Uncle John has such an ordinary name, maybe that's why he collectes other people's—and thing's. See if you can match the various identities (1–10) to their monikers (a–j).

____ 1. On *Scooby-Doo*, Shaggy's actual first name was…

____ 2. Jimmy Hoffa's middle name was…

____ 3. The first name of Howdy Doody's sister was…

____ 4. On *The Andy Griffith Show*, Barney Fife's middle name was…

____ 5. Donald Duck's middle name is…

____ 6. The first hurricane given a male name was…

____ 7. Little Red Riding Hood's first name is…

____ 8. On *Gilligan's Island*, Gilligan's first name was…

____ 9. The name of the monster in the novel *Frankenstein* is…

____ 10. On *Star Trek*, the name of Dr. McCoy's daughter (and who even knew he had one?) was…

a. Adam

b. Blanchette

c. Bob

d. Fauntleroy

e. Heidi

f. Joanna

g. Norville

h. Oliver

i. Riddle

j. Willy

ANSWER, PAGE 226

NOW *THAT'S* SLOW

Small crostic puzzles are solved just like the big ones (directions on page 13) but the first letter of the fill-in words **do not** spell out a hidden message.

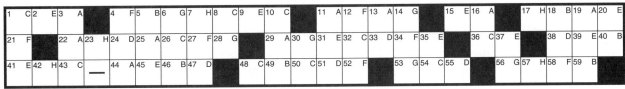

A. Pretty miffed (2 wds.)

29 19 25 22 3 11 13 44 16

B. Bring back to Broadway (or to life!)

59 18 5 49 46 40

C. Lead or gold, e.g. (2 wds.)

26 54 36 32 43 48 10 1 8 50

D. Hover on the brink

24 47 51 38 33 55

E. Most common place name in the U.S.

39 31 35 2 45 20 9 37 15 41

F. Biblical brother of Martha and Mary

34 58 21 4 12 27 52

G. Like a kid from Choate or Andover

14 30 6 53 28 56

H. Early anesthetic

23 42 17 57 7

ANSWER, PAGE 226

YO!

Pick one: The yo-yo is a (exotic animal, Polynesian coin, popular toy). Okay, enough of the easy ones. Can you figure out the true history of the yo-yo by picking the correct facts from the choices in parentheses?

The yo-yo is believed to be the second-oldest toy in the world, after (**dolls, building blocks, the hula hoop**). It goes back to prehistoric times, where Philippine hunters wrapped straps around rocks that they hurled at prey; if they missed, they could pull the rocks back and try again. In fact, the word "yo-yo" comes from a Filipino expression that roughly means (**"rock-rock," "come back," "try again"**).

Even the ancient Greeks played with yo-yos. Later, in the 1700s, yo-yo mania hit Europe; there's even a painting of (**Napoleon Bonaparte, King George IV of England, Lucrezia Borgia**) whirling a yo-yo. And there are accounts of French noblemen playing with yo-yos while (**sitting at sidewalk cafes, being hauled to the guillotine, constructing the Eiffel Tower**)!

The real turning point for yo-yos came in 1928, when Donald Duncan—an entrepreneur who is also known for inventing (**waxed dental floss, the electric pencil sharpener, the Eskimo Pie**)—met Pedro Flores, who owned his own yo-yo corporation. Duncan bought out Flores and named the company after himself. He began with just one model, called the (**Magical Spinning Amusement Device, Oy-Oy, O-Boy Yo-Yo Top**), but eventually developed a full line of them.

Duncan was a natural promoter; one of his techniques was to have photos taken of celebrities playing with his yo-yos. During World War II, he even talked a young singer named (**Frank Sinatra, Bing Crosby, Elvis Presley**) into singing songs about yo-yos, including such lyrics as "What is the dearest thing on earth, that fills my soul with joy and mirth? My yo-yo." Bet you won't find *that* among his greatest hits.

The yo-yo craze really took off in the 1960s. In 1962, 45 million yo-yos were sold; at the time, there were only (**10, 40, 100**) million kids in America. But the Duncan company had to file for bankruptcy in 1965; the trouble was (**they couldn't keep up with the demand because they never switched from wood to plastic, they lost their trademark on the word "yo-yo," they expanded too far and went into debt, all of the above**). Someone else bought the rights to the Duncan name, which still survives to this day. Duncan yo-yos currently account for about (**30, 65, 80**) percent of all yo-yos sold.

Yo-yos have been used in all sorts of unusual ways. In the early 1900s an Ohio man patented an (**edible, erotic, ermine-covered**) yo-yo. In 1977 a world record was set when a Virginia man yo-yoed for (**48, 120, 256**) hours straight. In 1980 the TV show *You Asked for It* unsuccessfully tried to launch a (**48, 120, 256**)-pound yo-yo called "Big-Yo" off a pier.

In 1984 the yo-yo was taken aboard the space shuttle, where it was discovered that in space, when a yo-yo reaches the end of its string, it (**bounces back up, "sleeps," just hangs in the air**). For a toy known for its ups and downs, that's probably as far up as it's ever gone!

ANSWER, PAGE 227

GREETINGS FROM EARTH

When NASA launched the twin Voyager 1 and 2 spacecraft in 1977, it sent along a message containing 115 images, a variety of natural sounds and musical selections from different cultures and eras, and spoken greetings in 55 languages. It may be a long time before it finds its way into the hands (or whatever they've got) of aliens, but in the meantime, why don't you find some of them yourself? First find the 26 photos and sounds listed below. Then read the leftover letters to spell out the message from India that was included in the mission.

```
                S
              W A E
              F W W
            A N I A R
            R N N R T
          L D E G E E H
          A Y S S I K H
          H N A P P R C
          A U H T R A E
          M R Y E H M E
          J S J T E R P
          A I O U Q E S
          T N H L R P E
          N G N F A U F
          A M N C P S F
          H O Y I U F O
          P T B G L O T
        N E H G A S O F R
        D L E O M A T I I
      H S E R O Y R S L V O
      T H U N D E R T O E U
    B R I   R E E H E   T A P
    P I P   Y F T H P   E U E
    R B S   B I R D S   R E A
```

The photos:
AUTO
BIRTH
EARTH
ELEPHANT
NURSING MOTHER
SEQUOIA
SUPERMARKET
TAJ MAHAL
VIOLIN

The sounds:
BIRDS
FIRE
FOOTSTEPS
HYENA
"JOHNNY B. GOODE"
KISS
LIFT-OFF
"(The) MAGIC FLUTE"
PULSAR

RAIN
RIVETER
SAWING
SHIPS
SPEECH
SURF
THUNDER
WIND

ANSWER, PAGE 227

GORE LORE

The BBC called him "America's eloquent WASP." Here's a page of pithy comments from author and extraordinary wit (and Jackie Kennedy's step-brother and Al Gore's eighth cousin), Gore Vidal. To read them, choose a letter from each column and drop it into its correct place in the grid.

1.

I	L		W	E		I	H	N	O	H	D	E	A	N		L	D		S
E	M	P	R	Y		I	F	P	E	P	E	A	V	I		E	O		S
O	H	E	E	H	I	C	O	C	O	L	U	M	N	U	U	R	O	D	L
T	M	V	L	D	D	D	S	A	S	U	L	D	D	O	S	B	E	B	
					I					I	M		O	T	P	B		L	

2.

T		B	R		W	H		H	V			A		O	S	
E	E	S	E		M	O	O	T	H	I	I	T	E	R	R	A
R	G	O	E	W	N	G	M	E	A	D	N	R	R	U	E	V
R	H	O	N	I	S	I	E	R	L	N	S	T	J	S	N	E
		F	E	I			N		I	G	A				D	
				S			H		E	S	M				R	
									S	O						

3.

A	P		I			T		E			E			O		
I	A		P		H	S	H	T	S	M	O	I	H	A	E	
H	P	L	R	S	E	A	L	F	T	E	D	H	A	N	N	W	P	P
O	R	L	F	E	O	E	I	D	R	V	E	E	L	T	P	E	E	E
O	T	E	F	R	N	F	V	E	E	E	A	A	O	F	E	D	S	F
									E	A	M	R	C		D		S	F
									N	M	N	H						

SUCH A NASTY PLACE!

At one point on our most recent visit to England, we cried out, "Nasty!" No, we weren't disappointed in our surroundings; we'd simply arrived at the village of Nasty, one of many strange but real places in that country. Also on our tour were such highlights as Ugley, Crackpot, Lickey End...and the 29 places listed below. See if you can fit all of them them into the grid so that they interlock like a crossword. Happy traveling!

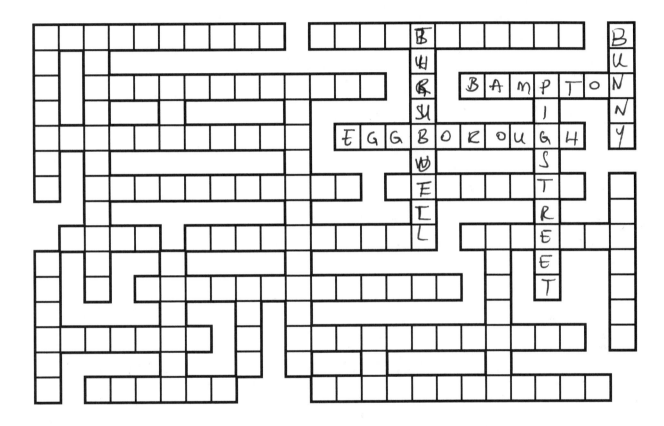

3-letter words
Ash
Ham

4-letter words
Dull
Pill

5-letter word
Bunny

6-letter words
Corney
Piddle
Pity Me

7-letter words
Bampton
Burpham
Dorking
No Place
Puddles
Upperup

8-letter word
Nempnett

9-letter words
Pig Street
Thrubwell

10-letter words
Bat and Ball
Bug's Bottom
Eggborough

11-letter words
Giggleswick
Haltwhistle
Shootup Hill
Slackbottom

12-letter words
Great Bulging
Great Snoring
Limpley Stoke
Nether Wallop

13-letter word
Yornder Bognie

ANSWER, PAGE 227

PERFECT 10 #2

Here are 10 more *almost* perfect statements. Remember that the numbers have been switched in *pairs*: If the 2 should replace 10, the 10 should also replace the 2. Can you restore the 10 to perfection?

The average beard grows **1** inch a year.

In her Oscar-winning *Midnight Cowboy* role, Sylvia Miles was onscreen for **2** minutes.

The average American worker has held **3** different jobs by age 40.

The most yolks ever found in one egg is **4**.

There are **5** time zones in China.

The average skywritten letter is **6** miles high.

The speed of a roller coaster increases an average of **7** mph when it's raining.

It costs **8** cents to make a dollar bill.

It takes **9** hours to hard-boil an ostrich egg.

There are **10** spikes in the Statue of Liberty's crown.

ANSWER, PAGE 227

AND A JIFFY AND A TRICE?

Small crostic puzzles are solved just like the big ones (directions on page 13) but the first letter of the fill-in words **do not** spell out a hidden message.

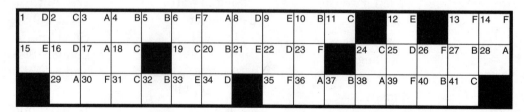

A. Join together

‾3‾ ‾38‾ ‾29‾ ‾17‾ ‾36‾ ‾7‾ ‾28‾

B. Sent off from Cape Canaveral

‾10‾ ‾20‾ ‾27‾ ‾5‾ ‾37‾ ‾4‾ ‾32‾ ‾40‾

C. Person whom Livingstone sought in Africa

‾41‾ ‾18‾ ‾24‾ ‾31‾ ‾19‾ ‾2‾ ‾11‾

D. He starred as Bulworth and Dick Tracy

‾25‾ ‾16‾ ‾8‾ ‾22‾ ‾1‾ ‾34‾

E. Soda shop orders

‾15‾ ‾12‾ ‾9‾ ‾33‾ ‾21‾

F. Kind of neglectful "sin"

‾14‾ ‾13‾ ‾30‾ ‾23‾ ‾35‾ ‾6‾ ‾26‾ ‾39‾

ANSWER, PAGE 227

ALL THAT JIVE

Cab Calloway was the ultimate hepcat; he even wrote a guide, published in the 1940s, on how to talk like a hipster. Herewith, some excerpts. Pay attention—you've been acting kind of geeky lately.

ACROSS

1 Bill's *Groundhog Day* costar
6 Private eye Spade
9 Zodiac critter for most of July
13 Earthquake
14 Something told on the way to Canterbury
15 Less calorie-rich, on some product labels
16 Pulsate
17 Corny, à la Calloway
19 Arrival at Ararat
20 Excessively widespread
22 Where the Renaissance took place
23 Apply yourself diligently, à la Calloway
26 Use one's scull
27 Table scrap, in Dickens stories
28 Liable (to do something)
31 House in Madrid
34 Military truant, for short
37 Ritzy kind of fur
39 Prefix meaning "high"
40 Pantyhose stuff
42 Callous cad
43 Derek and the Dominoes hit of 1972
45 Dynamic start?
46 Airline to Tel Aviv
47 Baking shortcut
48 "Spring ahead" abbr.
50 Oolong, for one
52 Applause, à la Calloway
58 Top-notch, as eggs go
61 Deeply engrossed
62 Where Elton reads *Uncle John*?
63 Very good dancer, à la Calloway
65 "Going to the dogs" is one
67 Actor Baldwin of *Prelude to a Kiss*
68 Hawaiian strings
69 ___ and desist (quit it)
70 Lucie's dad
71 End of a family business name, maybe
72 One to respect

DOWN

1 Take _____ at (attempt)
2 First prime minister of India
3 Bogarde and Benedict
4 Metric prelude?
5 Ultrasound picture, often
6 More secure
7 1936 candidate Landon
8 Shooting star
9 7-Eleven worker
10 Baseball's Petrocelli or Brogna
11 Sitting on
12 Actress Neuwirth
14 Vegetarian's high-protein staple
18 Goes after foxes
21 Davenport native
24 Lag behind
25 Film choice
28 Biblical brother
29 It may be entered in court
30 Spill the beans
31 Not frazzled
32 Jai ___
33 River to Hades
35 One of the Earps
36 Encouragement for a matador
38 Coming up
41 Still sleeping
44 Farewell
49 ___ quo
51 Play the siren
52 1701, in Roman numerals
53 Get all dolled up
54 Boat propellers
55 Trojan War epic
56 Gallows feature
57 One of Andy's TV cronies
58 Reunion attendee, for short
59 "Do unto others..." is a golden one
60 "Forever"
64 Ref's call, in boxing
66 "Runaway" singer Shannon

ANSWER, PAGE 228

WOULD WE LIE TO YOU, SPORT?

You bet we would! In this quiz, we explain the origins of some sports terms that you may have wondered about. The only trouble is, we're offering too many explanations. Can you find the one true answer in each set?

1. Why is zero called "love" in tennis?
   a. Because circles have symbolized love for centuries. (That's why we wear wedding rings, for instance.)
   b. In old tennis clubs, if a player went scoreless through an entire match, it was jokingly called a "love match" (implying that it had been a "happy pairing" for the winner). As a result, tennis players tended to equate "love" with zero.
   c. As it's used on tennis courts, the word "love" is actually a distortion of the French word *l'oeuf*, meaning "the egg," as in goose egg.

2. Why is a golfer's helper called a "caddie"?
   a. It's a variation on the word *caddy*, a device designed to hold something (such as a tea caddy). Equating a person to a device is hardly politically correct, but no one in the 1600s gave it much thought.
   b. It's a variation on the word *cadet*, a low-level aide who hangs around waiting to be assigned errands.
   c. It's Scottish dialect for *kiddie*, because caddying was originally done by young boys.

3. Why did Roger Staubach dub his famous 1975 touchdown pass a "Hail Mary"?
   a. Because it was "thrown high enough to reach heaven."
   b. Because it was "thrown up as a prayer."
   c. Because all the players trying to catch it "raised their hands like they were praying."

4. Why is that flat rubber disk that hockey players bat around called a "puck"?
   a. Puck is actually a variation on the word *poke*, which describes what hockey players continually do to pucks: "Poke: to thrust or push, as if with a stick."
   b. The first hockey pucks were produced by the Puck Rubber Company, which dutifully stamped its name onto each one.
   c. Nowadays hockey pucks are chilled before each game, but the earliest pucks (then called "flats") weren't. Warmer pucks tend to bounce higher and behave more erratically. So erratically, in fact, that people began calling them "pucks"—after Puck, a mischievous demon of folklore.

5. Nowadays a "second string" is a squad of replacement players, but what did the term originally refer to?
   a. A set of extra horses for a cavalry unit.
   b. A mountain climber's safety line.
   c. A second bowstring carried by archers, in case the first one broke.

ANSWER, PAGE 228

TALKIN' TRASH

Uncle John's been collecting wacky business slogans forever—like the window cleaning service that says, "Your pane is our pleasure." You can see why he likes them so much, can't you?

Anyway, we've got a dirty job for you. To solve this puzzle, you'll have to go through the trash can and find the 19 capitalized words and phrases on the list of businesses below (one of which happens to be a trash pickup service). Once you've found them all, you shall be rewarded: The leftover letters will reveal yet another business and its hilarious (no, really) slogan.

Then, if you're not too tired and dirty, have a go at matching each business (1–19) with its slogan (a–s).

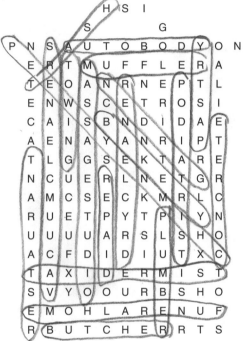

Sign on an electricians truck, let us fix your shorts

List of businesses:

F 1. AUTO BODY shop ✓
N 2. BAKERY ✓
A 3. BUTCHER ✓
H 4. CHIMNEY SWEEP ✓
Q 5. CONCRETE company ✓
M 6. DIAPER service ✓
J 7. DRY CLEANER ✓

R 8. FUNERAL HOME ✓
G 9. GARDEN shop ✓
E 10. MASSAGE STUDIO ✓
I 11. MUFFLER shop ✓
D 12. PASTRY shop ✓
S 13. PLUMBER ✓
K 14. PODIATRIST ✓

L 15. RESTAURANT ✓
O 16. TAXIDERMIST ✓
B 17. TOWING company ✓
P 18. TRASH service ✓
C 19. VACUUM CLEANERS ✓

Slogans:

a. Let me meat your needs.
b. We don't want an arm and a leg...just your tows!
c. Business sucks.
d. Get your buns in here.
e. It's great to be kneaded.
f. May we have the next dents?
g. Our business is growing.
h. We kick ash.
i. No appointment necessary. We'll hear you coming.
j. Drop your pants here.

k. Time wounds all heels.
l. Don't stand there and be hungry, come in and get fed up.
m. Let us lighten your load.
n. While you sleep, we loaf.
o. We really know our stuff.
p. Satisfaction guaranteed or double your trash back.
q. We dry harder.
r. Drive carefully, we'll wait.
s. A good flush beats a full house.

Completed by Sana N. on Feb. 22/2010 at 8:55pm

ANSWER, PAGE 228

WORDS AT PLAY

No, our typesetter hasn't been at the punch bowl again. And our proofreader is not on vacation. The clues that look a little funny at first glance are there for a reason. Trust your Uncle John.

ACROSS

1 Fashionable resorts
5 Big name in tractors
10 Margarita garnish
14 Approximately
15 Blend
16 Half a train?
17 **ALL 0**
20 Actress Kurtz
21 Capable of holding water?
22 You can get some at 1 Across
24 Letters on a headstone
25 Sing to the cops
29 Foray
31 EMT specialty
34 Cleanse
35 Heavenly ring
36 A room of Juan's own?
37 **L E G A L**
40 "Clan of the Cave Bear" author Jean
41 *Uno* plus *dos*
42 Sealy competitor
43 "You bet!"
44 At the home of
45 Best
46 Wednesday's child is full of it
47 Shorebird
49 Kneecap, to your doctor
53 Where to find most "all-news" stations
58 **STANDING   AN**
60 Give for a while
61 Exposed
62 Bouquet
63 Go to and fro
64 Put up with
65 Pea picker-upper

DOWN

1 What Henry VIII wanted
2 Figurehead's place
3 Concerning
4 Manhattan's artsy district
5 Elton John hit
6 Just beats, with "out"
7 GP's group
8 Schism
9 The outside
10 Metal for recycling
11 Gregory Peck role
12 Take it easy
13 Antique metalware
18 Sea of Galilee locale
19 Oklahoma city

23 Circus gizmo named for a back muscle
25 Spread out
26 Take-a-number alternative
27 Suggests strongly
28 Equal, to Yves
30 "What a pity!"
31 Mideast capital
32 Novel ingredients
33 Attacked
35 Roll call reply
36 Flower holder?
38 Napoleon was exiled there
39 In the back of the boat
44 Heartless

45 Messy, as a bed
46 Never Never Land visitor
48 Gave an assessment
49 Buds
50 One more time
51 Sushi ingredient
52 Iraqi, e.g.
54 Just ___ on the horizon
55 Conn of *Benson*
56 A party to
57 Shrek is one
59 Brew suffix

ANSWER, PAGE 229

TOM SWIFTIES: A VARIATION

Here's a version of Tom Swifties in which the sentence that "Tom said" is a familiar phrase or the words to a song. Can you match what Tom said (1–10) to the adverb (a–j) that will make the best Tom Swifty? (If Tom Swifites are new to you, see page 75.)

J   1. "Eat my dust!" Tom said...
I   2. "En garde!" Tom said...
E   3. "Hey, baby, I'm your handyman," Tom said...
B   4. "I vant to sock your blahd," Tom said...
D   5. "I'll see you on the dark side of the moon," Tom said...
F   6. "It's beginning to look a lot like Christmas," Tom said...
H   7. "Maxwell House. Good to the last drop," Tom said...
G   8. "Pants pressed while you wait," Tom said...
C   9. "To get to the other side," Tom said...
A   10. "What a long, strange trip it's been," Tom said...

a. acidly   c. crossly   e. fixedly   g. ironically   i. pointedly
b. bitingly   d. delightedly   f. frostily   h. perkily   j. winningly

ANSWER, PAGE 228

THAT'S A LOT OF PEPPERONI

Small crostic puzzles are solved just like the big ones (directions on page 13) but the first letter of the fill-in words **do not** spell out a hidden message.

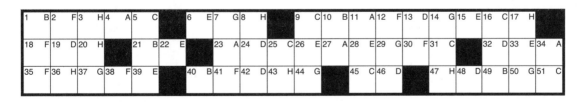

1 B	2 F	3 H	4 A	5 C		6 E	7 G	8 H		9 C	10 B	11 A	12 F	13 D	14 G	15 E	16 C	17 H
18 F	19 D	20 H		21 B	22 E		23 A	24 D	25 C	26 E	27 A	28 E	29 G	30 F	31 C		32 D	33 E	34 A
35 F	36 H	37 G	38 F	39 E		40 B	41 F	42 D	43 H	44 G		45 C	46 D		47 H	48 D	49 B	50 G	51 C

A. Sign at a highway entrance ramp

$\overline{27}\ \overline{23}\ \overline{4}\ \overline{34}\ \overline{11}$

B. Bowl over

$\overline{40}\ \overline{10}\ \overline{21}\ \overline{49}\ \overline{1}$

C. Mecca for auto racing fans in Florida

$\overline{31}\ \overline{9}\ \overline{5}\ \overline{25}\ \overline{45}\ \overline{16}\ \overline{51}$

D. Tinkerbell and friends

$\overline{46}\ \overline{19}\ \overline{13}\ \overline{42}\ \overline{48}\ \overline{32}\ \overline{24}$

E. Home state of James Dean and David Letterman

$\overline{26}\ \overline{39}\ \overline{6}\ \overline{33}\ \overline{28}\ \overline{22}\ \overline{15}$

F. *The Wapshot Chronicle* author John

$\overline{41}\ \overline{35}\ \overline{18}\ \overline{30}\ \overline{2}\ \overline{38}\ \overline{12}$

G. Montezuma's people

$\overline{7}\ \overline{50}\ \overline{29}\ \overline{37}\ \overline{14}\ \overline{44}$

H. Get ready to put into print

$\overline{36}\ \overline{8}\ \overline{47}\ \overline{43}\ \overline{17}\ \overline{3}\ \overline{20}$

ANSWER, PAGE 229

KURT REJOINDERS

What does Uncle John read in the bathroom? Here are a few thoughts from one of his favorite cynics, novelist Kurt Vonnegut, Jr.

1.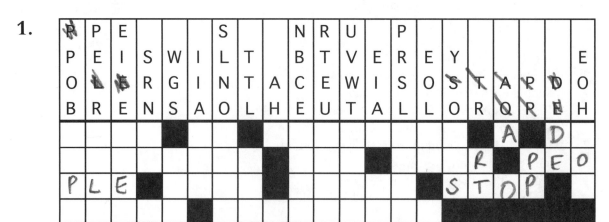

ANSWER, PAGE 229

HONK IF YOU LOVE REARRANGING THINGS

We've broken up these bumper sticker sayings into consecutive three-letter strings and rearranged the three-letter groups into alphabetical order. The numbers that follow signify the number of letters in the original. For instance, if the bumper sticker read HONK IF YOU LOVE ME, the scrambled version would look like this: EME HON KIF LOV YOU (4 2 3 4 2).

[handwritten: IF YOU'RE HAPPY AND YOU KNOW IT, CLANK YOUR CHAINS]

1. AND CHA CLA EHA IFY INS KNO NKY OUR OUR PPY WIT YOU (2 3'2 5 3 3 4 2, 5 4 6.)

[handwritten: ASK ME ABOUT MY VOW OF SILENCE]

2. ASK BOU ILE MEA NCE OFS TMY VOW (3 2 5 2 3 2 7.)

[handwritten: I DRIVE WAY TOO FAST TO WORRY ABOUT CHOLESTEROL]

3. BOU FAS IDR IVE OLE RQL RYA STE TCH TOQ TTO WAY WOR (1 5 3 3 4 2 5 5 11.)

[handwritten: RED MEAT ISN'T BAD FOR YOU. FUZZY GREEN MEAT IS.]

4. ADE EEN MEA MEA NTB ORY OUF RED TIS TIS UZZ YGR (3 4 3'1 3 3 3. 5 5 4 2.)

[handwritten: NEVER D]

5. EOP ERD ERW HEP ITH KSF LAY LEY NEV OCA ORT OUP POK RDT RIC (5 2 4 6 3

3 6 3 4 5 4.)

ANSWER, PAGE 229

WHAT? IT'S NOT?

Small crostic puzzles are solved just like the big ones (directions on page 13) but the first letters of the fill-in words **do not** spell out a hidden message.

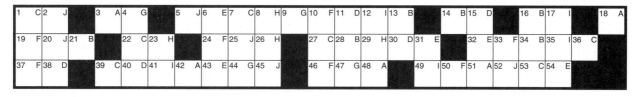

A. Limoges product

$\overline{42}\ \overline{18}\ \overline{3}\ \overline{48}\ \overline{5}$

B. Queen Victoria's consort

$\overline{34}\ \overline{13}\ \overline{16}\ \overline{21}\ \overline{28}\ \overline{14}$

C. This may give you high overhead?

$\overline{39}\ \overline{36}\ \overline{1}\ \overline{53}\ \overline{22}\ \overline{7}\ \overline{27}$

D. Nicholson title role of 1992

$\overline{40}\ \overline{15}\ \overline{38}\ \overline{11}\ \overline{30}$

E. Author of *We Were the Mulvaneys*

$\overline{6}\ \overline{43}\ \overline{31}\ \overline{54}\ \overline{32}$

F. Taught privately

$\overline{33}\ \overline{50}\ \overline{24}\ \overline{37}\ \overline{10}\ \overline{19}\ \overline{46}$

G. Atari rival

$\overline{4}\ \overline{9}\ \overline{44}\ \overline{47}$

H. Garden in Genesis

$\overline{29}\ \overline{8}\ \overline{26}\ \overline{23}$

I. Very

$\overline{49}\ \overline{12}\ \overline{41}\ \overline{35}\ \overline{17}$

J. Deserving of respect

$\overline{5}\ \overline{45}\ \overline{20}\ \overline{2}\ \overline{25}\ \overline{52}$

ANSWER, PAGE 229

YOU KNOW THE OLD SAYING

Debunking a few of those overworked myths from the wonderful world of animals.

Blind as a bat:

EODW   OZFU'D   EBHUY   OUY   CTWD   WKFPHFW   TS

EODW   POU   WFF   NFZM   GFBB,   DJOUI   MTR.   ERD

EODW   DJOD   JRUD   DHUM   HUWFPDW   OD   UHQJD

YTU'D   ZFBM   TU   DJFHZ   NHWHTU.   HUWDFOY,   DJFM

ZFBM   TU   KFZWTUOB   WTUOZ,   TZ   "FPJTBTPODHTU."

You can't teach an old dog new tricks:

HT,   FRI   FHD   EZV.   AHPI   EZV   YRZBV   NBCESI   ZN

ZVF   ZPR,   CX   NTRF'BR   ILZBN   RVHDPT.   HXNRV   CN'I

UBRRA,   BZNTRB   NTZV   ZPR,   NTZN   TRYJI   Z   AHP

YRZBV.   *UHBARB   EHYYCRI,   JHHAYRI,   *PRBLZV

ITRJTRBAI   ZVA   PHYARV   BRNBCRWRBI   ZBR   IZCA   NH

YRZBV   NBCESI   NTR   XZINRIN.

Sweat like a pig:

XTNB   PUJZ   YR   BOZUL   NEUYFB   UYF   USZ   CYUDEZ

LR   BOZUL.   TYBLZUF,   LPZA   OUEERO   TY   ICF   LR

QRRE   FROY.   LPZTS   ICQGA   UXXZUSUYQZ   NTJZB

XTNB   U   SZXCLULTRY   VRS   BERJZYETYZBB.   UQLCUEEA,

XTNB   USZ   BRIZ   RV   LPZ   QEZUYZBL   UYTIUEB

USRCYF.

ANSWER, PAGE 229

PARK IT!

Every car on the list below has been waiting for someone like you to come along. Can you drive all 40 autos into their assigned parking spaces in the grid so that they all fit, crossword-style?

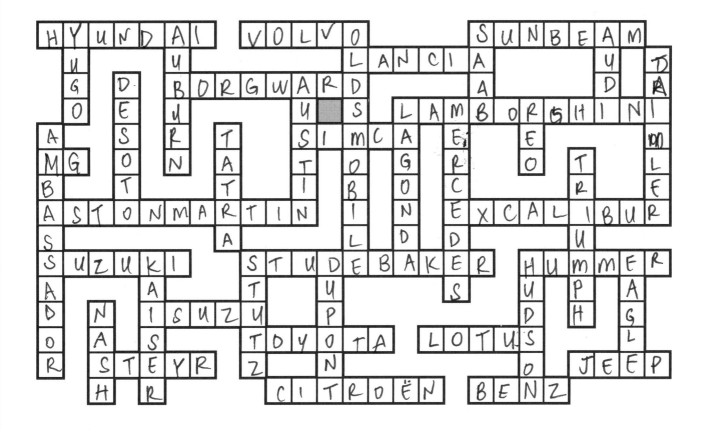

2-letter word
✓MG

3-letter word
✓Reo

4-letter words
✓Audi
✓Benz
✓Jeep
✓Nash
✓Saab
✓Yugo

5-letter words
✓Eagle
✓Isuzu
✓Lotus
✓Simca
✓Steyr
✓Stutz
✓Tatra
✓Volvo

6-letter words
✓Auburn
✓Austin
✓Desoto
✓DuPont

✓Hudson
✓Hummer
✓Kaiser
✓Lancia
✓Suzuki
✓Toyota

7-letter words
✓Citroën
✓Daimler
✓Hyundai
✓Lagonda
✓Sunbeam
✓Triumph

8-letter words
✓Borgward
✓Mercedes

9-letter word
✓Excalibur

10-letter words
✓Ambassador
✓Oldsmobile
✓Studebaker

11-letter words
✓Aston Martin
✓Lamborghini

ANSWER, PAGE 230

WORD GEOGRAPHY

The eight words hidden in the grid come from all over the planet. Figure out what the words are from the clues about their origins, find them in the grid, and the leftover letters will reveal something you might not know about the origins of another word. The eight hidden words are listed on the answer page.

1. In 1516, the city fathers of Venice decreed that all of the city's Jews had to live on the island of Geto. The practice spread throughout Europe, and the Jewish quarters of every city came to be known as a ___.

2. According to the Bible, the ancient people of Babylon once tried to build a mighty tower (the Tower of Babel) to reach the heavens. But the Lord was not happy with this and "confounded the tongues of the people that they might not understand one another's speech." The result provides us with the English word ___, a meaningless confusion of words and sounds.

T	T	O	H	E	E	F	I	R	S
R	E	Z	T	L	E	S	C	C	T
N	B	N	B	T	A	U	O	G	A
T	L	B	O	H	E	A	L	Y	D
E	A	W	A	Y	C	H	O	S	P
B	R	R	R	H	A	O	G	D	U
C	N	E	I	D	I	B	N	N	N
A	E	U	G	F	A	T	E	U	C
K	Y	C	O	N	F	N	E	C	T
I	C	U	T	I	N	1	9	3	7

3. The first was invented in Kocs, Hungary, in the 15th century, and its use quickly spread throughout Europe because it provided cheap transportation for commoners who couldn't afford their own conveyances. A century later, the word ___ became synonymous with English university tutors, apparently because they, too, carried their students along, albeit educationally.

4. In 1602, an Irishman by the name of Cormack McCarthy sweet-talked the British, who had encircled his castle (located in the town this word is named for) into delaying its takeover indefinitely. McCarthy's verbal success subsequently resulted in the term ___, meaning "smooth, flattering talk."

5. In 50 AD, a city in Germany was founded by the Romans and named Colonia Agrippina (Agrippina's Colony) because it was the birthplace of Agrippina, the wife of the Roman emperor. The name of the city was later shortened to Colonia. And while the German word for the city is now Köln, during its French occupation it was called ___ and gave its name to the perfumed water produced there since 1709.

6. The Spanish seaport of Tarifa, a one-time Roman settlement, was controlled by African pirates during the Moorish occupation of Spain. The Mediterranean freebooters forced ships passing through the Straits of Gibraltar to pay duties, a form of blackmail that came to be known as a ___.

7. According to legend, a dagger called a ___ was manufactured in Bayonne, France, in 1490. The name was later used for a knife that is attached to the muzzle of a rifle.

8. A source of naturally sparkling mineral water was found in Niederselters (Lower Selters), Germany, in the mid-18th century. The name for this bubbly water first appeared as *Selterser Wasser* (Selters water), which was ultimately Anglicized and lowercased to ___.

ANSWER, PAGE 230

SCAREDY-CATS

Everybody's afraid of something. See if your phobia is lurking in here somewhere.

ACROSS

1 Trajectory shapes
5 *J'accuse* author
9 Like some commitments
14 Eeyore's ursine pal
15 Pressing need?
16 Movement in a sonata
17 *Fashion Emergency* host
18 What a ligyrophobe is afraid of
20 Constitutional Amendment XXI, commonly
22 Cereal "for kids"
23 Yale Bowl attendee
24 "___ You Come Back to Me"
26 New Testament letter
28 Root cellar veggies
31 Stitch
32 Dwight, informally
33 Not appropriate
35 Cobb, for one
39 Ingredient in refried beans
41 Heir, perhaps
43 Lawrence Berra's nickname
44 Big name in disinfectants
46 King of Judea, 37–4 BC
48 Keanu's *Matrix* role
49 Gymnast's bottom?
51 What a xenophobe is afraid of
53 Pesto ingredient
57 Disseminate
58 "Evil Woman" rock grp.
59 Summertime pest
61 Role models
64 What a taphephobe is afraid of
67 ___ Major (the Big Dipper)
68 Famous firefighter Red ___
69 Sooner, in the Depression
70 June 6, 1944
71 Socially awkward
72 Rocker Turner
73 "What you see is what you get"

DOWN

1 Imitator
2 Capital on the Tiber River
3 What a cyberphobe is afraid of
4 TV's Queen of the Jungle
5 More than a few... much, much more
6 Gold, in Guatemala
7 Oaf
8 Previn or Agassi
9 Substitutes
10 Louis XIV, *par exemple*
11 Atlas close-up
12 Nancy of *Access Hollywood*
13 The Jetsons' robot maid
19 Pinches off
21 Westernmost Aleutian island
25 Cary Grant's real last name
27 Persuade
28 Apothecary preparation
29 Authorize
30 Moles, e.g.
34 First-year law course
36 What a hippopotomonstrosesquippedalio phobe is afraid of
37 Tommie of the Mets
38 A-line designer Christian
40 Rotunda
42 German Ocean, today
45 British actress Lillie
47 Challenge
50 Fix a piano
52 Chilean Nobel poet Pablo ___
53 Pie nut
54 ___ France
55 Baseball's Garciaparra
56 Deck with a Magician card
60 *Kon-*___
62 He plays Esteban on PBS's *American Family*
63 Simon ___
65 ___ al-Fitr (end of Ramadan)
66 Teutonic pronoun

ANSWER, PAGE 230

OF ALL THE LUCK!

Whether it's crossing your fingers or carrying a rabbit's foot, people will do just about anything to attract a little luck, and the rich and famous are no exception. Can you guess these celebrity superstitions?

1. Jimmy Connors wouldn't compete in a tennis match unless he had this tucked into his sock:
   a. a note from his grandmother
   b. a list of insults to yell at the umpire
   c. a crisp $1 bill

2. Meanwhile, on the other side of the court, John McEnroe had his own quirks. Not only wouldn't he step on a white line on the court, he thought it was bad luck to play on:
   a. Groundhog Day
   b. any day after an eclipse
   c. Thursday the 12th

3. Auto racer Mario Andretti won't give you an autograph if you do this to him:
   a. tell him that *your* name is also Mario
   b. hand him a green pen to write with
   c. make silly "vroom vroom!" noises

4. Just before filming begins, Jack Lemmon whispers this to himself:
   a. "Magic time!"
   b. "Well, here goes nothing..."
   c. "Mommmmyyyyyy!"

5. General Stonewall Jackson always charged into battle doing this, for "psychic balance":
   a. holding his second-in-command's hand
   b. holding his left hand over his head
   c. repeatedly shifting his sword from one hand to the other

6. Kichiro Toyoda, founder of Toyota, does this at the advice of a fortuneteller:
   a. only uses car names that begin with the letter C
   b. avoids making new models in odd-numbered years
   c. gives his children the same names as his cars

7. When John Madden was coach of the Oakland Raiders, he wouldn't let his team leave the locker room until running back Mark van Eeghen did this:
   a. sang "Danny Boy"
   b. punched him in the stomach
   c. belched

8. The Barrymores—Lionel, Ethel, and John—always gave each other one of these on the night of a show's premiere:
   a. an apple
   b. a ham sandwich
   c. a crisp new dollar bill

9. John Wayne's luckycharm was a person. The Duke considered it good luck to be in a movie with was:
   a. Maureen O'Hara
   b. Ward Bond
   c. His son Patrick

ANSWER, PAGE 230

AND HOW ABOUT A RUSTY NAIL?

Directions for solving are on page 13.

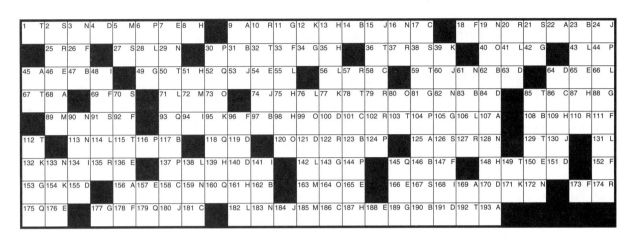

A. Motivation for an invention, it's said

‾68‾ ‾45‾ ‾125‾ ‾9‾ ‾193‾ ‾156‾ ‾22‾ ‾169‾ ‾107‾

B. Star guitarist of a self-named band (3 wds.)

‾14‾ ‾47‾ ‾162‾ ‾31‾ ‾97‾ ‾190‾ ‾108‾ ‾62‾ ‾146‾ ‾117‾ ‾123‾ ‾83‾ ‾23‾

C. Shrinks from the heat

‾186‾ ‾158‾ ‾101‾ ‾86‾ ‾58‾ ‾181‾ ‾17‾

D. Actor in *Diner* and *Body Heat* (2 wds.)

‾121‾ ‾100‾ ‾140‾ ‾64‾ ‾151‾ ‾155‾ ‾84‾ ‾119‾ ‾170‾ ‾4‾ ‾63‾ ‾191‾

E. Broadway belter born in Astoria, Queens (2 wds.)

‾136‾ ‾157‾ ‾176‾ ‾54‾ ‾46‾ ‾150‾ ‾165‾ ‾188‾ ‾166‾ ‾7‾ ‾65‾

F. *Christina's World* painter (2 wds.)

‾69‾ ‾26‾ ‾33‾ ‾96‾ ‾147‾ ‾18‾ ‾173‾ ‾92‾ ‾111‾ ‾152‾ ‾178‾

G. Dean Koontz spine-tingler of 1976 (2 wds.)

‾88‾ ‾189‾ ‾11‾ ‾143‾ ‾177‾ ‾49‾ ‾153‾ ‾81‾ ‾34‾ ‾42‾ ‾105‾

H. Missouri home of the Harry S. Truman Library

‾139‾ ‾8‾ ‾187‾ ‾161‾ ‾98‾ ‾51‾ ‾13‾ ‾109‾ ‾35‾ ‾148‾ ‾75‾ ‾87‾

I. Tie, link; core of the matter

‾134‾ ‾141‾ ‾168‾ ‾94‾ ‾48‾

J. Side show operators; swindlers

‾24‾ ‾184‾ ‾180‾ ‾130‾ ‾53‾ ‾15‾ ‾60‾ ‾74‾

K. Dog originally bred to hunt underground

‾39‾ ‾154‾ ‾171‾ ‾95‾ ‾12‾ ‾77‾ ‾132‾

L. Like debris at Roswell, New Mexico, maybe (4 wds.)

‾66‾ ‾138‾ ‾56‾ ‾114‾ ‾43‾ ‾71‾ ‾28‾ ‾41‾ ‾182‾

‾142‾ ‾131‾ ‾76‾ ‾106‾ ‾55‾

M. Tenth-part offering

‾89‾ ‾5‾ ‾163‾ ‾72‾ ‾185‾

N. Students who perform better than expected

‾19‾ ‾113‾ ‾3‾ ‾16‾ ‾133‾ ‾183‾ ‾90‾ ‾61‾ ‾29‾ ‾82‾ ‾172‾ ‾159‾ ‾128‾

O. Everyone else

‾40‾ ‾99‾ ‾164‾ ‾73‾ ‾80‾ ‾120‾

P. Kingsley Amis's comic first novel (2 wds.)

‾124‾ ‾104‾ ‾6‾ ‾116‾ ‾144‾ ‾137‾ ‾44‾ ‾30‾

Q. Shreds

‾118‾ ‾52‾ ‾145‾ ‾175‾ ‾179‾ ‾160‾ ‾93‾

R. Daughter of Jawaharlal Nehru (2 wds.)

‾25‾ ‾127‾ ‾79‾ ‾174‾ ‾20‾ ‾122‾ ‾135‾ ‾37‾ ‾10‾ ‾110‾ ‾57‾ ‾102‾

S. Blunders

‾2‾ ‾167‾ ‾38‾ ‾27‾ ‾126‾ ‾21‾ ‾91‾ ‾70‾

T. Title role player in *'Breaker' Morant*, 1980 (2 wds.)

‾36‾ ‾32‾ ‾85‾ ‾1‾ ‾50‾ ‾115‾ ‾67‾ ‾103‾ ‾129‾

‾112‾ ‾78‾ ‾149‾ ‾192‾ ‾59‾

ANSWER, PAGE 231

YUPPIE PUPPIES

If your dog has had its fill of filet mignon, and is now seeking new luxuries, here are a few products to consider. Not all of them are real, though. Can you separate the authentic puppy treats from the times where we had a ball and pretended to throw it, but then didn't throw it after all?

BOW-LINGUAL DOG TRANSLATOR

This device (from Japan...where else?) analyzes your dog's barks, growls, and whines and translates them into emotions, using a 200-word vocabulary. With a tiny microphone that attaches to the dog's collar, this pager-sized device generates sentences like "I feel lonely" and "Mega happy day!" It also stores a record of your dog's last hundred barks, so you don't have to worry about forgetting any requests your dog may have made earlier in the day.

DOG DOORBELL

For owners who can't bear to have their dogs suffer the indignity of scratching at doors, Hammacher Schlemmer offers this device, which Fido can use to indicate he wants to go out by stepping on a paw-shaped radio transmitter. The transmitter activates a remote chime, letting master know that nature is calling.

OH MY DOG! EAU DE TOILETTE SPRAY

It's the world's first top-quality fragrance crafted especially for canines, and it's available at Saks Fifth Avenue (where the dogs aren't allowed in for a test spritz, sadly). "Top notes of rosewood and orange leaves suggest happy barking while the heart notes evoke a boisterous tussle in the grass." Also available: Oh My Cat!

DOG'S BEST FRIEND

Is your dog lonely, staying home all day while you're at the office? You might consider investing in Dog's Best Friend, essentially a motorized stuffed toy on wheels (not unlike a robotic vacuum cleaner), which will periodically zoom around your house and bark playfully, offering your house-bound hound a little mechanized companionship. But if you come home to a broken lamp, don't be surprised if your dog blames the robot.

DELIGHTED DOGGY PET TUNES

Another product meant to keep stay-at-home dogs happy, this one ostensibly works by mellowing your pooch out to the mellifluous sounds of classical composers like Bach, Brahms, and Chopin. It also suggests you and your dog have a little music appreciation session: "Try sitting and listening together—you'll both benefit from relaxing and hearing these timeless selections." But what if your dog prefers the Sex Pistols?

DOGGY-GO-ROUND

Everyone knows how much hamsters love to run in their little plastic wheels. Why wouldn't dogs like to do the same? Well, the wheels are too small. But if they were *much bigger*? This is the perfect product for someone who has both a tiny backyard and a dog who likes to run like crazy. The manufacturers recommend the wheel for small dogs only, but since small dogs are also the most hyper, that works out fine.

IONIC BATH PET BRUSH

If you love your puppy but not his smell, this brush showers your pet with ozone particles, which neutralize odors and condition his fur...using science! Science has been shown in many scientific studies to be much less traumatizing to dogs than bath water.

ANSWER, PAGE 219

COLOR ME GULLIBLE

Every color has a subliminal effect on our moods and appetites. Find out what researchers have proven—and what product designers do with that information so that we'll do exactly what they want us to do. For further instructions and hints on how to solve, see page 7.

Pink: ZCHVJNZ   ZIDA   CIMC   FNDFEN   MEGDZC   MEAMOZ

QNEJNWN   "FMZCLJNZ   ULDG   M   FJPX   QDR   CMZCN

QNCCNL   CIMP   ULDG   MPO   DCINL   BDEDL   QDR."

Blue: LXRD   NVSNLNAW   ASD   ZDWNTD   AG   DIA;   NV

OIBA,   TDWDITBSDTW   WIC,   "EDGEXD   ADVZ   AG   DIA

XDWW   OTGF   LXRD   EXIADW."

Orange: AIMVSP   YR   M   XJYGO   MCCPVCYAV-SPCCPI,   MVW

LTPV   YC'R   JRPW   AV   M   FIAWJGC,   YC   "NAJWNZ

FIAGNMYBR   CTMC   CTP   FIAWJGC   YR   DAI   PUPIZAVP."

Green: UTAAY   BR   MRAN   OX   RAHH   DAUAOIWHAR   IYN

VQAJBYU   UMZ.   WMO   KAXKHA   IDXBN   MRBYU   BO   OX

RAHH   ZAIO,   WAVIMRA   BO   TAZBYNR   VXYRMZATR   XE

ZXHN.

ANSWER, PAGE 230

NAME DROPPINGS

It's little wonder that actor Albert Brooks (*Broadcast News*, *The Muse*) decided to change his name. You might have too if your folks, Mr. and Mrs. Einstein, had named you "Albert." In this puzzle you'll meet eight other people who, for their own reasons, decided, yeah, a new name would be just the ticket.

ACROSS
1 Wipe clean
6 Tokyo mats
13 Brew choice
19 ___ blanche
20 Elevated standing
22 Deli buy
23 Charles Buchinski's new name
25 Clog
26 Mrs. Hoggett, in *Babe*
27 "It's a Sin to Tell ___"
28 Mozart's "Cosi fan ___"
30 "No thanks"
31 *East of Eden* girl
33 Thomas Mapother IV's new name
35 Open-backed truck
38 Restaurateur Toots
40 Long lunches?
41 TV's *Doctor* ___
44 Shows to a seat, slangily
45 1930s boxer Max
46 Have chits out
47 "___ out!" (ump's call)
48 Disparaging word
49 Hungarian stew
52 MPG raters
53 Glitch
54 Jiff
55 Ralph Lifshitz's new name
57 Margaret Thatcher adherent
58 Sarah Hughes, e.g.
61 Evenings in Paris
62 Cautionary advice
63 Pen point
64 "___ you see that?"
67 OJ trial judge
69 Noisy clamor
70 Soccer chauffeurs?
71 Brooks Brothers buys
75 Moneybags
78 Trash in Eden?
79 Joyce Frankenberg's new name
83 Gig
85 Tribal hand-me-downs
86 Don't just stand there
87 Sign the check on the back
88 Preserve with salt
89 Former White House spokesguy Fleischer
90 Wisk rival
91 Fourth piggy's share
92 Rapper/record producer
93 "Indubitably"
94 Greek sorceress
97 Fix up
98 Initial, as a voyage
99 Elias Bates's new name
101 Pinball problem
102 It's a good thing
105 Quinn of *Legends of the Fall*
106 Bad boy of the Bible
108 Jazz singer Fitzgerald
112 Actress Marlee
114 Eleanor Gow's new name
117 Land of the Blessed, in myth
118 Big name in whiskey
119 Liz Taylor-James Dean film
120 Tranquil
121 Sondheim's ___ *Todd: The Demon Barber of Fleet Street*
122 Billionaire Bill

DOWN
1 Behold, to Brutus
2 Stadium cheers
3 Composer Khachaturian
4 Oscar crasher of the '70s
5 Slippery type
6 Inventor Nikola
7 Prefix with "dextrous"
8 Poop out
9 365 *dias*
10 One with a protégé
11 "To recap…"
12 Chivas Regal, e.g.
13 Balky beast
14 *The Piano Lesson* painter
15 Natural incline
16 Spanish appetizer
17 Ostrich relatives
18 "Hot ___" Houlihan
21 ___ nous (confidentially)
24 He said he slew Johnny Ringo
29 Norway's continent
32 Where Rosa Parks made her mark
33 Hebrew scrolls
34 Des Moines native
35 Kisser
36 The British ___
37 Carlos Ray's new name
38 The first king of Israel
39 The Beach Boys' "___ Me, Rhonda"
41 Christina Ciminella's new name
42 Locket shape
43 Bawdy party
45 Get on the boat
49 Test for college srs.
50 ___-mo (instant replay speed)
51 "Bali ___"
52 Prefix for "while"
53 Long-suffering

56 Spoon-bender Geller
59 Actress Anouk
60 It's about three tsp.
62 Pesticide first tested in Colorado in 1939
65 "Well, ___ that special!"
66 Scheduled to arrive
68 Serviceable
70 Dinty or Demi
72 British ending for "real"
73 Perfect score in gymnastics
74 Aussie port
76 Exist
77 Yankees manager Joe
78 Ruben's runner-up in 2003's *American Idol*

79 Actor Leto
80 Maine national park
81 ___ music (soothing sounds)
82 Words that sometimes follow 93 Across
84 Existed
88 Standards
90 Love or hate
92 Indian sauce for rice
95 Adams and Falco
96 Mixes up
97 Go back on one's word
98 Ho Chi ___ City
99 *Beauty and the Beast* heroine

100 Steven Bochco series
101 Stewed
102 "He loves," in Latin 101
103 Sock away
104 Top banana
106 James of *The Godfather*
107 High point
109 Future atty.'s exam
110 Word with wolf or Ranger
111 Hill insects
113 Tampa-to-New York dir.
115 Desert Storm eats for a GI
116 Heckler's missile

ANSWER, PAGE 231

THE TIME IT TAKES #3

Put the following time-takers in order from the least amount to the most amount of time they take.

____ The length of time in a snail's life span

____ The length of time in the life expectancy of a Neanderthal man

____ The time it takes an adult to walk one step

____ The time it takes for 50 people to be born

____ The time it takes for a slow boat to get to China from New York

____ The time it takes to completely recover from jet lag

____ The time it takes to reach an actual person when calling the IRS during tax time

____ The time it would take for the Earth to fall into the Sun if it lost its orbit

____ The time it would take to reach the nearest star, Proxima Centauri, in a car going 65 mph

____ The time span from a new moon to a new moon

ANSWER, PAGE 231

THAT SETTLES THAT

Small crostic puzzles are solved just like the big ones (directions on page 13) but the first letter of the fill-in words **do not** spell out a hidden message.

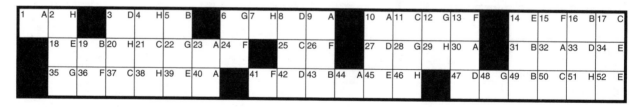

A. Get happy at the thought of

___ ___ ___ ___ ___ ___ ___ ___
10 44 1 23 32 9 30 40

B. Wood shop or electronics tool

___ ___ ___ ___ ___ ___
19 43 5 31 16 49

C. Taqueria order

___ ___ ___ ___ ___ ___
25 21 17 37 50 11

D. Vice president from Wyoming

___ ___ ___ ___ ___ ___
47 27 33 8 42 3

E. Attractive item?

___ ___ ___ ___ ___ ___
34 18 45 52 39 14

F. Author of *The Sorrows of Young Werther*

___ ___ ___ ___ ___ ___
41 26 24 13 15 36

G. Beach rental for privacy

___ ___ ___ ___ ___ ___
6 28 35 48 22 12

H. Teacher's pet

___ ___ ___ ___ ___ ___ ___ ___
2 7 29 4 20 51 38 46

ANSWER, PAGE 229

YOU'VE BEEN WARNED!

Manufacturers are so afraid of being sued that they've started to attach some really dumb warning labels...like the ones below. First, work back and forth between the blanks and the grid to fill in the missing words and phrases. (The number of blanks tell you the number of letters in each word or phrase, and the missing words in the list are in alphabetical order. That should help.) Once you've found all the missing words and phrases in the grid, the leftover letters will reveal a stupid warning label we might have attached to this puzzle. (Warning: If you need help, the complete word list is on the answer page.)

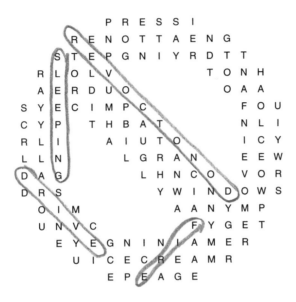

```
              P R E S S I
            R E N O T T A E N G
            S T E P G N I Y R D T T
    R   L O L V         T O N H
    A E R D U O         O A A
  S Y E C I M P C       F O U
  C Y P T H B A T       N L I
  R L I A I U T O       I C Y
  L L N L G R A N       E E W
  D A G L H N C O       V O R
  D R S Y W I N D O W S
  O I M A A N Y M P
  U N V C F Y G E T
  E Y E G N I N I A M E R
    U I C E C R E A M R
    E P E A G E
```

1. On a vacuum cleaner: "Do not use to pick up anything that is currently __ __ __ __ __ __ __ __."

2. On a CD player: "Do not use the Ultradisc 2000 as a projectile in a __ __ __ __ __ __ __ __ __ __."

3. On a pair of shin pads: "Shin pads cannot protect any part of the body they _D_O_ _N_O_T_ _C_O_V_E_R_."

4. On a cardboard sunshield for a car: "Do not _D_R_I_V_E_ with sunshield in place."

5. In a microwave oven manual: "Do not use for __ __ __ __ __ __ __ __ __ __ __ __."

6. On a toner cartridge: "Do not __ __ __ __ __ __ __ __ __ __."

7. On a Duraflame fireplace log: "Caution—Risk of _F_I_R_E_."

8. On a plastic, 13-inch wheelbarrow wheel: "Not intended for __ __ __ __ __ __ __ __ __ use."

9. On a bottle of hair coloring: "Do not use as an __ __ __ __ __ __ __ __ __ topping."

10. On a box of rat poison: "Warning: Has been found to cause cancer in laboratory __ __ __ __."

11. On a toilet bowl cleaning brush: "Do not use __ __ __ __ __ __ __."

12. In the instructions for a digital thermometer: "Do not use orally after using __ __ __ __ __ __ __ __ __ __."

13. On a laser pointer: "Do not look into laser with __ __ __ __ __ __ __ __ __ __ __ __."

14. On a portable stroller: "__ __ __ __ __ __ __ __ __ __ __ __ __ __ __ __ __ __ before folding for storage."

15. On a propane blowtorch: "Never use while _S_L_E_E_P_I_N_G_."

16. On a Batman costume: "Warning: Cape does not enable user _T_O_ _F_L_Y_."

17. On an air conditioner: "Avoid dropping air conditioners out of __ __ __ __ __ __ __ __."

ANSWER, PAGE 232

COMING CLEAN WITH THE STORY

Directions for solving are on page 13.

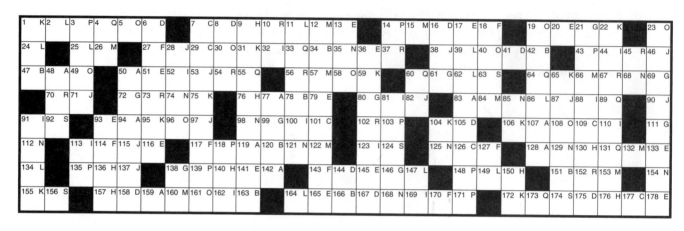

A. Author of the cop novel *Badge of Honor* (4 wds.)

$\overline{77}$ $\overline{142}$ $\overline{128}$ $\overline{159}$ $\overline{50}$ $\overline{94}$ $\overline{83}$ $\overline{119}$ $\overline{107}$ $\overline{48}$

B. Innate ability

$\overline{78}$ $\overline{34}$ $\overline{166}$ $\overline{47}$ $\overline{163}$ $\overline{120}$ $\overline{151}$ $\overline{42}$

C. Word with team or holy

$\overline{177}$ $\overline{101}$ $\overline{109}$ $\overline{7}$ $\overline{126}$ $\overline{29}$

D. Formative years

$\overline{175}$ $\overline{167}$ $\overline{158}$ $\overline{41}$ $\overline{16}$ $\overline{144}$ $\overline{8}$ $\overline{105}$ $\overline{6}$

E. "The house that Ruth built" (2 wds.)

$\overline{79}$ $\overline{51}$ $\overline{17}$ $\overline{116}$ $\overline{145}$ $\overline{36}$ $\overline{178}$ $\overline{141}$ $\overline{165}$
$\overline{13}$ $\overline{20}$ $\overline{133}$ $\overline{93}$

F. Rice flavored with broth and spices

$\overline{117}$ $\overline{27}$ $\overline{127}$ $\overline{170}$ $\overline{18}$ $\overline{143}$ $\overline{114}$

G. English inventor of the spinning jenny

$\overline{80}$ $\overline{99}$ $\overline{21}$ $\overline{138}$ $\overline{146}$ $\overline{61}$ $\overline{69}$ $\overline{111}$ $\overline{72}$

H. Celebs, luminaries, etc.

$\overline{136}$ $\overline{140}$ $\overline{130}$ $\overline{76}$ $\overline{157}$ $\overline{150}$ $\overline{176}$ $\overline{9}$

I. Specialist who'll really set you straight!

$\overline{169}$ $\overline{32}$ $\overline{113}$ $\overline{91}$ $\overline{100}$ $\overline{88}$ $\overline{44}$ $\overline{81}$ $\overline{110}$
$\overline{123}$ $\overline{162}$ $\overline{52}$

J. Norah Jones's 2003 Record of the Year (3 wds.)

$\overline{137}$ $\overline{71}$ $\overline{28}$ $\overline{97}$ $\overline{46}$ $\overline{87}$ $\overline{115}$ $\overline{90}$ $\overline{38}$
$\overline{53}$ $\overline{82}$

K. McMurtry sequel to *Terms of Endearment* (with *The*) (2 wds.)

$\overline{22}$ $\overline{106}$ $\overline{1}$ $\overline{59}$ $\overline{155}$ $\overline{75}$ $\overline{95}$ $\overline{172}$ $\overline{104}$
$\overline{65}$ $\overline{31}$

L. Ballpark figures?

$\overline{25}$ $\overline{24}$ $\overline{134}$ $\overline{164}$ $\overline{149}$ $\overline{147}$ $\overline{39}$ $\overline{86}$ $\overline{11}$
$\overline{2}$ $\overline{62}$

M. The whole enchilada

$\overline{26}$ $\overline{66}$ $\overline{122}$ $\overline{84}$ $\overline{153}$ $\overline{132}$ $\overline{57}$ $\overline{15}$ $\overline{12}$ $\overline{160}$

N. Roger Clemens or Nolan Ryan, e.g. (hyph.)

$\overline{74}$ $\overline{85}$ $\overline{121}$ $\overline{154}$ $\overline{35}$ $\overline{125}$ $\overline{129}$ $\overline{68}$ $\overline{98}$
$\overline{112}$ $\overline{168}$

O. Film critic author of *Laughing Matters* (2 wds.)

$\overline{49}$ $\overline{30}$ $\overline{5}$ $\overline{161}$ $\overline{108}$ $\overline{96}$ $\overline{58}$ $\overline{19}$ $\overline{40}$ $\overline{23}$

P. Prime-time players covet this (2 wds.)

$\overline{118}$ $\overline{3}$ $\overline{171}$ $\overline{103}$ $\overline{148}$ $\overline{43}$ $\overline{135}$ $\overline{139}$ $\overline{14}$

Q. Jackie Chan-Chris Tucker problem of 1998 (2 wds.)

$\overline{55}$ $\overline{33}$ $\overline{89}$ $\overline{131}$ $\overline{64}$ $\overline{4}$ $\overline{173}$ $\overline{60}$

R. Credited in print

$\overline{152}$ $\overline{70}$ $\overline{10}$ $\overline{45}$ $\overline{67}$ $\overline{102}$ $\overline{73}$ $\overline{56}$ $\overline{54}$ $\overline{37}$

S. Bops on the bean

$\overline{174}$ $\overline{92}$ $\overline{124}$ $\overline{63}$ $\overline{156}$

ANSWER, PAGE 231

WHERE AM I?

Imagine if you went to bed one night in Quinnipiac, Connecticut, and woke up the next day in New Haven. You might think you were crazy—but if you consulted Uncle John, he'd tell you it happens all the time: It's just because the city fathers and mothers got tired of their old name and decided to change it. We've scrambled the letters of some of the old names of U.S. cities. Your job is to put them back in the right order. And don't worry; there isn't a Quinnipiac in the bunch. Would we do that to you? Well, maybe, but not this time.

1. Miami, Florida: F O R T   D A L L A S
   OFRT   LADLAS

2. Truth or Consequences, New Mexico: H O T   S P R I N G S
   THO   GRINSPS

3. Chicago, Illinois: F O R T   __ __ __ __ __ __ __ __
   TRFO   BORDANER

4. Lincoln, Nebraska: __ __ __ __ __ __ __ __ __
   SCATERNAL

5. Atlanta, Georgia: __ __ __ __ __ __ __ __
   SMUTREIN

6. Baltimore, Maryland: __ __ __ __ __ ' __   H A R B O R
   SLOCE   BRORAH

7. Austin, Texas: __ __ __ __ __ __ __ __
   TEALOWOR

8. Wilmington, Delaware: __ __ __ __ __ __ __ __ __ __ __
   GINWILTWOLN

9. Charleston, South Carolina: __ __ __ __ __ __   P O I N T
   ROYSET   NIPOT

10. New York, New York: N E W   __ __ __ __ __ __ __ __ __ __
    WNE   LATERNNHED

11. Minneapolis, Minnesota: A L L   S A I N T S
    LAL   TANISS

12. Reno, Nevada: L A K E   C R O S S I N G
    KELA   SNICSROG

13. Cleveland, Ohio: N E W   C O N N E C T I C U T
    EWN   NICOTNECUTC

14. Concord, New Hampshire: __ __ __ __ __ __ __
    FRUDMOR

ANSWER, PAGE 233

SIMPLY MAUVELOUS!

In 1993 the Crayola people introduced a red-purple color they called "Mauvelous." Here are a few more creatively named colors that the Binney & Smith company has come up with over the years. Do try to stay inside the lines.

ACROSS

1 Bottomless pit
6 Nectarine's ancestor
11 Table of honor
15 Disney's ___ and the Detectives
19 Call from the flock
20 Open-air rooms
21 Big role for Ingrid
22 The Right Stuff org.
23 Pale pink introduced in 1998
25 Dark pink introduced in 1949
27 They may be natural
28 Danny's Mrs.
30 Walked into the wings
31 Canon camera name
32 Mother of Hermes
34 Peter or Alexander
35 Get hung up (on)
39 Color renamed in 1990, formerly called Ultra Red
45 Slave away
46 Dramatist of The Playboy of the Western World
47 Popular Valentine's Day buy
48 Beatle wife
49 Purplish fluorescent color introduced in 1972
52 Sell hot tickets
53 Fatty treat for birds
54 WSW's opposite
55 They're girded, in purple prose
56 The original Anita of West Side Story
57 ___ voce
58 Cinnamon candies
60 View from Notre Dame
61 Parish cleric
62 Fluorescent color introduced in 1990, formerly called Ultra Orange
66 Witch's magic brew
69 Hubbub
70 Reluctance to move

74 Babushka
75 In unison
76 Euro fractions
78 Traveler's stop
79 Runs smoothly
80 Copycat's forte
81 Orange shade introduced in 2003
83 Spy TV host Landry
84 Squiggle on señor
85 Handled
86 The clink, in Canterbury
87 Azure shade introduced in 2003
90 Pure as the driven snow
92 CD-___ (computer storage media)
93 Was remorseful
94 One might go for a buck
95 Master jewel thief Lupin
98 Echinacea, e.g.
100 Wimbledon worker
105 Medium yellow introduced in 1958
107 Pale yellow introduced in 1998
110 Pull at the earth's surface
111 Heavy book
112 Subsided
113 Sir John of England
114 Miami-___ County
115 British gun
116 Speak disparagingly of
117 What epicures prize

DOWN

1 The basics
2 Group with a purpose
3 Abominable Snowman
4 Fill full
5 Sir Mick and group
6 Counts out for a duel
7 LAX guesstimates
8 Son of Prince Valiant

9 Spanish hero El ___
10 Wagon outing
11 Grungy eatery
12 Inter ___ (among other things)
13 Cousin of equi-
14 Avon lady, for one
15 Whole
16 Trading center
17 "Gotcha"
18 Laura Dern's mom Diane
24 Enlisted personnel of rank (abbr.)
26 Diagnostic tests
29 Hem's partner
32 Money makers
33 Pond growth
34 Croatian-born inventor
35 Survey choice
36 Cumberland Gap trailblazer
37 Positioned
38 Spiral-grained wood
39 Ed who played Uncle Albert in Mary Poppins
40 Making a trajectory
41 How some things fit
42 Yahoos
43 ___ a customer
44 Cancelled, as an airing
46 Earthquake
50 Many
51 Was sympatico (with)
52 Sparkle
53 More achy
56 Stop
57 Having the most marbles
59 They're found in the brush
60 Lead of The Police
61 Kind of bean or pony
63 Not alfresco
64 Boxer Gerry, a.k.a. The Great White Hope
65 All-Starr Band leader
66 "Poppycock!"
67 Eyes

68 Language of Sri Lanka
71 Yothers and Chow
72 Bar of gold
73 Green (sometimes) lizard
75 Top grade
76 Made a birdcall
77 ___'acte
80 Hypochondriac's list
81 Identified, in police slang
82 ___ Khan
84 Steak choice

85 Gave the cold shoulder
88 Coat with flour
89 Bobby of hockey legend
90 Soda machine selection
91 Batter's protection
94 Fine partner
95 "How like ___," says Hamlet
96 Dishy Barrett
97 Rare sale in Florida
98 Neck of the woods
99 First lady's residence

100 Boxer Buddy
101 Festive event
102 Football stats
103 Thigh-slapping funny
104 Bowler's zone
106 Go bad
108 Playwright Burrows
109 Peacock network

ANSWER, PAGE 233

WOULD WE LIE TO YOU AGAIN?

Oh, yeah. In this quiz, we explain some everyday phenomena that have been puzzling us for a long time—perhaps you've been similarly perplexed...? And once again, we're offering too many explanations, all of which sound perfectly reasonable. Can you figure out the one true answer in each set?

1. Why don't spiders get caught in their own webs?
   a. Because not every strand of a web is sticky, and spiders know where to step to avoid getting stuck.
   b. Because spiders coat their legs with an oily spittle to make them nonstick.
   c. Because spiders are just walking on the webs. To get really stuck, you have to *fly* into a web.

2. Why are children's coin banks traditionally shaped like pigs?
   a. Frugal people in the Middle Ages saved their coins in kitchen jars made out of *pygg*, a dense orange clay. The name "pygg jar" (later simplified to "pig jar") persisted, and eventually potters began casting coin banks in pig shapes, to fit the common name.
   b. The earliest piggy banks were openable only with a hammer; they were specifically designed to encourage kids to save money. The idea behind the pig shape was that the bank, being a "greedy pig," was always willing to take your money but not so willing to give it back.
   c. The choice of a pig was largely practical. Toy makers wanted kids' coin banks to look like *something*, and pigs were a good shape: round and fat, with small supporting legs. The first "piggy banks" sold briskly, and the pig shape became a tradition.

3. Why aren't cashews ever sold in their shells?
   a. Because cashews don't have shells. In fact, they're not nuts at all; they're seeds from a pear-shaped fruit.
   b. Because cashew shells are mildly poisonous, and cashew companies don't want to get sued if some idiot eats them.
   c. Actually, you *can* buy unshelled cashews in certain gourmet food stores. But they're not very popular, because the shells are heavy and hard to open.

4. Why is June such a popular month for getting married?
   a. Outdoor weddings were very fashionable in old England, but rain always threatened to dampen the festivities. To minimize the chance of having one's wedding spoiled by weather, couples scheduled their ceremonies for June, the sunniest month.
   b. In the 1800s, university students in the U.S. were taught in two sessions: one from January through May, the other from mid-July through mid-December. (These sessions would later be shortened, creating the summer vacation that we all know and love.) Since students had no classes in June, it was a logical time to schedule a wedding.
   c. This tradition actually dates back to ancient Roman times: June weddings were meant to honor Juno, queen of the gods and goddess of women. Winning Juno's favor meant that your marriage would last longer and childbirth would be easier.

5. You've seen birds pecking at the soil, but how do they know where to find those juicy worms?
   a. They look for holes in the ground where worms have surfaced recently.
   b. They feel the vibrations of the worms with their incredibly sensitive feet.
   c. They don't know exactly where the worms are, but they know which soils are likely to contain worms, so they just keep pecking until they find one.

ANSWER, PAGE 232

MIND YOUR MANNERS, PART ONE

Thank goodness for books of etiquette! How else would we know how to behave? If you need directions on how to solve this puzzle, see page 13.

1.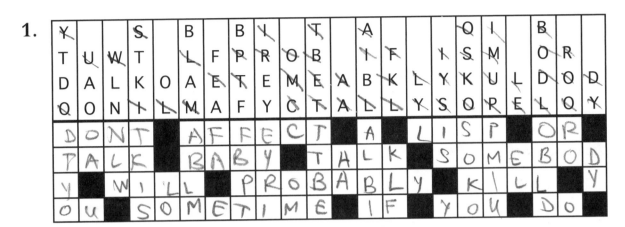

2.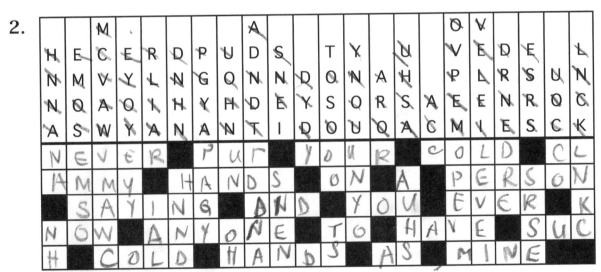

3.

ANSWER, PAGE 232

PERFECT 10 #3

More of those *almost* perfect statements, except that the 10 numbers have been switched. Don't forget that the numbers have been exchanged in *pairs*—that is, if the number 3 replaces the 10, the 10 should replace the 3. Can you make the 10 perfect again?

The ashes of the average cremated person weigh **1** pound.

The average American eats **2** pounds of "artificial flavorings, colorings and preservatives" each year.

The average yawn lasts **3** seconds.

A pelican's beak can hold **4** gallons.

The average Ph.D. candidate spends **5** years on his/her dissertation.

Babe Ruth's jersey number was **6**.

You dream an average of **7** times each night.

The average speed of traffic in New York City during the 1980s was **8** mph.

A coffee tree yields about **9** pounds of coffee in a year.

The average grocery shopper stands in line **10** minutes.

SHOOTING UP

Small crostic puzzles are solved just like the big ones (directions on page 13) but the first letter of the fill-in words **do not** spell out a hidden message.

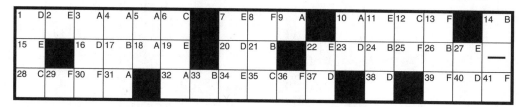

A. Flattering on you, as clothes

　4　31　18　5　3　32　9　10

B. Lone Star State capital

　14　17　21　26　24　33

C. Foot that goes clop

　35　12　6　28

D. Caribbean resort destination

　1　40　23　38　16　20　37

E. Somewhat grating, as a voice

　15　7　11　2　22　34　19　27

F. "Road" to the garage

　39　25　29　30　36　13　8　41

HAVE YOU HERD?

Not all animals gather into such sensible-sounding groups as "herds" or "flocks." There's a leap of leopards, a murmuration of sandpipers, and an unkindness of ravens. Can you fit all of the other actual animal groups into the grid, crossword-style? Both capitalized words in each entry should be entered separately in the grid.

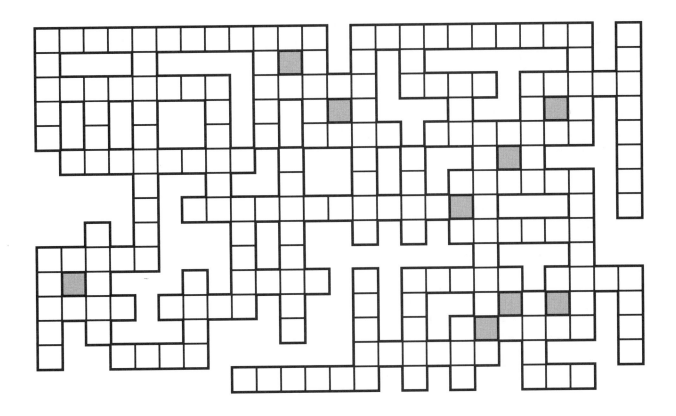

a TROOP of APES
a PACE of ASSES
a SINGULAR of BOARS
an ARMY of CATERPILLARS
a RAG of COLTS
a MURDER of CROWS
a DOLE of DOVES
a TEAM of DUCKS
a GANG of ELK
a BUSINESS of FERRETS
a SKEIN of GEESE
a TRIP of GOATS

a SIEGE of HERONS
a DRIFT of HOGS
a DECEIT of LAPWINGS
a NEST of MICE
a PARLIAMENT of OWLS
an OSTENTATION of PEACOCKS
a NYE of PHEASANTS
a CRASH of RHINOCEROS
a BEVY of ROEBUCKS
a BED of SNAKES
a KNOT of TOADS
a RAFTER of TURKEYS

ANSWER, PAGE 233

I DO SOLEMNLY SWEAR

This is the way a nebbish tells somebody off...

ACROSS
1 British VIPs
4 Elmo of polling fame
9 Model plane stick-on
14 Curbside pickup
18 Date ___ (attractive single)
19 Speed skater ___ Anton Ohno
20 Battery pole
21 Ski bum's Colorado hangout
22 Sign on a shoppe
23 "Gag me with a spoon!"
24 Light bulb unit
25 "Take Five" jazzman Brubeck
26 Part 1 of a sworn statement
30 ___ Time Crooks
31 Flu shots, e.g.
32 Alpacas' cousins
36 "Huzzah!"
37 Film director Lee
40 Category in Twenty Questions
45 "Never Enough" rocker Patty
46 Skedaddles
49 And others, in Latin class
51 Aqua Velva competitor
52 Sworn statement, part 2
55 March Madness org.
57 City that's an anagram of Tokyo
58 Hit the trails
59 Water cooler?
60 Comic strip shrieks
61 Sister, in Sausalito
62 Be an omen of
65 First step in grilling, usually
67 "I'm not ___ complain, but..."
69 Sworn statement, part 3
73 Van Gogh liked to paint there
76 Ibn ___ (Mideast dynasty founder)
78 "___ jungle out there!"
79 Docs' bloc

81 Senior lobbyist org.
82 Withdraw, with "out"
84 Man of La Mancha
87 Almost out of
89 Yearly celebration, for short
90 Sworn statement, part 4
95 Filler in a florist's arrangement
96 Cheer-ful places
97 Fly with a serious bite
98 Cares for
100 Displays contempt
102 "Well, lah-di-___!"
103 Marge, in the Simpson family
106 Beginnings
108 The "I" in I.M. Pei
111 Cognizant
113 End of the sworn statement
120 Silly fool
123 Up and about
124 Fortuneteller's card
125 Ancient concert halls
126 Seabiscuit nail-biter
127 See 112-Down
128 Kooky Kovacs of old TV
129 "Buenos ___"
130 George's answer to "Who chopped down that cherry tree?"
131 Lowly workers
132 Bridge positions
133 Designer monogram

DOWN
1 Picasso's designer daughter
2 When Mother's Day falls, roughly
3 Romance novelist Danielle
4 Popular sauce brand

5 Grand Ole place in Nashville
6 Some toy bears
7 Girlfriend mentioned in the song "Cabaret"
8 Speakers' platforms
9 Tyne or her brother Tim
10 Plenty, informally
11 Command to Fido
12 Arabian gulf
13 Czech tennis great Ivan
14 CSI, Cold Case, and others
15 High bond rating
16 14 in old Rome
17 Land in la mer
18 Assertive and then some
27 Candied, as fruits
28 Tressed like a lion
29 Golfer Ernie
33 Eliza Doolittle, titlewise
34 Cobwebby area
35 Lamp prettifier
38 Cozy corners
39 "I've ___ Under My Skin"
41 Señor follower?
42 Rowdy disorder
43 Second part of a court game?
44 Chain part
46 California peak
47 Garden hazard
48 Stage backdrop
50 Summer quenchers
52 Alternates
53 Sci-fi maid, maybe
54 Bean sprout?
55 Keanu, in The Matrix
56 100 yrs.
63 Raised-eyebrow remarks
64 ___ for Murder
66 Fit for growing
68 Eject
70 Tongue-lashing

71 Cries out loud
72 Acted like in a melodrama
74 Noteworthy period
75 Le Carré character
77 Webster's entries (abbr.)
80 *Rapture* singer Baker
82 "We're ___ see the ..."
83 Doll up
85 Crackers
86 *The Good Earth* wife
88 Ump's call
91 Grateful
92 Never, in Nürnberg

93 "Splish Splash" guy
94 "I don't buy it!"
99 R–V connection
101 Parlor piece
103 Tuesdays, to Thérèse
104 Trying time
105 Monument Valley sights
107 Backpack feature
109 *Pal Joey* author
110 Times Square noisemakers
112 With 127-Across, author of the sworn statement

114 Cleo's river
115 Capital on a fjord
116 High-schooler
117 Bed-and-breakfasts
118 Linda Ellerbee's *And ___ Goes*
119 Followers of *printemps*
120 Prefix with athlete
121 Roll of bucks
122 Here, in Le Havre

ANSWER, PAGE 234

ODD JOBS

Looking for an exciting new career? Here are some of the most unusual-sounding occupations we could find. There's just one little catch—actually *three* little catches—all these jobs are real except for three. Your job is to find the hoaxes amidst the real jobs.

Killer Bee Hunter: Your mission is to track down Africanized "killer" bees, which are migrating north from Central America, and destroy them before they can take up residence in North America.

Chicken Shooter: Fire dead chickens out of a cannon at aircraft to see what kind of damage it causes.

Mother Repairer: It's not what you think. It actually entails cleaning metal phonograph record "mothers" (the master from which records are pressed) by removing dirt and nickel particles from the grooves.

Scum Sucker: Several varieties of algae are a good source of phytoalexins, plant compounds that help fight disease. The most effective way of collecting it is to suck it up with long flexible straws, and then transfer it to a collecting jar. (Try not to swallow!)

Anthem Man: A unique profession. King Alfonso of Spain was tone deaf...he employed one man whose job was to alert him when the Spanish national anthem was playing (so he would know when to salute).

Peephole Plugger: Little holes keep mysteriously appearing in the dressing-room walls of a clothing-store chain that's popular with teens. Your job is to find those sneaky little peepholes and plug 'em up with wood putty. No peeking allowed!

Worm Collector: Get ready to crawl through grass at night with a flashlight, to catch the best worms for fishing. Tip: Grab them in the middle to avoid bruising.

Weed Farmer: If you like gardening, here's a change of pace: grow weeds...then sell them to chemical companies for pesticide research.

Pig Manure Sniffer: Workers try to recognize chemical markers in manure so researchers can determine which foods make pig manure so foul-smelling. Women only for this job, because estrogen increases sensitivity to smell.

Sewage Diver: Put on a diving suit and plunge into a sewage-containment vat.

Animal Chauffeur: We've heard of only one—a guy named Stephen May. His "limousine" is equipped with, among other things: a blanketed floor, eight-inch color television, stereo speakers, and silk flowers.

Flush Tester: A gold star from Uncle John to the gallant professionals who test toilet-bowl standards by trying to flush rags down various toilets.

Ho Counter: That's what they call themselves. Hawaiian entertainer Don Ho, the "Tiny Bubbles" guy, likes to keep count of the customers in his club, the Island Grill. Local kids keep tabs as each customer enters. They get 50 cents per customer, which motivates them to spread the word to tourists on the street about visiting the club. So next time you're looking for a Ho in Honolulu, just ask for Bubbles!

Armpit Sniffer: Enough said.

ANSWER, PAGE 228

WISE WOMEN

Some thoughtful observations that we've translated into simple letter-substitution code for your solving pleasure. For further instructions and hints on how to solve, see page 7.

RITA MAE BROWN
1. *YNFP *GPI KYZRW: "NU FLI RZYSB RIYI P

SZDNHPS XSPHI, GIW RZVSB YNBI ONBIOPBBSI."

HELEN KELLER
2. *GFZFB *HFZZFI: "DGF GFIFCP QA QBF KWF

RFNQJFC DGF QIDGQYQVP QA DGF BFVD."

KATHERINE MANSFIELD
3. *XYNUZCSGZ *VYGATSZQL: "CZRCZN SA YG

YWWYQQSGR KYANZ ET ZGZCRP; PEF BYG'N

MFSQL EG SN; SN SA EGQP REEL TEC

KYQQEKSGR"

ANNA FREUD
4. *IXXI *UBNVO: "LBNIGFCN AFXOK PICN ISEIZK

YNNX RXWEX GW KVBCFCN IXZ RFXO WU YIO

GBIFXFXM."

ERICA JONG
5. *UHTYV *CXFM: "TI WXD RXF'S HTBG VFWSATFM,

WXD HTBG UNUF ZXHU."

ANSWER, PAGE 233

ESPERANTO...

The international language known as Esperanto was the life's work of L.L. Zamenhof, who unleashed his brainchild on the world in 1887. Thousands of people speak Esperanto today, but a worldwide embrace of the language is yet to come. Which doesn't mean we can't have a little fun with it.

Your task on this page is to match all the Esperanto terms (1–40) with their English meanings (a–nn). It's not as hard as it looks: For example, BUTIKO sounds like "boutique" (hint, hint). You've got all the TEMPO in the world, so just use your KAPO and you'll get the hang of it. Scoring: 20 is good; 25 is very good; 30 is excellent; 35 is superb; all 40 is awesome in any language!

1. AKVOFALO
2. BESTOGARDENO
3. BUTIKO
4. DIAMANTOIDO
5. DISKOGURDO
6. DOMO
7. FANTOMO
8. GLACIAJO
9. GLACIO
10. HEROO
11. HUNDO
12. INFANETO
13. JOGO
14. JUNA
15. KONSTANTA FRIZO
16. KORO
17. KRISPA
18. KVARKO
19. LAKTO
20. MALBELA
21. MALBONO
22. MANGBASTONETOJ
23. NAZO
24. NOKTOMEZO
25. NUTRAJO
26. OKULO
27. PLUMO
28. PORKO
29. REGO
30. SAKSAFONO
31. SCRIBOTABLO
32. SINJORINO
33. SORCITA KADAVRO
34. SPEKTACLO
35. TERO
36. TRAFIKO
37. TRIFOLIETO
38. VIVO
39. VIZAGO
40. X-RADIO

- _12_ a. baby
- ___ b. chopsticks
- ___ c. desk
- ___ d. dog
- ___ e. earth
- ___ f. evil
- ___ g. eye
- _39_ h. face
- ___ i. feather
- ___ j. food
- _7_ k. ghost
- ___ l. heart
- _10_ m. hero
- ___ n. house
- _9_ o. ice
- _8_ p. ice cream
- _5_ q. jukebox
- ___ r. king
- ___ s. kinky
- ___ t. lady
- _38_ u. life
- ___ v. midnight
- _19_ w. milk
- _23_ x. nose
- ___ y. pageant
- ___ z. permanent wave
- _28_ aa. pig
- ___ bb. quark
- ___ cc. rhinestone
- _30_ dd. saxophone
- ___ ee. shamrock
- ___ ff. shop
- _36_ gg. traffic
- ___ hh. ugly
- _1_ ii. waterfall
- _40_ jj. x-ray
- ___ kk. yoga
- ___ ll. young
- _33_ mm. zombie
- ___ nn. zoo

ANSWER, PAGE 234

...IT MEANS THE WORLD TO ME

Now find all 40 Esperanto words and phrases from the previous page hidden in the globe-shaped grid below, running horizontally, vertically, or diagonally, but always in a straight line. When you've found all the entries, the unused letters will spell out a hidden message, an appropriate quip from the 17th century by one Aphra Behn.

```
                                    O
              O  K  I  T  U  B          N     M
           M  O  O  I  O  D  N  U  H  E          O
        N  L  E  Y  N  S  R  P  E  D  E  A          D
     P  U  T  R  A  F  I  K  O  R  K  D  R  S          I
     K  O  N  S  T  A  N  T  A  F  R  I  Z  O          A
  O  O  S  R  E  P  N  N  G  S  N  E  S  I  L  O     M
  P  N  T  A  K  L  E  O  K  R  A  V  K  A  A  G     A
  L  O  Z  E  M  O  T  K  O  N  Z  N  O  F  F  A     N
  U  G  U  A  I  S  O  G  T  E  O  A  G  A  O  Z     T
  M  A  L  B  E  L  A  O  J  A  R  T  U  N  V  I     O
  O  O  L  B  A  T  O  B  I  R  C  S  R  T  K  V     I
     I  S  A  K  S  A  F  O  N  O  L  D  O  A        D
     L  D  L  N  P  A  T  I  I  O  O  O  M  N        O
        S  A  S  I  N  J  O  R  I  N  O  O        I
           I  R  U  O  G  E  R  T  N  D        C
           R        X  O  T  K  A  L        A
        K                             L
           E  O  G  O  J  A  I  C  A  L  G
                    U  V
                    I  N
  M  A  L  B  O  N  O  R  V  A  D  A  K  A  T  I  C  R  O  S
  R  S  J  O  T  E  N  O  T  S  A  B  G  N  A  M  T  A  N  D
```

A TRULY GAUCHE PUZZLE

At one time it was very uncool to be left-handed. In fact, the condition was so associated with being awkward, unlucky, or downright evil that words like *gauche* and *sinister* both originally meant "left" or "on the left side." Harumph, we say. We think you'll agree that the famous lefties in our puzzle are more than "all right." And that's no left-handed compliment.

ACROSS

1 Deputy ___ (cartoon canine)
5 "Shucks"
9 Abbey accommodation
13 Locust tree
19 Pilot's word for "E"
20 Cultural prefix
21 Diva's big moment
22 Turbine turners
23 Lefty of *Hollywood Squares*
26 Sacking
27 Agreeable response
28 Most free of errors
30 Property claims
31 Abbr. on some envelopes
33 Brian of rock fame
34 Arrive (at)
36 The basics
40 Lefty author of
   The Ponder Heart
45 Great gallery of NYC or SF
48 Androcles' friend
49 Some steaks
50 Marked with ridges, like
   corduroy
52 Stimpy's pal
53 Drink for Dracula
55 She rescued Ulysses from
   drowning
56 Super-wide shoe size
57 ___ Joe's (diner sign)
59 Lefty creator of the Mad Hatter
63 Chihuahuas, usually
65 Outcome
66 Europe/Asia boundary
68 Bill of *Groundhog Day*
69 Family "map"
70 Short snooze
71 Open-mouthed
73 It measures flying distance

77 Places for window boxes
79 Become aware of
82 Asylum seekers
84 Lefty star of *Analyze That*
87 Article of faith
88 Frigate's front
90 Small batteries
91 Broil on a hibachi, say
93 Pester
94 Dish's fellow runaway, in
   rhyme
96 Kind of pig or hen
99 Relinquish
100 Years, in the Yucatan
102 Lefty who played Dorothy
104 Yachting, perhaps
105 Word with Miss or chocolates
107 18-wheeler
108 *Best in Show* participant
110 Daisy's look-alike
112 Yadda, yadda, yadda…
117 ___ judgment (be hasty)
122 Magic spells
124 Lefty brainiac
126 Sucker for a vehicle?
127 Offstage aide
128 Agatha's contemporary in
   mysteries
129 Cubic Rubik
130 Separate wheat from chaff
131 Dick Tracy's love interest
   Trueheart
132 Auction ender
133 Church service

DOWN

1 Like morning grass
2 Workout woe
3 "___ on first?"
4 Sludgy substances

5 The height of fashion for
   lunch ladies
6 Lay an ___ (fall flat)
7 Nile denizen, for short
8 *A View to a ___* (Bond flick)
9 Poolside dressing rooms
10 Before this time
11 Old Milano moola
12 Falls behind
13 Wall Street trader, briefly
14 *The Little Engine That ___*
15 Open courtyard
16 Lefty composer of
   Anything Goes
17 Turkey's neighbor
18 Egyptian cobras
24 Treat from Mrs. Smith
25 Name on many a tractor
29 Big name in tea
32 Partitioned work space
35 Bill ___, the Science Guy
36 Priest's robe
37 Month's-end mail
38 Dove, for one
39 Aptly named senator from
   Maine
41 Is charitable
42 ___ about (approximately)
43 *The Seven Year Itch*
   costar Tom
44 Ka ___ (southernmost point of
   Hawaii)
46 Ben Stiller's mom, Anne
47 Jittery
51 Flooding
54 Bends out of shape
56 Go by
58 Earth Day mo.
60 Burst of voltage
61 Be almost out

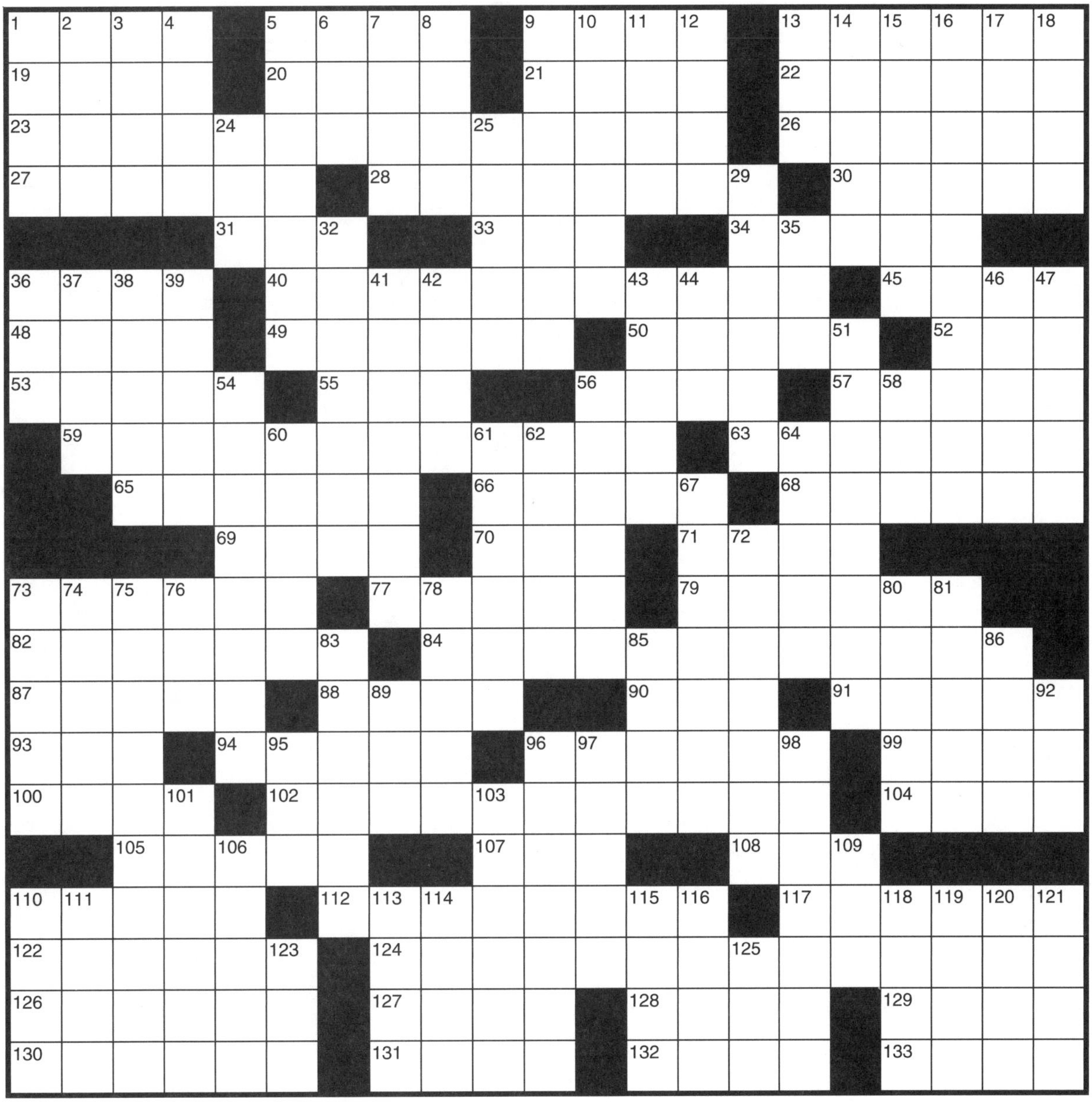

[Crossword grid]

62 Toothbrush brand
64 Chew the scenery
67 Latin-rock guitarist Carlos
72 Windfall
73 Hartford rival
74 "That is to say..."
75 Lefty of the Fab Four
76 T-shirt size (abbr.)
78 Wry humor
80 About, in historical time
81 Northeastern Indians
83 Legal partner
85 Racetrack fence

86 Ye ___ Curiosity Shoppe
89 Drapery holder
92 Actress Thompson
95 Nightwear, informally
96 Old-fashioned footwear
97 Insistent one
98 Trimmed the tree
101 Go off course
103 Aquatic birds
106 La Douce and Rombauer
109 Gloomy guy
110 It's got your number (abbr.)
111 He occupied the Peacock Throne

113 Diplomat's skill
114 These very words
115 Hwys. on a map
116 Space opening?
118 Beanstalk, e.g.
119 Mrs. Zeus
120 Items in a Brit supermarket
121 Lennon's in-laws
123 UCLA is one
125 Badly

ANSWER, PAGE 235

HOW TO DRIVE PEOPLE NUTS

Some truly bizarre practical jokes, translated into simple letter substitution code. For further instructions and hints on how to solve, see page 7.

1. QL DGS VQNNZS RH DGS LQIGD, LRQOOZJ AEFJ W HEZZJ NFSOOSN VWLLSYEQL QL JREF AWKB-JWFN. WFFWLIS ZWXL HEFLQDEFS RL DGS HFSOG VRELN WLN OQD NRXL QL QD YEQKBZJ XGSL DGS CRZQKS WFFQUS.

2. LWVV FTR *Z-FYDA LEAFQURC ARCBYLR KEUNRC WKM AWP FTWF QKR QJ FTR LQFFQK AIWN DWCFA GEAF LWUR QJJ YK PQEC RWC. ITRK FTRP CRDVP, ORRD ATQEFYKX, "ITWF? ITWF? ITWF MYM PQE AWP?"

3. JNFG BINJFWKT RI RGW *WJ YEQ WOCKYVE RI RGW EVZGR ENJFW RGYR BIN SWJW JWFRVEZ IE BINJ KWZ TIJ Y KIEZ RVXW YEQ EIS VR TWWKF KVMW CVEF YEQ EWWQKWF. YFM VT RGWB'KK GYAW RI YXCNRYRW.

4. OW JW JIZ MWHRQ TZRQ ZSXHWPDQZ RJ JIZ KWW RSF PIWDJ, "*X'CWS, *HRQQB. JRUZ WVV JIRJ XWPJDCZ RSF XWCZ TRXU JW JIZ WVVNXZ."

MONOGRAMS

Plenty of famous people have initials that lend themselves to self-descriptive phrases, like Regis Philbin, who could be described as "Ripa's Partner," or Charles Dickens, a.k.a. "Created Dorrit" or even "Created Drood."

First try to identify the famous people who fit the monograms below. As you figure them out, circle their names in the shirt-shaped grid. Once you've found them all, read the leftover letters from left to right to spell two more sets of monograms and the people they describe. If you need some help initially…ahem…we name names on the answer page.

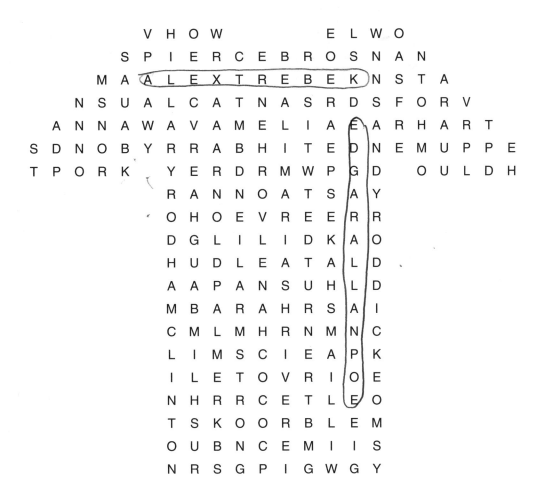

```
            V  H  O  W        E  L  W  O
         S  P  I  E  R  C  E  B  R  O  S  N  A  N
      M  A  A  L  E  X  T  R  E  B  E  K  N  S  T  A
      N  S  U  A  L  C  A  T  N  A  S  R  D  S  F  O  R  V
   A  N  N  A  W  A  V  A  M  E  L  I  A  E  A  R  H  A  R  T
S  D  N  O  B  Y  R  R  A  B  H  I  T  E  D  N  E  M  U  P  P  E
T  P  O  R  K     Y  E  R  D  R  M  W  P  G  D     O  U  L  D  H
            R  A  N  N  O  A  T  S  A  Y
            O  H  O  E  V  R  E  E  R  R
            D  G  L  I  L  I  D  K  A  O
            H  U  D  L  E  A  T  A  L  D
            A  A  P  A  N  S  U  H  L  D
            M  B  A  R  A  H  R  S  A  I
            C  M  L  M  H  R  N  M  N  C
            L  I  M  S  C  I  E  A  P  K
            I  L  E  T  O  V  R  I  O  E
            N  H  R  R  C  E  T  L  E  O
            T  S  K  O  O  R  B  L  E  M
            O  U  B  N  C  E  M  I  I  S
            N  R  S  G  P  I  G  W  G  Y
```

1. Asks Trivia
2. Aviatrix Extraordinaire
3. Aces Regularly
4. Awesome Putter
5. Blasts Baseballs
6. Classic Couturiere
7. Eerily Authored Poems
8. Highly Recognizable Congresswoman
9. Mrs. Schwarzenegger
10. Married Bancroft
11. Notable Astronaut
12. Plays Bond
13. Riles Liberals
14. Surrealist Dandy
15. Signifies Christmas
16. Television Titan
17. Wrote Sonnets

ANSWER, PAGE 235

THE BAD BOOK

Directions for solving are on page 13.

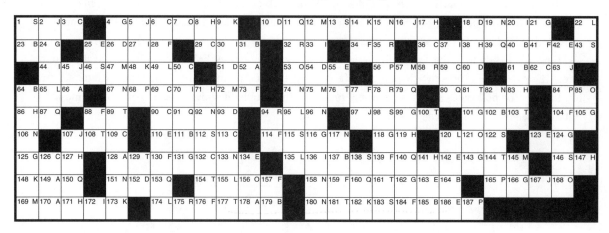

A. Sitting Bull and Geronimo, to their tribes

$\overline{149}$ $\overline{170}$ $\overline{178}$ $\overline{66}$ $\overline{52}$ $\overline{128}$

B. Electrolux extras

$\overline{61}$ $\overline{179}$ $\overline{31}$ $\overline{102}$ $\overline{40}$ $\overline{111}$ $\overline{137}$ $\overline{185}$ $\overline{23}$ $\overline{64}$ $\overline{164}$

C. Youngest ever Senate Majority Leader, 1953–61 (2 wds.)

$\overline{59}$ $\overline{113}$ $\overline{6}$ $\overline{109}$ $\overline{36}$ $\overline{62}$ $\overline{90}$ $\overline{29}$ $\overline{126}$ $\overline{132}$ $\overline{69}$ $\overline{3}$ $\overline{50}$

D. Opportunity to evade a law, so as to profit

$\overline{93}$ $\overline{26}$ $\overline{152}$ $\overline{10}$ $\overline{54}$ $\overline{51}$ $\overline{18}$ $\overline{60}$

E. Angler's bait of choice

$\overline{55}$ $\overline{42}$ $\overline{163}$ $\overline{110}$ $\overline{134}$ $\overline{25}$ $\overline{123}$ $\overline{186}$ $\overline{142}$

F. Definite Top 10 in late-night comedy (2 wds.)

$\overline{157}$ $\overline{34}$ $\overline{130}$ $\overline{41}$ $\overline{28}$ $\overline{114}$ $\overline{159}$ $\overline{88}$ $\overline{184}$
$\overline{73}$ $\overline{77}$ $\overline{176}$ $\overline{139}$ $\overline{104}$

G. Major tourist stop in the City of Light (3 wds.)

$\overline{21}$ $\overline{166}$ $\overline{24}$ $\overline{131}$ $\overline{118}$ $\overline{124}$ $\overline{116}$ $\overline{162}$ $\overline{4}$
$\overline{125}$ $\overline{105}$ $\overline{101}$ $\overline{143}$ $\overline{99}$

H. 2003 Chris Rock movie (3 wds.)

$\overline{147}$ $\overline{127}$ $\overline{71}$ $\overline{141}$ $\overline{8}$ $\overline{38}$ $\overline{17}$ $\overline{119}$ $\overline{171}$ $\overline{83}$ $\overline{86}$

I. Marked by great striving; labored

$\overline{44}$ $\overline{33}$ $\overline{37}$ $\overline{136}$ $\overline{27}$ $\overline{70}$ $\overline{20}$ $\overline{30}$ $\overline{172}$

J. Bernstein's Watergate partner

$\overline{2}$ $\overline{5}$ $\overline{167}$ $\overline{63}$ $\overline{97}$ $\overline{107}$ $\overline{16}$ $\overline{45}$

K. Feel in one's bones; sense

$\overline{148}$ $\overline{9}$ $\overline{173}$ $\overline{182}$ $\overline{48}$ $\overline{14}$

L. Train, to a tot (hyph.)

$\overline{135}$ $\overline{95}$ $\overline{22}$ $\overline{49}$ $\overline{174}$ $\overline{65}$ $\overline{120}$ $\overline{155}$

M. Poker pots

$\overline{72}$ $\overline{57}$ $\overline{47}$ $\overline{145}$ $\overline{12}$ $\overline{75}$ $\overline{169}$

N. Television, movies, theater, and the like

$\overline{15}$ $\overline{82}$ $\overline{117}$ $\overline{96}$ $\overline{158}$ $\overline{133}$ $\overline{180}$ $\overline{92}$ $\overline{74}$ $\overline{67}$ $\overline{19}$ $\overline{151}$ $\overline{106}$

O. Minnesota city that's home to the Great Lakes Aquarium

$\overline{7}$ $\overline{168}$ $\overline{156}$ $\overline{121}$ $\overline{53}$ $\overline{85}$

P. Teensy

$\overline{56}$ $\overline{68}$ $\overline{84}$ $\overline{165}$ $\overline{187}$

Q. 1965 John Wayne movie (3 wds.)

$\overline{39}$ $\overline{140}$ $\overline{150}$ $\overline{160}$ $\overline{11}$ $\overline{87}$ $\overline{80}$ $\overline{153}$ $\overline{91}$ $\overline{79}$

R. "When a Man Loves a Woman" crooner Michael

$\overline{58}$ $\overline{32}$ $\overline{78}$ $\overline{94}$ $\overline{175}$ $\overline{35}$

S. Meg, Jo, Beth, and Amy (2 wds.)

$\overline{183}$ $\overline{46}$ $\overline{122}$ $\overline{1}$ $\overline{43}$ $\overline{112}$ $\overline{146}$ $\overline{98}$ $\overline{138}$ $\overline{115}$ $\overline{13}$

T. The Count of Monte Cristo (2 wds.)

$\overline{129}$ $\overline{100}$ $\overline{177}$ $\overline{89}$ $\overline{144}$ $\overline{181}$ $\overline{161}$ $\overline{76}$ $\overline{108}$ $\overline{154}$ $\overline{81}$ $\overline{103}$

ANSWER, PAGE 236

EH TWO, CANADA?

O, Canada. In *Uncle John's Unstoppable Bathroom Reader*, we reported on the surprising variety of categories in which Canada—the 35th most populous country in the world—comes in second. Can you figure out what countries listed below are number one to Canada's number two? Australia is the answer to two of the questions; each of the other countries is used once.

1. Canada was the 2nd country to legalize medical marijuana. The first was _____.

2. Canada is the country with the 2nd coldest national capital: Ottawa. The first is _____.

3. Canada has the 2nd largest oil reserves in the world. The 1st is _____.

4. Canada has the 2nd highest proportion of immigrant population. The 1st is _____.

5. Canada has the 2nd highest amount of gum chewed per capita. The 1st is _____.

6. Canada is the 2nd largest country in the world. The 1st is _____.

7. Canada has the 2nd highest water quality. The 1st is _____.

8. Canada was the 2nd country to develop a jet airplane. The 1st was _____.

9. Canada is the 2nd largest exporter of red meat. The 1st is _____.

10. Canada is the 2nd most workaholic nation in the world. The 1st is _____.

Australia (twice)	Great Britain	Russia
Belgium	Japan	Saudi Arabia
Finland	Mongolia	United States

ANSWER, PAGE 232

* * * * *

UNCLE OSCAR'S BIG NIGHT #3

More scrambled Oscar-winning stars and the Oscar-winning films they won for. For complete directions on how to solve, see page 46.

The Stars	The Films
1. OFFHAND, I'M NUTS (6 7)	a. ADROIT GAL (9)
2. ORLON ARMBAND (6 6)	b. ANY EMU BACTERIA (8 6)
3. ORWELL'S CURSE (7 5)	c. RV MAKER'S REMARK (6 2 6)
4. PESKY CAVE-IN (5 6)	d. FROG HAD TEETH (3 9)

ANSWER, PAGE 235

ON THE CAMPAIGN TRAIL

Some people will say anything to get elected....

ACROSS

1 Book before Nahum
6 Practice for the ring
10 Clockmaker Thomas
14 1957 Literature Nobelist
19 Pueblo material
20 Dance that tells a story
21 Cut down to size
22 Companion-free
23 "A leader, for a change" (1976)
26 The Catskills or Cascades, e.g.
27 Resistance unit
28 T-shirt size (abbr.)
29 Little flower?
30 Split
31 Cause of many an accident
34 Qatar neighbor
35 After-hours music combo
36 Like Cheerios
37 Three-___ sloth
38 Give a hoot
39 Pipe rim
42 "Roosevelt for ex-president" (1940)
48 Canal features
49 Debate side
50 Love-'em-and-leave-'em guys
51 Work for
52 Asian mountain range
53 Jump right in
56 Homer's neighbor on *The Simpsons*
57 Bundled hay
58 "Return to normalcy" (1920)
61 *Gunsmoke* star
62 Lynn ___, MVP of Super Bowl X
63 Actress Salonga of *Miss Saigon*
64 Make an assumption
66 Drawer scent item
69 "A chicken in every pot and a car in every garage" (1928)
74 Am or America start
75 Be in hock
77 Phoenician or Arab, e.g.
78 Article of merchandise
79 Yorkshire river
80 Cat Nation members
82 Corp. VIP
83 Scoops out
84 "In your heart you know he's right" (1964)
88 Trumpet relative
89 ___ W (root beer brand)
90 Noncommittal response
91 Yvonne's Munster mate
92 "Sorry, I must refuse"
96 Nearly never
97 Entranceway prop
101 Arkansas chain
102 Slew
103 A time to remember
104 Playwright Levin
105 Flick
106 "A full dinner pail" (1900)
110 Licoricelike flavoring
111 ___ *fixe*
112 Tennis win
113 Brunch slice
114 Throws out a sentence?
115 They must be crazy, in a Botswana film title
116 Some ballot markings
117 Sheriff's band

DOWN

1 College student's decision
2 The Gem State
3 Feature of this clue, notably
4 Actor Vigoda
5 "___ a Rebel"
6 Scooby-Doo's pal
7 Blender setting
8 Half and half?
9 Masked scavenger
10 Butter knife
11 Downed
12 Arduous journey
13 One of LBJ's beagles
14 Mars bar center
15 Oft-useless theft deterrents
16 Actor Markham
17 Madison's housemate
18 Burpee buys
24 Give a lift
25 Ready to fight
30 The City of Light
32 Rock concert host
33 Dusting items
35 Yammered
37 Kind of saxophone
38 Big help for *CSI* staffers
39 It may be tragic
40 Kinks hit
41 Rent-___
42 God in *Das Rheingold*
43 Have cravings
44 Crowd home plate
45 Leafy veggie
46 Fits of pique
47 Concludes
49 Pacino role in HBO's *Angels in America*
53 Nearly invisible pest
54 Just hanging around
55 Wedding cake features
57 Zest for life
59 Rams' dams
60 Local theater, in *Variety*

61 *Off the Court* author
64 Snoop
65 Snorkel's pooch
66 Run through
67 Selection from *Verdi's Greatest Hits*
68 Mystery writer who created Dr. Gideon Fell
69 Pay attention to
70 Ryan Seacrest, e.g.
71 Carly's "You're So ___"
72 T'ai chi guru Montaigue
73 Staff symbol

75 University of Maine setting
76 Card or cat lead-in
80 "Zounds!"
81 Defrauds
83 Orange Free State settler
85 Steinbrenner's squad
86 Computer character set
87 Like the Ninja Turtles
88 Sound froggy
91 Coalition ___ (group in Iraq)
92 One who won't settle down
93 Protective global layer
94 Nitpick

95 Get up
96 Snockered
97 *The Silence of the Lambs* director
98 Cash storers
99 Nabisco cookies
100 "Band of Gold" singer
102 Prank
106 Lose it, with "out"
107 The Grinch's dog
108 Little devil
109 Opposite of paleo-

ANSWER, PAGE 237

THAT MAN IN THE WHITE HOUSE

Questions about the presidents that probably won't show up on pop quizzes in American History 101.

1. Thomas Jefferson invented…
   a. the swivel chair
   b. the rocking chair
   c. the indoor toilet

2. The president who called Richard Nixon "a no-good lying bastard" was…
   a. Harry Truman
   b. Lyndon Johnson
   c. Dwight Eisenhower

3. Herbert Hoover was the only president who gave his entire salary…
   a. to his wife
   b. to charity
   c. to the U.S. Treasury

4. During his youth, Bill Clinton performed in a three-person jazz combo called…
   a. The Three Blind Mice
   b. The Arkansas Shades
   c. Darkness at Noon
   …so named because they all wore sunglasses.

5. George Washington once had to borrow $600 from a neighbor to…
   a. replace his false teeth
   b. attend his own inauguration
   c. pay his vice president

6. Ulysses S. Grant was once arrested and fined for…
   a. littering
   b. speeding
   c. spitting
   …on the streets of Washington, D.C.

7. Always a man ahead of his time, Abraham Lincoln told an Illinois newspaper in 1836 that…
   a. women
   b. slaves
   c. Native Americans
   …should have the right to vote.

8. Warren G. Harding, an enthusiastic, but not especially good, poker player would often bet (and lose)…
   a. treasury bonds
   b. American flags
   c. White House china
   …when he was low on cash.

9. Theodore Roosevelt coined the famous advertising slogan…
   a. "The pause that refreshe."
   b. "Good to the last drop"
   c. "All the news that's fit to print"

10. David Rice Atchison, president pro tempore of the Senate, became president for one day in 1849 because Zachary Taylor…
    a. was too religious to be inaugurated on a Sunday
    b. had laryngitis and couldn't recite the oath of office
    c. misremembered the date of his inauguration and didn't show up

ANSWER, PAGE 235

SOMETHING'S BREWING

Considering a career as a fortuneteller? Uncle John knows all about that stuff. He even made you a cup of tea so you can practice reading tea leaves. There are 43 traditional symbols hidden in the teacup, and to help you interpret them, we've put them into alphabetical order, giving you the first letter of each word or phrase, followed by the number of letters it contains and what the symbol means. When you've found them all, the leftover letters will reveal a quote about a city that some might call "Tea Central."

If you need a little extra help, the complete word list is on the answer page.

```
            I D N A H N L O E C N E F L O W E R S E N D O
              N A R O T A G I L L A R W L N H N G N I R
              O V I U M B R E L L A O Q E A A E N V D S
    F E A T H E R C A G O A T R G U N K D C E E A L
    I           T W G P N A R T R W E E E C B E L L O
    S           N O L A L S R A E Y I S P I D E R O I
    H T         D R A E L A D D E R S T R E P D T P V
      H A     E M S D E P N B B E S I C H A I N E
        G R A S S H O P P E R T S O A H W S E E
              T E N L I Z A R D N E D E R S
                O E F T N C T M T P E
                  A J O C H O A A N
        O E L P O E P I T C H F O R K I T E L T S A C
        S B Y L F R E T T U B G K N I F E O R N E
```

A_____ (5)	Good health, good luck	H_____ (4)	Friendliness
A_____ (8)	Unexpected journey; if wings are shattered, danger	H_____ (5)	A letter or lover is coming
		H_____ (9)	Danger nearby
A_____ (9)	Strength and power	K_____ (4)	Trip that will lead to a valuable friendship
A_____ (5)	Good news, luck in love		
A_____ (5)	Long life, gain in business	K_____ (5)	Danger
A_____ (5)	A letter; if bent, bad news	L_____ (6)	Success, travel
B_____ (4)	Good news, wedding	L_____ (6)	Treacherous friends
B_____ (4)	Friendly visitor	P_____ (6)	Good omen
B_____ (9)	Frivolous pleasure	P_____ (9)	Deceitful member of the opposite sex
C_____ (6)	Marrying into money	Q_____ (8,4)	Beware all major decisions
C_____ (5)	Early marriage; if broken, an unhappy one	R_____ (4)	Marriage
		S_____ (5)	Enemy, threat
D_____ (5)	A new love	S_____ (6)	Unexpected inheritance
E_____ (8)	Good luck, health, happiness	S_____ (4)	Achievement and success
E_____ (8)	Good news; if blurred, bad news	T_____ (4)	Unknown enemy
F_____ (7)	Frivolity, lack of responsiblity	T_____ (4,6)	Better health
F_____ (5)	Obstacles	U_____ (8)	New opportunities
F_____ (4)	Good news from far away	V_____ (7)	Major upheaval
F_____ (7)	Loyal friends, happy marriage, success	W_____ (5)	Unexpected gift or inheritance
F_____ (4)	Beware excessive pride	W_____ (5)	A strange occurrence
G_____ (4)	You're surrounded by enemies	W_____ (5)	Secret enemies
G_____ (6)	Happiness		
G_____ (11)	A friend will leave, perhaps never to return		

ANSWER, PAGE 236

LA MARSEILLAISE

It's the sort of thing that keeps Uncle John awake at night: Why is the battle cry of the French Revolution—which took place in Paris, for goodness sake—named after Marseilles, a city that's hundreds of miles away? While he was wondering, Uncle John took apart the first verse and created the 37-word list you see below. Can you put "The Marseillaise" back together again, crossword-style? Allons, enfants!

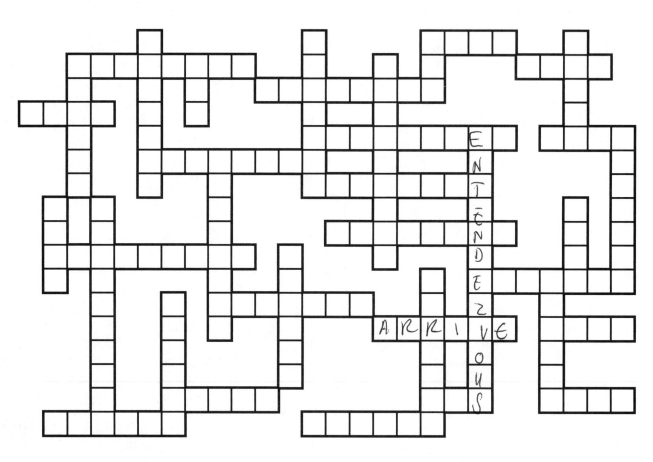

3-letter words
Est
Nos
Vos

4-letter words
Bras
Dans
Fils
Jour
Levé
Nous
Qu'un
Sang

5-letter words
Impur
Mugir

6-letter words
Allons
Arrivé
Contre
Formez
Gloire
Jusque
Patrie

7-letter words
Abreuve
Égorger
Enfants
Féroces
Sillons
Soldats

8-letter words
Aux armes
Citoyens
Marchons
Sanglant
Tyrannée
Viennent

9-letter words
Campagnes
Compagnes
L'Étandard

10-letter word
Bataillons

12-letter word
Entendez-vous

ANSWER, PAGE 237

KATE THE GREAT

Katharine Hepburn's best quotes were made without benefit of a script. To see them, choose a letter from each column and drop it into its correct place in the grid.

1.

I		I	N			W		A		M		L	Y			R			N	X
T		F	U	N		P	W	O	N	Y		H	S		S	I	M			L
Y	C	B	L	T	D	A	O	S	A	A	L	A	E	K	O	W		N	X	O
A		T	I	Y	A	M	N	M	T	N	D	N	Y	T	E	N	S	E	N	O

2.

	O				D		E		B	D		S		I	D			I			T	O	R
L	I	U	N	E	T	B	S	B	P	E	Y	I	E	Y	T		I	S	T	L	O	R
N	F	I	E	O	B	O	L	U	W	A	R	T	H	A	N	G	R	S	Y	E	I
Y	G	F	T	D	S	E	O	O	O	E	O	W	V	L	L	U	B	F	G	F	U
	H	A	V	H	S	M		N	T	P	R	T	E		U				E	O	
					I			I		Y		E									

3.

A		D		O	O	M			I		A		D				H					
T	O	M		S	I	M	E	S	R	A	T	N	L	Y	S	R	I	E		E	U	O
A	C	V	D	L	T	H	E	N	E	X	R	O	P	P	O	R	A	D	M	S	H	E
U	N	D	E	W	I	T	E	R	W	E	W	L	D	D	T	H	N	Y	I	T	N	S
S	L	H	I	T	I	V		N	N	P	A	H	A	N	E	E	F	U	J			

ANSWER, PAGE 236

SHORT BUT SWEET

In *Uncle John's Supremely Satisfying Bathroom Reader* we listed some of the two-letter words that are permitted in the game of Scrabble. Since two-letter words are a no-no in crossword puzzles, we decided to turn the tables. See if you can figure out how these two-letter words—some familiar, some obscure—are defined.

ACROSS
1 Borden spokescow
6 OF
10 Fetch
15 Diner lunch order
18 Tart candies
19 Old Italian bread?
20 AX
21 ___ Dawn Chong
22 JO
24 Boxer's combo punch
25 ICU hookups
26 Dicts. from abroad
27 1150, in old Rome
28 "No thanks"
30 ___ Mater (Latin hymn)
32 Captured again
34 High school jr.'s exam
35 Campfire confection
36 Obsolescent form of address
37 AL
42 Giuliani and Vallee
45 Whispers' companion, in an Ingmar Bergman title
46 Algerian seaport
47 Helpful thing from Heloise
48 Sweeping in scope
49 Duffer's tools
50 Sistine Chapel image
51 Disney World gateway Lake ___ Vista
52 ___ colada
53 Beatty and Rorem
54 Bit of wine sediment
55 Former ABC exec Jamie
56 Buying everything in sight
58 Video game name
59 Watering hole
60 OR
65 Vintage British sports cars
66 Sky light

67 Place that's off-limits
70 Emmy-winning sportscaster Bob
74 State trooper's beat (abbr.)
75 Agatha's colleague
76 Monthly bill for some
77 ___ left field (far-fetched)
78 Sledding site
79 Like model plane parts
80 Mediterranean Strip
81 Computer image
82 Whisky mixer
83 Children's Dr.
84 Fish dish garnish
85 AI
88 Speed up (abbr.)
89 *Le Fifre* artist
90 West Wing worker
91 They preceded the Stuarts
94 "Bam!" chef Lagasse
96 Dorian Gray's creator
98 Business card info
99 Make origami
101 Buckley book ___ *and Man at Yale*
102 Gathers
104 OY
107 Prefix meaning "bird"
108 OM
109 Letter from Athens
110 Former New York City mayor Abe
111 Novelist Deighton
112 Craggy ridge
113 BO
114 Madrileño's title

DOWN
1 Gas from the past
2 Berth option
3 Kid with a nap?

4 Argument-ending phrase
5 Body shop no.
6 Tiny piece
7 Iranian money
8 Eight-time Norris Trophy winner
9 *Window at Tangier* and *Jazz Icarus* e.g.
10 Bakeshop trayful
11 Auto map abbrs.
12 *The Addams Family* cousin
13 TV anchor
14 Connecticut submarine base site
15 Illicit payoffs
16 AA
17 Use for the Bonneville Salt Flats
20 Raccoon's tropical cousin
23 Managed care gps.
29 Tiny butter portions
31 Guinevere's hubby
33 Hosp. areas
34 Diligent effort
35 *The King and I* setting
37 Ate away at
38 "Forget it"
39 Schlep
40 -trix relative
41 JFK postings
42 Auctioned car, maybe
43 ___ the air (undecided)
44 Washington of jazz
45 Wicker baskets
49 Hardly dapper
50 Odorless gas
51 Hindi title of courtesy
54 Fake drake
55 Pulled hard
57 Spin doctor
58 Look from Scrooge

59 Lowly workers
61 "That makes me happy!"
62 Surge
63 Dunkin' Donuts order
64 Dance feature in *Oklahoma!*
68 Singer Stuarti
69 ___ impasse (stuck)
70 Landmark tower of San Francisco
71 "That hurts!"
72 Raided like gangbusters
73 Liability for a music major

74 Lie low
75 Rinse, as with a solvent
78 Catcall
79 Like Buckminster Fuller's dome
82 Dazzling
83 Lost traction
84 Digital readout, initially
86 Baffling riddle
87 Dip with zip
88 "___ Lang Syne"
91 Coffee break time

92 *Laugh-In* cohost
93 Replay option
94 Same, on the Somme
95 GO
96 Light bulb unit
97 Memo opener
98 Garb for Pavlova
100 Natty Bumppo's quarry
103 NYC-to-Boston dir.
105 Reaction to a trapeze artist
106 Delivery room docs

ANSWER, PAGE 238

LOONEY LAWS REVISITED

Ignorance of the law is no defense. How would you behave if you were visiting these places?

1. In Carmel, California, it's against the law for a woman to...

    a. take a bath
    b. be referred to as "sir"
    c. do jumping jacks

    ...in a business office.

2. In Fruithill, Kentucky, any man who comes face to face with a cow on a public road, must...

    a. escort it to the nearest police station.
    b. remove his hat
    c. refrain from feeding it

3. It's against the law to feed...

    a. margarine instead of real butter
    b. personalized birthday cakes
    c. less than two side dishes at dinner

    ...to prisoners in Wisconsin.

4. It's illegal in California to...

    a. leave dirty clothes under the bed
    b. play the xylophone
    c. peel an orange

    ...in your hotel room.

5. In Hawaii it's against the law to put...

    a. coins
    b. aspirin
    c. bugs

    ...in your ears.

6. In Oxford, Ohio, a woman may not remove her clothing while standing in front of...

    a. a picture window
    b. a picture of a man
    c. the mayor

7. You're breaking the law in South Dakota if you...

    a. speak above a whisper
    b. fall asleep
    c. remove your shoes

    ...in a cheese factory.

8. In Idaho it's illegal to fish for trout while...

    a. sitting on the back of a giraffe
    b. wearing a clown suit
    c. pregnant

9. It's against the law in Garfield County, Montana, to...

    a. install black
    b. build a house without
    c. draw funny faces on

    ...window shades.

10. It's illegal in Roanoke, Virginia, to...

    a. spit tobacco on
    b. advertise on
    c. tie one's dog to

    ...a tombstone.

ANSWER, PAGE 237

LUCKY SEVENS

Lots of people consider the number seven to be lucky, which might explain why so many things come in sets of seven. We've hidden seven groups of seven in the grid below, but we've only given you the categories, leaving it to you to remember what seven things go in each group. When you've found them all, the leftover letters will reveal yet another set of sevens. So what do you say—feeling lucky?

```
N M A S J A A S B R Y N N E R T C H A R I T Y R
E C N E D U R P E O P R O F E S S O R N A M U T
S Q S O C O S G T T P C G A R P R H E T O R I C
E U P N T E N T R R A D C L I F F E G N Y E O R
D E N A G I L L I G H O N C U O A O O R R P P E
Y E N H G U A V R C I T E M H T I R A W T P J
O N E C N A R E P M E T H N G L T E N A E I E
                        N S H O V M M K
                        M A R Y A N N O S
                        G U S R G R Y E I
                      S P R I D E L R G
                    S E A C I G O L B O
                    N M E P O H M W L
                  V M A L L T D Y U
                Y A A C L N S C F H
                R I O S U R R H A
              G A B L O S A S N
            S H U E M P T A A R
            D R A N R A B D R
          A N N D D H E K Y
        E B U C H H O L Z S
        L R A Y T O W E N
      Y E L S E L L E W
    H T A R W W E N L R
    X C E T Y H S E L
  E M E I R P C U R
D Y S H E S M I T H
F O R T I T U D E
L L E W O H S R M
Y P E E L S V G E
B R O N S O N N
```

The 7 Actors Who Played the Title Characters in *The Magnificent Seven*
The 7 Cardinal Virtues
The 7 Castaways on *Gilligan's Island*
The 7 Deadly Sins
The 7 Dwarfs
The 7 Liberal Arts
The 7 Sisters Colleges

ANSWER, PAGE 239

UNDER THE INFLUENCE

Directions for solving are on page 13.

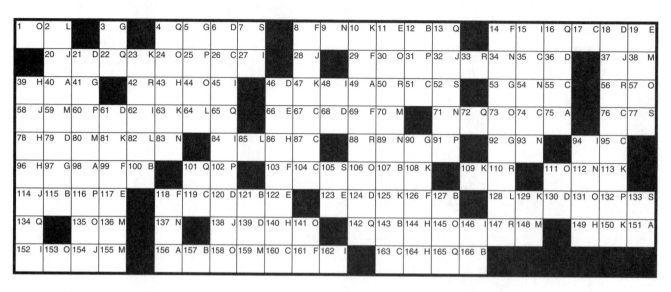

A. Possible enemy aircraft

$\overline{156}$ $\overline{151}$ $\overline{75}$ $\overline{98}$ $\overline{40}$ $\overline{49}$

B. THIS, but not this

$\overline{157}$ $\overline{143}$ $\overline{166}$ $\overline{107}$ $\overline{12}$ $\overline{121}$ $\overline{115}$ $\overline{100}$ $\overline{127}$

C. Partner of this quote's focus (3 wds.)

$\overline{87}$ $\overline{160}$ $\overline{67}$ $\overline{163}$ $\overline{119}$ $\overline{74}$ $\overline{51}$ $\overline{35}$ $\overline{95}$

$\overline{76}$ $\overline{26}$ $\overline{17}$ $\overline{104}$ $\overline{55}$

D. Creator of *Dick Tracy* (2 wds.)

$\overline{46}$ $\overline{124}$ $\overline{6}$ $\overline{79}$ $\overline{120}$ $\overline{18}$ $\overline{130}$ $\overline{68}$ $\overline{139}$ $\overline{61}$ $\overline{36}$ $\overline{21}$

E. Language heard in the Knesset

$\overline{122}$ $\overline{11}$ $\overline{66}$ $\overline{19}$ $\overline{117}$ $\overline{123}$

F. Small, tart fruit (2 wds.)

$\overline{29}$ $\overline{8}$ $\overline{69}$ $\overline{118}$ $\overline{99}$ $\overline{103}$ $\overline{14}$ $\overline{126}$ $\overline{161}$

G. Oakland, California's county

$\overline{53}$ $\overline{97}$ $\overline{92}$ $\overline{90}$ $\overline{5}$ $\overline{41}$ $\overline{3}$

H. Carved art mentioned in *Moby Dick*

$\overline{78}$ $\overline{140}$ $\overline{144}$ $\overline{43}$ $\overline{39}$ $\overline{86}$ $\overline{164}$ $\overline{96}$ $\overline{149}$

I. Mythical reptile thought to live in fire

$\overline{48}$ $\overline{94}$ $\overline{84}$ $\overline{62}$ $\overline{152}$ $\overline{15}$ $\overline{146}$ $\overline{27}$ $\overline{45}$ $\overline{162}$

J. The psyche, if you're a guy (2 wds.)

$\overline{20}$ $\overline{114}$ $\overline{154}$ $\overline{58}$ $\overline{138}$ $\overline{32}$ $\overline{28}$ $\overline{37}$

K. *Jeopardy!* special (2 wds.)

$\overline{108}$ $\overline{47}$ $\overline{125}$ $\overline{23}$ $\overline{150}$ $\overline{81}$ $\overline{129}$ $\overline{109}$ $\overline{10}$ $\overline{63}$ $\overline{113}$

L. Two-masted sailing vessels

$\overline{82}$ $\overline{85}$ $\overline{128}$ $\overline{64}$ $\overline{2}$

M. Giving a quick once-over

$\overline{148}$ $\overline{159}$ $\overline{38}$ $\overline{70}$ $\overline{136}$ $\overline{80}$ $\overline{59}$ $\overline{155}$

N. Stephen Foster's most popular song (2 wds.)

$\overline{9}$ $\overline{112}$ $\overline{93}$ $\overline{71}$ $\overline{83}$ $\overline{137}$ $\overline{54}$ $\overline{34}$ $\overline{89}$

O. One of *The Jungle Book*'s heroes (hyph.)

$\overline{30}$ $\overline{145}$ $\overline{131}$ $\overline{44}$ $\overline{135}$ $\overline{158}$ $\overline{73}$ $\overline{141}$ $\overline{106}$

$\overline{153}$ $\overline{111}$ $\overline{1}$ $\overline{57}$ $\overline{24}$

P. Go into detail for the IRS

$\overline{132}$ $\overline{60}$ $\overline{91}$ $\overline{116}$ $\overline{31}$ $\overline{25}$ $\overline{102}$

Q. Peter Straub tale that was later a movie (2 wds.)

$\overline{134}$ $\overline{101}$ $\overline{22}$ $\overline{72}$ $\overline{4}$ $\overline{142}$ $\overline{13}$ $\overline{165}$ $\overline{16}$ $\overline{65}$

R. Have an effect (on)

$\overline{33}$ $\overline{42}$ $\overline{110}$ $\overline{50}$ $\overline{88}$ $\overline{147}$ $\overline{56}$

S. Comic strip star whose pal is Sluggo

$\overline{133}$ $\overline{77}$ $\overline{7}$ $\overline{105}$ $\overline{52}$

ANSWER, PAGE 237

UNITED STATES

Uncle John's gone postal. We've combined the state abbreviations below to spell out words and phrases. For example, the clue "Conceal a delivery from the post office" would be HIDE MAIL (HI for Hawaii, DE for Delaware, MA for Massachusetts, and IL for Illinois). The blanks that follow each clue tell you how many letters are in that answer and how the words break. And keep in mind that while some of the answers are straightforward enough, others are as peculiar as a disgruntled employee.

1. An implement for shaving

   __ __   __ __ __ __ __

2. Yours truly is a nerd

   __ __   __ __ __   __ __ __ __ __

3. Relating to a tropical disease spread by mosquitoes

   __ __ __ __ __ __ __ __ __ __

4. The largest moon in our solar system; also the cupbearer to the gods in Greek myth

   __ __ __ __ __ __ __ __ __ __

5. Preparing a hot dinner, for example

   __ __ __ __ __ __ __ __   __ __   __ __ __ __ __

6. Baseball's Boggs gave a fee to a child

   __ __ __ __   __ __ __ __ __   __ __   __ __ __ __

7. That man's pit for excavating precious gemstones

   __ __ __ __   __ __ __ __ __ __ __ __ __ __   __ __ __ __ __

8. Singer Morrison slices bottle plugs in a Colorado ski town

   __ __ __ __   __ __ __ __ __ __   __ __ __ __ __ __ __   __ __ __   __ __ __ __ __ __

9. Chablis is capable of causing damage to ice-skating ovals

   __ __ __ __ __ __ __ __ __ __ __ __ __ __ __ __ __ __   __ __ __   __ __ __ __ __ __ __

10. Georgia city auto highway path generates fear in a lot of female parents

   __ __ __ __ __   __ __ __ __   __ __ __ __   __ __ __ __ __ __ __ __

   __ __ __ __ __   __ __ __ __ __ __

STATE ABBREVIATIONS

AL	CT	IL	ME	MO	NM	OR	TX	WI
AK	DE	IN	MD	MT	NY	PA	UT	WY
AZ	FL	IA	MA	NE	NC	RI	VT	
AR	GA	KS	MI	NV	ND	SC	VA	
CA	HI	KY	MN	NH	OH	SD	WA	
CO	ID	LA	MS	NJ	OK	TN	WV	

ANSWER, PAGE 238

THE SAME, ONLY DIFFERENT

There's naval commander Matthew Perry and *Friends* star Matthew Perry... explorer Sebastian Cabot and old TV actor Sebastian Cabot... Jock Ewing portrayer Jim Davis and "Garfield" creator Jim Davis. Ten more examples of such famous "double identities" are spotlighted in this puzzle.

ACROSS

1 Some poets
7 Tickles
13 Popular Navy legal eagles show
16 Actress Anna ___ Wong
19 "Relax"
20 *Being and Nothingness* writer
21 Alfalfa and pals
23 Former Mets player and hotelier
25 Trapper's work
26 Be grandiloquent
27 Cash register stack
28 *SCTV* comedian and fast food king
30 Magic Johnson was one
32 French bean?
33 Drain
34 Go back on
37 Sighed words
39 Flat-topped hills
43 *Dr. Quinn* actress and Henry VIII's third wife
46 Ebonics, for example
48 ___ *Sharkey* (TV oldie)
49 Finishes the yardwork
50 *Loot* playwright Joe
52 Be patient
54 No-win situation?
55 Inventor and Reagan cabinet member
59 Medium setting
60 Cost
63 Avoid a shutout
65 Type data for the computer
66 Gets one's bearings
70 Looking like a villain
72 Eloise's hotel

75 Heads out to sea
77 Rots
81 Deal with one darned thing after another?
83 Former Illinois senator and singer/songwriter
87 It may be found in the woods
88 Displays clearly
90 Chop finely
91 Garment attachment
93 Cribbage need
94 "___ Crime?" (Sade song)
97 Pasha of Egypt and great boxer
100 Notable tower in Chicago
102 Eggnog topping
104 Hashhouse clients
105 Blood-typing system
107 Couples
108 Abu ___
110 Scandal-plagued baseball player and rock singer
114 Algerian port
115 Epicure's pride
120 Embassy aide
121 English explorer and Welsh actor
124 Royal spouse
125 Candlestick on the wall
126 Bouncer's request
127 Mauna ___
128 Amount after expenses
129 They're forbidden
130 Medieval tales of adventure

DOWN

1 ___ Rios, Jamaica
2 Word with step or stop

3 Early presidential caucus state
4 Chair back feature
5 Unflagging
6 Criterion (abbr.)
7 Unanimously
8 *Politically Incorrect* host
9 Coffee servers
10 John, Paul, and George, but not Ringo (abbr.)
11 Chipped away at
12 Lawmaking assemblies
13 Rosemary's first hubby
14 Members of the extended family
15 English novelist and Oneida Indian actor
16 Seriously wound
17 *Black Beauty* author Sewell
18 Silly Putty containers
22 Reach for in the dark
24 One of the Smurfs
29 Osso buco meat
31 Personal ad datum, often true
32 Intentionally loses
34 Tesla, not Marconi, invented it
35 Georgia of *The Mary Tyler Moore Show*
36 Once-named
37 Reveals, in a way
38 WWII fliers
40 Something in the air
41 Quickly
42 More achy
43 Vinny Testaverde's team
44 Popular tattoo word
45 It's picked out
47 Discouraging words

51 Table salt, chemically speaking
53 Stooge Moe's hairstyle
55 TV actress Lansing
56 Bellicose god
57 Placekicker's pride
58 *Uno + due*
61 Box of doughnuts contents, usually
62 Modern painter and 17th-century philosopher
64 Therefore, in logic
67 Forty winks
68 ___ Maria liqueur
69 Candidate for urban renewal
71 It has a small charge
72 Gets ready for the OR
73 Breakwater

74 Band of Pain's "Que ___?"
76 Primordial oozes
78 Celeste's husband, in kiddie lit
79 Figure-skating jumps
80 It can make a hero
82 ___ Plaines, Illinois
84 One size too small
85 I, in Innsbruck
86 ___ culpa
89 Moral lapse
91 Leeway
92 Fruity beverage
95 Makes "shame, shame" sounds
96 If nothing goes right
98 "___ Mrs. Jones"
99 Queen of the fairies

101 Punjab potentates
103 Name in the news, 1998
106 Earth tone
108 Severe lawmaker of ancient Athens
109 Racetrack dogs' "carrots"
110 Tire-changing need
111 Missouri River tribe
112 European erupter
113 *Etta* ___ (old comic)
114 Cry after a spill
116 Lobs' paths
117 Quickly, in the ER
118 Went quickly
119 They may be loose or tight
122 Male swan
123 Magnanimous

ANSWER, PAGE 238

WORDS YOU DON'T SEE EVERY DAY

You won't find these words in everyday conversation, but at least you have an opportunity to find them in the grid below. After you've tracked down all 38 of them, the leftover letters will reveal a quote about one of the words. Which will make you a more well-rounded individual (but not in the callipygian sense).

```
P G C U G G E R M U G G E R A R I
O D Y L E L H P M Y N A R A P O T
G E N U G L Y P H I C S M P O S A
O A C N G I U S P I T B H O U U L
N G I A H L T P P I I P T D O W B
I R B S L E I D N V E A I R I H O
P V E E E L K F E J I N N I Y E H
D F T R C H I R U O M D T P H O T
E U F K A X T P R R E I O N T C H
G C C H N A H S Y R F C R O N K D
T A U T O N Y M E G O U P D G E A
B L L L S S B E A R I L R U O O S
L E R O C L O O I O A A K R D N M
U G Z O O N O S E S Z T N O A U I
M O O C P T M F T Z O E R D R T L
B N T H Y E E Y I L I V E W A R E
A O O L Y D R A G W A D T E P R T
```

AMBIVERT: A person who's half introvert and half extrovert.
BACKCLIPPING: Shortening a longer word into a smaller one, like "chrysanthemum" to "mum."
BLUMBA: A certifying metal tag attached to kosher meat.
BOOMER: A male kangaroo.
CALLIPYGIAN: Having shapely buttocks.
COOLTH: Coolness.
CRONK: A horse made sick so it will lose a race.
CUGGERMUGGER: Gossiping done in a low voice.
DEDANS: The part of a tennis court used by spectators.
FURFURRATE: What dandruff does when it falls from your scalp.
GARDYLOO: A word used as a warning cry back when it was customary to throw slops from windows into the streets.
GEGG: A joke or hoax.

GENUGLYPHICS: Painting or decorating a person's knees to make them more erotic.
HYPOCORISM: Baby talk.
INFIX: A word placed inside another word to change its meaning, as in "fan-freakin'-tastic."
IZZARD: The name of the letter "z."
JINNIYEH: A female genie.
KITH: Your friends.
LECANOSCOPY: The act of hypnotizing yourself by staring into a sink filled with water.
LIVEWARE: People who work with computer software and hardware.
NIDUS: A place where bacteria multiplies.
OBLATI: Willing slaves of the church.
OTOPLASTY: A surgical procedure to fix ears that stick out.
PANDICULATE: To yawn.
PARADOG: A military dog that's been trained to parachute out of airplanes.
PARANYMPH: The bridesmaid or best man at a wedding.

PICA: A desire to eat non-foods (like dirt).
POGONIP: An icy winter fog producing pneumonia when inhaled, peculiar to the Sierra Nevadas.
PRINGLE: To tingle annoyingly.
PULLET: A female chicken one year old or younger.
PUWO: An animal that's half poodle and half wolf.
SCOON: To skip on the surface of the water.
SMILET: A little smile.
TARESTHESIA: The tingling sensation you get when your foot falls asleep.
TAUTONYM: A word consisting of two identical parts, like "tutu."
THOB: To rationalize one's beliefs (from THink + Opinion + Believe)
UCALEGON: A neighbor whose house is burning down.
ZOONOSES: Diseases humans can get from animals.

ANSWER, PAGE 238

HABLA ES-PUN-OL?

What a difference a letter makes. We've taken 16 foreign phrases and changed just one letter in each so that it translates into a very silly statement. Take *MENAGE A TROIS*, for instance. When it becomes *MONAGE A TROIS*, it means: "I am three years old." See if you can figure out which letter in each saying was changed, based on its new translation.

VENI, VIDI, VICI
   I came, I'm a very important person, I conquered.

COGITO ERGO SUM
   I think; therefore I waffle.

RIGOR MORTIS
   The cat is dead.

RESPONDEZ S'IL VOUS PLAIS
   Honk if you're Scottish.

QUE SERA SERA
   Life is feudal.

LE ROI EST MORT—VIVE LE ROI
   The king is dead. No kidding.

FELIZ NAVIDAD
   Our cat has a boat.

HAUTE CUISINE
   Fast French food.

PARLEZ-VOUS FRANCAIS
   Can you drive a French motorcycle?

VENI, VIDI, VICI
   I came, I saw, I partied.

QUID PRO QUO
   Fast retort.

ALOHA OE
   Love; greetings; farewell; from such a pain you would never know.

VIVA LA FRANCE
   Don't leave your chateau without it.

L'ETAT, C'EST MOI
   I'm bossy around here.

ICH BIN EIN BERLINER
   He deserved it.

E PLURIBUS UNUM
   Out of any group, there's always one asshole.

ANSWER, PAGE 233

* * * * *

I'LL BUY THAT

Are these stories about the origins of brand names true or false? If you buy them, put a T in the blank; if not, mark the blank with an F.

___ **Pennzoil:** The motor oil company originally called itself "Pennsoil" with an s (short for William Penn's Oil). But people kept pronouncing it "Penn soil," so they changed the *s* to a *z*.

___ **Dial Soap:** The name refers to a clock or watch dial. The reason: It was the first deodorant soap, and Lever Bros. wanted to suggest that it would prevent B.O. "all around the clock."

___ **Mazda:** The company's Japanese founder chose the word *Mazda* because it was the name of the Zoroastrian god of good and light.

ANSWER, PAGE 237

SUBURBAN LEGENDS

They say human beings use only 10 percent of their brains. Come on, people! You in the back row there! Wake up! Okay. Now that we've got your attention, we intend to clarify the following urban and suburban legends for your edification. All you have to do is answer True or False.

_____ 1. There are only "six degrees of separation" between any two people.

_____ 2. Scientists dug up an oversized "velociraptor" after Steven Spielberg created one for *Jurassic Park*.

_____ 3. Rice thrown at a wedding will get eaten by birds and swell up in their stomachs and make them explode.

_____ 4. Flea circuses are real.

_____ 5. People can get so frightened that their hair turns white overnight.

_____ 6. Chocolate is toxic to dogs.

_____ 7. Cats will always land on their feet.

_____ 8. You can be blinded by looking at a solar eclipse without a filter.

_____ 9. Tomatoes are a fruit.

_____ 10. Plowing a field at night will reduce weeds more than plowing during the day.

_____ 11. A fire in the fireplace makes the house colder.

_____ 12. Hot water freezes faster than cold water.

ANSWER, PAGE 240

HONK IF YOU LOVE
MORE ANAGRAMS

Rearrange the sets of three letters to form the bumper sticker sayings we found in the parking lot across the street. For complete instructions on how to solve, see page 117.

1. ACA BLE HEW INT IWA KEL NDI NGU NOE NTT OMA ORS OVE PIN SSI STA

    TPO WAY (1 4 2 4 4 2 3 5 8 3 — 8 2 2 1 5.)

2. ACY ART DIP EEL EON ETT ETY ING LOM OFL OUR SEG SOM THE WAY (9: 3 3

    2 7 7 4 3 4 3.)

3. EEL FON FOR HUK IXR MEE RKT TON YWU (4 2 5 5 5 3 3!)

ANSWER, PAGE 238

HOW MOSQUITOES CHANGED HISTORY

In *Uncle John's Bathroom Reader Plunges into History* we traced the progress of the small but powerful mosquito with an eye toward how it had manipulated the course of human history. Look at the dates and places below and, using your extensive knowledge of history and geography—and a large dollop of common sense—see if you can figure out which mosquito factoid matches up with each time and locale. We're itching to see how well you do.

___	**Africa, 1,600,000 BC**	___	**New Orleans, 1802**
___	**India, 500 BC**	___	**Stockholm, 1902**
___	**Babylon, 323 BC**	___	**Panama, 1905**
___	**Rome, 410 AD**	___	**Colorado, 1939**
___	**Africa, 1593**	___	**Dutch East Indies, 1942**
___	**England, 1658**	___	**Vietnam, 1965–1975**
___	**Barbados, 1690**	___	**Geneva, 1995**

1. Bitten by a possibly Royalist mosquito, Oliver Cromwell dies of malaria, paving the way for the return of the monarchy.

2. Brahmin priest Susruta deduces that mosquitoes are responsible for the spread of malaria. No one pays any attention for the next 2,400 years.

3. British army surgeon Dr. Ronald Ross receives the Nobel Prize for establishing the link between mosquito bites and malaria.

4. DDT is tested and found to control mosquitoes and other insects. Mosquitoes eventually develop resistance to the chemical; humans don't.

5. Japanese troops seize the islands that provide most of the world's quinine, the only reliable malaria therapy known at the time, hoping mosquitoes will become a weapon against Allied forces. Nearly half a million American troops in the East are hospitalized with malaria between over the next four years.

6. Marauding Visigoths finish off the once-great empire, already undermined by a fifth column of malaria-spreading mosquitoes in the low-lying areas surrounding the capital. Shortly afterward, Alaric, leader of the vanquishers, is vanquished in his turn by a treacherous mosquito.

7. Mosquitoes almost succeed in halting construction of the canal, as panicked workers flee a yellow fever epidemic.

8. Mosquitoes spread malaria to as many as 53 American soldiers in a thousand every day.

9. Napoleon sends a force of 33,000 to reinforce France's claim to Louisiana and put down a slave rebellion in Haiti. A whopping 29,000 of the soldiers are killed by mosquito-borne yellow fever. Shortly thereafter, Louisiana is turned over to the U.S. and Haiti becomes an independent republic.

10. Our ancestors take their first upright steps. Thanks to mosquitoes, they are already infected with malaria.

11. The lowly mosquito fells its first world-famous victim: Alexander the Great dies of malaria at the age of 33. His dream of a united Greek empire collapses within a few years, and widespread malarial infection further contributes to the decline of Greek civilization.

12. The spread of yellow fever halts a British expedition en route to attack the French in Canada.

13. The World Health Organization (WHO) declares mosquito-borne dengue fever a "world epidemic," while deaths from malaria rise to nearly 3 million a year.

14. Yellow fever and malaria spread via the slave trade, laying the basis for epidemics that will decimate both colonial and aboriginal populations.

ANSWER, PAGE 242

SCREEN DEBUTS

Because everybody has to start somewhere…

ACROSS

1 Slide at a water park
6 Used a stiletto on
13 Pile
18 Nobles like Macbeth
19 Puff the Magic Dragon's land
20 Actresses Dern and San Giacomo
22 Kevin Costner's screen debut, 1974
24 Diamond-patterned sock
25 Internet note
26 Recesses in a cathedral
27 Actor John ___-Davies
29 Offer from a sorority
30 U. of Maryland player
31 Babysitter's tormentor
32 Roughly
34 Dopey
36 Imogene's longtime partner
37 Lucy Liu's screen debut, 1996
41 He looks out for Smokey
42 Caught in a trap
44 Apple pie baker's utensil
45 ___ matter (brains)
47 Range part
48 In top shape
49 Bullfrog or raven, at times
52 Dinah, to Alice in Wonderland
55 ___-Tiki
56 Publishes
59 Equi- kin
60 Govt. workplace watchdog
61 Mark with a branding iron
63 Motorcycles around a limo, perhaps
64 Shaq's alma mater
65 Memorial stone pillar
67 Sigourney Weaver's screen debut, 1976
69 Small bay
71 Little bit

72 Moving in one of two directions
74 Maiden
76 Nota ___ (note well)
77 Season on the Seine
78 Martha's Vineyard, e.g.
79 Mies Van ___ Rohe
80 Covered with mother-of-pearl
82 Part of I.R.S.
84 Opposite of *unter*
86 Dangler on a fishhook
87 Don Juan's mother
88 Killer whales
90 Termite predator
94 With proficiency
96 Charles Bronson and Lee Marvin's screen debut, 1951 (a.k.a. *You're in the Navy Now*)
99 "___ Mir Bist Du Schön" (Andrews Sisters hit)
100 Monument Valley sights
102 Leaders of the pack?
103 Battering weapons
104 B.A. holder
105 Bobby of hockey fame
106 Ballet swan's skirt
108 "... that bloom in the spring, ___"
110 Statement of belief
111 John of *Full House*
113 Ronald Reagan's screen debut, 1937
117 Be a pickpocket
118 Wanted-poster names
119 Fashion designer Johnson
120 Chipped in chips
121 Two-___ (short films)
122 Sports pg. reports

DOWN

1 Add one's 2 cents
2 Obstacles on a golf course
3 Open, as a jacket
4 Swiss archer of legend
5 Pt. on a compass
6 *True West* playwright Sam
7 Warm and cozy
8 Clear ending?
9 Cries of disgust
10 "Nel ___, dipinto di..." ("Volare" line)
11 Some M.I.T. degrees
12 Letter opener
13 Bump off
14 Ankles, to a med student
15 Mo. named for a Caesar
16 Jack Nicholson's screen debut, 1958
17 Baseball Hall-of-Famer Al
18 Dreaded fly
21 Passover feast
23 Unproductive, and then some
28 Where land meets sky (abbr.)
31 Frenchy caps
32 Like Shrek
33 Have second thoughts about
35 March Madness org.
37 Diner pour
38 Thom ___ of shoe fame
39 "You've got mail" announcer
40 Everglades wader
43 Sought-after label for dieters
46 Martini partner
48 Impose oneself
49 Permanent results
50 Ancient Semite
51 Vanquished
52 Movie lobby ad
53 You can't take it with you
54 John Travolta's screen debut, 1975
55 Doting Milne mother
57 Worker in a fish store

58 Kind of energy
62 Two under par
63 Brain chart, for short
66 Online mag
68 Brings on
70 Leno's network
73 Rodeo maker
75 Warnings from Bowser
79 Work space
81 Candy striper, for one
83 "Only Time" singer
85 Call to Bo-Peep
86 Riddler's nemesis

88 Smooch-related
89 AAA plan
90 Stumped
91 Side by side
92 Sets up
93 "Muskrat Ramble" trombonist
94 "It's ___ unusual day…"
95 Big ___ (WWI German cannon)
97 H.S. senior's exam
98 Handy puzzle solving aid?
101 Potbelly item

104 Nine-time marathon champ Waitz
107 Pre-owned
108 Greenish blue
109 Soufflés do it
110 Guitar virtuoso Atkins
112 Satisfied
114 Corrida cry
115 "C'est la ___!"
116 Atlanta-based Superstation (abbr.)

ANSWER, PAGE 239

WHAT DID YOU CALL ME?

Hidden in the baseball-shaped grid below are 20 legendary stars of the game, each of whom has a well-known nickname. Instead of giving you the names of the players (c'mon, that'd be *way* too easy!), we're giving you a list of their nicknames. And because we're not *totally* mean, we're even telling you how many letters are in their first and last names. (If you get stumped, you can find the line-up on the answer page.) When you've found them all in the grid, the leftover letters will tell you about a few other such athletes. Have a ball!

```
                  E   I   N   T
              E   R   E   L   S   T   I   T
          L   N   G   L   Y   N   T   I   O   C   F   K
          H   O   N   U   S   W   A   G   N   E   R   N   W   A
      W   M   U   E   D   B   A   S   Y   E   A   B   A   A   L   Y
    L   H   P   G   L   A   Y   E   P   R   N   X   M   S   L   H   E   A
    T   I   V   E   D   E   A   E   L   K   N   X   S   Y   T   O   V   I
  N   R   T   C   H   L   O   R   U   I   D   O   O   E   E   E   Y   O   D   M
  O   I   E   R   R   D   E   N   E   E   C   S   F   A   S   R   K   C   I   T
H   R   S   Y   G   I   Z   E   F   M   E   F   W   E   I   O   J   J   C   O   N   G
E   R   S   F   B   G   R   R   O   W   A   N   E   I   S   R   O   H   M   I   B   O
E   T   P   O   Z   Z   I   E   S   M   I   T   H   M   L   E   H   E   E   S   M   B
S   J   E   R   O   S   E   E   J   A   C   K   T   M   D   T   N   S   I   O   N   T
  O   A   D   C   M   T   E   J   R   C   R   A   I   I   E   S   F   L   I   C
  S   K   H   W   E   A   V   E   A   R   Y   M   J   N   P   O   H   L   A   M
      E   M   T   I   E   R   I   N   C   A   Y   H   A   G   N   N   I   K
      R   A   A   U   L   R   O   N   G   K   T   O   S   T   L   A   W   N
          T   H   E   R   L   M   G   A   N   S   M   U   U   S   Y   I
          A   L   A   E   I   N   D   J   I   O   I   N   M   C
              A   T   O   B   A   F   I   R   S   N   H   G
              H   U   A   M   N   H   T   E
                  R   B   S   C
```

BEAST (6, 4)	FORDHAM FLASH (7, 6)
BIG DOG (4, 5)	GEORGIA PEACH (2, 4)
BIG SIX (7, 9)	GREY EAGLE (4, 7)
BIG TRAIN (6, 7)	IRON HORSE (3, 6)
CHAIRMAN OF THE BOARD (6, 4)	MR. OCTOBER (6, 7)
CHARLIE HUSTLE (4, 4)	SPLENDID SPLINTER (3, 8)
COMMERCE COMET (6, 6)	STRETCH (6, 7)
CYCLONE (2, 5)	SULTAN OF SWAT (4, 4)
DONNIE BASEBALL (3, 9)	WIZARD OF OZ (5, 5)
FLYING DUTCHMAN (5, 6)	YANKEE CLIPPER (3, 8)

ANSWER, PAGE 243

HELL ON WHEELS

Directions for solving are on page 13.

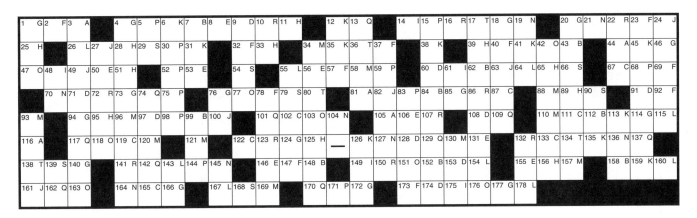

A. Uncool one; nerd

‾‾‾ ‾‾‾ ‾‾ ‾‾ ‾‾‾
116 81 3 44 105

B. Quasimodo's Gypsy friend

‾‾ ‾‾‾ ‾‾‾ ‾ ‾‾ ‾‾ ‾‾‾ ‾‾ ‾‾‾
99 148 158 7 84 62 152 43 112

C. What Stephen King aims to do

‾‾‾ ‾‾‾ ‾‾‾ ‾‾ ‾‾ ‾‾‾ ‾‾‾ ‾‾‾
122 111 133 87 67 119 102 165

D. Hale and healthy (3 wds.)

‾‾‾ ‾‾‾ ‾ ‾‾‾ ‾‾ ‾‾ ‾‾ ‾‾ ‾‾‾
153 128 9 108 97 60 71 91 174

E. Tree-creeping bird often seen upside down

‾ ‾‾‾ ‾‾‾ ‾‾‾ ‾‾ ‾‾ ‾‾ ‾‾‾
8 106 155 146 56 53 50 131

F. Mahogany-red hunting dog originally from Cork (2 wds.)

‾‾‾ ‾‾ ‾‾ ‾‾ ‾ ‾‾‾ ‾‾ ‾‾ ‾‾ ‾‾ ‾‾
147 40 78 69 2 173 92 23 32 37 57

G. 1960s TV show that inspired Will Smith's 1999 oater (4 wds.)

‾‾ ‾‾‾ ‾‾‾ ‾‾ ‾ ‾‾‾ ‾‾‾ ‾‾‾ ‾‾
46 114 177 76 4 124 140 172 85

‾‾ ‾‾‾ ‾‾ ‾‾ ‾‾ ‾
73 166 94 18 20 1

H. Large member of the oboe family also called a "cor anglais" (2 wds.)

‾‾ ‾‾ ‾‾ ‾‾‾ ‾‾ ‾‾ ‾‾ ‾‾‾ ‾‾ ‾‾ ‾‾
51 65 39 125 89 25 95 156 33 11 28

I. Immature stage of an insect

‾‾ ‾‾ ‾‾ ‾‾‾ ‾‾‾
61 48 14 149 175

J. Hankered or longed (for)

‾‾ ‾‾ ‾‾ ‾‾‾ ‾‾ ‾‾ ‾‾‾
63 24 27 161 49 82 100

K. *My Big Fat Greek Wedding* star (2 wds.)

‾‾ ‾‾‾ ‾‾ ‾ ‾‾ ‾‾‾ ‾‾ ‾‾ ‾‾‾ ‾‾ ‾‾‾
45 159 38 6 35 135 31 41 126 12 113

L. Legal possession

‾‾‾ ‾‾ ‾‾‾ ‾‾‾ ‾‾‾ ‾‾‾ ‾‾‾ ‾‾ ‾‾
143 26 154 115 160 178 167 64 55

M. Peter Bogdanovich's 2002 thriller starring Kirsten Dunst (3 wds.)

‾‾‾ ‾‾ ‾‾ ‾‾‾ ‾‾‾ ‾‾ ‾‾‾ ‾‾ ‾‾‾ ‾‾‾ ‾‾
130 88 96 110 121 58 169 34 157 120 93

N. Catch from behind

‾‾‾ ‾‾ ‾‾‾ ‾‾ ‾‾‾ ‾‾‾ ‾‾ ‾‾‾
136 70 145 19 104 164 21 127

O. Like Maine, Montana, or Minnesota

‾‾‾ ‾‾‾ ‾‾‾ ‾‾‾ ‾‾ ‾‾‾ ‾‾ ‾‾
118 151 163 176 77 103 47 42

P. She was called "Little Sure Shot" (2 wds.)

‾‾ ‾ ‾‾ ‾‾ ‾‾ ‾‾ ‾‾ ‾‾‾ ‾‾ ‾‾‾ ‾‾
83 5 75 68 30 15 52 144 98 171 59

Q. Johnny Cash song of 1963 (3 wds.)

‾‾‾ ‾‾‾ ‾‾‾ ‾‾‾ ‾‾‾ ‾‾ ‾‾‾ ‾‾ ‾‾‾ ‾‾‾
137 117 170 129 162 13 101 74 142 109

R. One of Shirley MacLaine's bio books (4 wds.)

‾‾ ‾‾‾ ‾‾‾ ‾‾ ‾‾ ‾‾ ‾‾ ‾‾‾ ‾‾‾ ‾‾‾
10 123 107 72 86 22 16 150 132 141

S. Enduring; not evanescent

‾‾ ‾‾ ‾‾ ‾‾ ‾‾‾ ‾‾‾ ‾‾
79 54 90 29 168 139 66

T. Magic or Shaq, e.g.

‾‾ ‾‾‾ ‾‾ ‾‾ ‾‾‾
17 138 36 80 134

ANSWER, PAGE 243

MANGIA! MANGIA!

Did you know that in Italian the plural of *pasta* is *paste*? Well, don't eat any of that, okay? Have some of our *paste* instead. See if you can fit all 37 varieties into the grid, crossword-style. Then have a look at the answers, where we've translated all these delicious dishes for you.

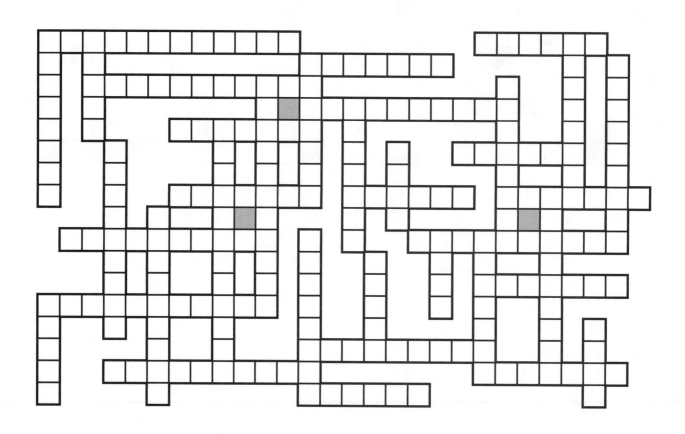

4-letter words
Nidi
Orzo
Ziti

5-letter words
Gigli
Penne
Ruote

6-letter words
Anelli
Eliche
Ondine
Rotini

7-letter words
Cubetti
Gemelli
Gnocchi
Lasagne
Orsetti
Ravioli
Rotelli
Spirali
Torchio

8-letter words
Avemarie
Fettucce
Linguine
Stelline

9-letter words
Ballerine
Cavatappi
Manicotti
Quadrucci
Radiatori

10-letter words
Fettuccine
Maccheroni
Margherite
Tortellini

11-letter words
Orecchiette
Pappardelle
Tagliatelle

12-letter words
Semi di melone
Strozzapreti

ANSWER, PAGE 244

MIND YOUR MANNERS, PART TWO

More helpful etiquette advice from days gone by. These are more challenging than the last set, so please mutter those rude comments under your breath instead of shouting them. Thank you very much. If you need directions on how to solve this puzzle, see page 5.

1.

2.

3.

ANSWER, PAGE 242

FAMOUS LAST WORDS

What some famous people had to say at the threshold of death's door.

ACROSS

1 Far from bulging, as eyes
8 "Better you ___ me!"
12 Places for soaking
16 Jan. 15 honoree
19 Takes off a spool
20 Gilbert Gottfried's *Aladdin* role
21 ___ mater
22 Hammer's location in the body
23 "Leave the shower curtain on the inside of the tub."
25 Contradicts
27 Movie whose working title was *Star Beast*
28 Number
30 Feeling of disquiet
31 ___ Bo (fitness program)
32 Bumped into
34 "I see black light."
37 Alphabetized, e.g.
38 It held the record for most Oscar wins until *Titanic*
39 Groan from Charlie Brown
40 Voter ___ (election year problem)
43 Whatsit
44 Lock
45 "Am I dying or is this my birthday?"
49 Keats' "Ode ___ Nightingale"
50 Descriptive word (abbr.)
51 Spirit that inhabits an object
52 Remove, as a campaign button
54 Teen's first major purchase, maybe
57 Places (ahem) for a public discussion?
60 Edith, to Archie
63 Journalist who founded a weekly newspaper named after himself
65 "Why do you weep? Did you think I was immortal?"
67 Amused chat room comment

68 "God damn the whole friggin' world and every one in it but you, Carlotta."
69 Some swing sites
70 A macho guy claims to be one
72 Pope known as "the Great"
73 Stop along the line (abbr.)
74 Prefix for mural
76 Uncharacteristically fertile area
78 Sell-out sign
80 Watson and Crick described its structure
81 "I must go in, the fog is rising."
86 Herman and Lily's son
89 City in Italy or Florida
90 Los Angeles suburb
91 Method of enforcing debt repayment
92 Volume controls, of a sort
93 "Face Dances" band
96 "All right then, I'll say it. Dante makes me sick."
98 Word with control or missile
99 Canadian Thanksgiving mo.
102 Smith-___
103 Parroting another's opinion
105 Purpose of some prenatal doctor visits, for short
107 Hurts your eardrums, maybe
109 "Why not? Why not? Why not? Why not? Yeah."
111 Penultimate Greek letter
112 Step 1 in steak grilling
113 Spotted
114 Birds related to the chickadee
115 Was introduced to
116 Mrs. Krabappel, to her friends
117 See
118 Marbles, e.g.

DOWN

1 Old coin of Venice
2 ___ *Gay*
3 Orange-skinned Muppet
4 Father, to François
5 P. Diddy's clothing line
6 Days of yore, in days of yore
7 Sightseer's souvenir
8 Competed in a joust
9 Detested
10 Super-excited
11 It's not worth writing home about
12 Melissa Gilbert is its pres.
13 *The Comedy of Errors* was based on his work
14 Key equivalent to C major
15 Having more cards in one's deck, say
16 Firm rule for a tailor or a baker
17 Birds do it
18 Rapper ___-One
24 Concerning, on a memo
26 Las Vegas casino that features the Casbar Lounge
29 Peal
33 Indo-European
35 Make butter the old-fashioned way
36 Cries of surprise
37 Bachelor pad, stereotypically
38 Twice, in music
40 In the style of
41 Sirius Black's alter ego, in Harry Potter tales
42 Opt to reconvene later
43 What a participle mustn't do
44 "Ectomy" that earns an ice cream reward
46 One with no tan lines
47 904, to Octavian
48 Longing
49 Spat
53 Eat out?
54 Big statues

55 It keeps a log?
56 Home addr.
58 Ocasek of The Cars
59 Take ___ to (grow to like)
61 Fluffy neckpiece
62 Brass and steel, e.g.
64 Where to start golfing
65 CDs' predecessors
66 Gabrielle was her sidekick
68 "What ___ saying...?"
70 Destructive spree
71 Magazine run by "the usual gang of idiots"
75 Aptly named Victorian novelist

77 Distorts, as facts
79 *Grapefruit* author Yoko
80 Clams or cabbage
82 Not marked by good performances
83 WKRP newsman Nessman
84 "... ___, 'til death do us part"
85 Sgt., for one
86 Building extension
87 Bishop's district
88 Part of FDIC
89 Andre Agassi, for one
92 Wrote
93 Part in an old amplifier
94 Safari, traditionally

95 Crazy ___
97 Drench
98 Cupid's neighbor
99 How happy people walk
100 The original "men are pigs" woman
101 *Getting* ___ (business advice book)
104 Casual greeting
106 Greedy kid's cry
107 Turntable speed stat.
108 Mrs., in Mallorca
110 Startled cry from Spot

ANSWER, PAGE 243

THE AVENGERS

Some fascinating facts you didn't know about the British TV cult phenom of the '60s. For instructions and hints on how to solve, see page 7.

1. *MQBWKPF   *JQPSYY   VQC   QS   QCCKCBQSB

   MWRXOPYW   RS   *YSENKCZ   *BH   VZYS   ZY   VQC

   RLLYWYX   BZY   NYQX   WRNY.   ZY   CQV   ZKC

   LOBOWY   KS   MWRXOPBKRS,   SRB   QPBKSE,   CR   ZY

   QCFYX   LRW   Q   WKXKPONROCNI   ZKEZ   CQNQWI   BR

   XKCPROWQEY   BZY   RLLYW.   BR   ZKC   CZRPF,   BZYI

   QPPYMBYX.

2. *YJRJH   *OCITVKIR   XCILFS   *BQFFS'B   UWHBQ

   BWSFVWTV,   IRS   *QE'B   UWHBQ   "BGXFHNJKIR"—IR

   IRQYHJXJCJAWBQ   IRS   MGSJ   FDXFHQ.   BYF   ZGWQ

   QJ   OFTJKF   I   KJEWF   BQIH   NYFR   BYF   NIB

   JUUFHFS   QYF   HJCF   JU   *XGBBL   *AICJHF   WR

   *AJCSUWRAFH.

3. EIB   FGZOYTBGV   KXSYGBO   EIBXG   ZCPJ   VIZE   QE

   VBPPXCS   EIB   VIZR   XC   *QUBGXTQ   RQV   EZ   ZKKBG

   VZUBEIXCS   EIQE   *IZPPJRZZO   TZYPOC'E—*BCSPQCO.

   VZ   EIBJ   FYGFZVBPJ   IQUUBO   XE   YF   RXEI   EIXTH

   *WGXEXVI   QTTBCEV,   VPQCS   QCO   VTBCBGJ.

ANSWER, PAGE 245

WOULD WE LIE TO YOU ONE MORE TIME?

Yes, and we love every minute of it! But after this, we'll never lie to you again—we promise. This time, the subject is phrase origins and where the heck they came from in the first place. Find the one true answer in each set.

1. Why is something that's worthless said to be "for the birds"?
    a. It's an old farmer's expression. When a particular portion of a crop came in so badly that it wasn't even worth harvesting, the farmer would leave it "for the birds."
    b. Magpies and other crowlike birds are known for hoarding shiny objects, most of which have no real value. Since birds don't know or care if an object is valuable, anything that's "for the birds" is worthless.
    c. Before the advent of the automobile, city streets contained a fair amount of horse manure. The undigested oats in the manure were frequently eaten by sparrows. So to say that something was "for the birds" was a polite way of calling it horse manure.

2. A risky situation is often described as being "touch and go." Why?
    a. When two stagecoaches passed each other on a narrow road, their wheels would often become entangled, wrecking both vehicles. If the drivers were lucky, however, the wheels would merely "touch and go."
    b. In bullfighting, it's always a bad idea for the *torero* to touch the bull as it charges past; the bull will usually halt its charge and circle back to the area where it felt the touch. But if the *torero* is lucky, the touched bull will simply continue its charge—a "touch and go."
    c. To demolitions experts, "touch and go" means to arm an explosive device and then get to minimum safe distance before it detonates. Needless to say, any mission involving a "touch and go" is very risky.

3. To be "not up to scratch" is to be inadequate. Where did that come from?
    a. A person who's starting from scratch (in other words, an absolute beginner is expected to do a poor job. Anyone who performs *beneath* these low expectations is said to be "not up to scratch."
    b. Before there were bells to start the rounds in boxing matches, the referee would scratch a line on the ground between the fighters, and the next round would begin when both men stepped over it. A boxer who was too worn-out to cross the line was "not up to scratch."
    c. "Scratch" is one of Satan's many nicknames. If you're so bad that even the devil won't take you, you're "not up to Scratch."

4. Why is a short-lived success called a "flash in the *pan*"?
    a. Old-time photographers would produce a flash by igniting a pan full of flash powder. A "flash in the pan" is therefore a single photograph—and if your success is over after a single photograph, you obviously weren't very successful.
    b. In flintlock muskets of the 1700s, sparks from the flint ignited the gunpowder in the *pan*, which in turn ignited the main charge in the barrel. However, occasionally the gunpowder in the pan would burn without igniting the main charge, producing a "flash in the pan" but no actual bullet.
    c. A *flash* is a very brief moment, and *pan* is a slang term for "face." So to call something a "flash in the pan" is to say that it only appeared in front of your face for the merest instant.

5. Why is a "fly in the ointment" a detrimental factor? What are flies doing in the ointment anyway?
    a. Ointment used to mean a sweet-smelling cosmetic. The phrase comes from a verse in the Bible, Ecclesiastes 10:1: "Dead flies make the perfumer's ointment give off an evil odor."
    b. Ointments for venereal disease in the Victorian age sometimes contained Spanish fly, a well-known aphrodisiac. If the medicine that was supposed to cure your affliction was instead tempting you to further sexual excesses, you were suffering from "fly in the ointment."
    c. The expression is a loose translation of a Middle English phrase, *fliege en unguen*, that means "flies in the grease"—a much more logical place to find flies than in ointment.

ANSWER, PAGE 237

DOROTHY PARKER SEZ...

Translate these wisecracks by figuring out the simple letter substitution code. For further instructions and hints on how to solve, see page 7. Meanwhile, let's start with a little poetry...

1. *FIC *GI *KUUH TG T *XUOO

   *IZ, OEPU EG T YOISEIJG QBQOU IP GIFY,

   *T LUKOUB IP UVCULHISTFUT;

   *TFK OIAU EG T CZEFY CZTC QTF FUAUS YI

      XSIFY;

   *TFK E TL *LTSEU IP *SIJLTFET.

2. U'B SRJRF OEUSO QE HR WIBEMZ. BX SIBR LUYY

   SRJRF HR LFUQ YIFOR ES QTR FEZQRF EW *QTEZR

   *LTE *CE *QTUSOZ. U CES'Q CE ISXQTUSO. SEQ

   ESR ZUSOYR QTUSO. U MZRC QE HUQR BX

   SIUYZ, HMQ *U CES'Q RJRS CE QTIQ ISXBEFR.

3. J LJFHWLWLOWH DQP YJHFE DGF UHNWB WZPNXQ

   EP ZNHENHW EQW UPUTEGJB VGHER JZEP BJYW.

   ONE VWHQGVF JE DPNBM OW ZPE EPP LNUQ EP

   FGR, JZ YGUE JE DPNBM OW ZPE WZPNXQ EP

   FGR, EQGE JE DGF ZPE DPHEQ EQW EHPNOBW.

SCIENCE DICTION

A few nonscientific comments on the subject of science.

1.

2.

3.

ANSWER, PAGE 244

TECHNOSLANG

Get hip to 21st century jive.

ACROSS

1 Jimmy Carter's home
7 Acid found in milk
13 Puts off
19 Examines narrowly
20 Author Fallaci
21 Biblical landfall
22 Some doors do it
23 Big expensive homes packed in tight rows
25 *The Lord of the Rings*, e.g.
26 Bit of encouragement
28 Nancy Drew's author
29 Used a spade
30 The area around a computer where you display all your trinkets
35 Squeaker or squealer
36 Johnny Mathis hit
38 Takes too much
39 Ostrich relative
40 "...feast ___ famine"
42 Hardcore fitness freak who looks down on the less fit
44 War winner
45 Comment ending
46 Masseurs' stock
47 Actor Cariou
48 Physical world, as opposed to cyberspace
55 *La Vie Boheme* musical
56 Adidas rival
57 Type of glove
58 Kind of contract
62 Old hirsute sitcom creature
63 *Death in Venice* author
64 Hip-hop enthusiast
66 Love to pieces
67 Whacking a device to get it going
73 "Double Delight" snacks
74 First name of the Church Lady
75 Perry's creator
76 Colonial descendants' org.
77 Impersonates

78 Name at a notions counter
81 "*Dies ___*"
82 Actress Freeman
83 Secretive about one's cosmetic surgery
88 Nicole's role in *Cold Mountain*
91 Image on a monitor
92 Merkel and O'Connor
93 Wrecker
94 TV or radio fundraiser
96 ___ in xylophone
97 Dinghy thingies
99 Midafternoon refresher
102 Goof-ups
103 Pennington and Hardin
105 Sexploitation film featuring lots of women in bikinis
108 Brooklyn conclusion
109 Rotelle or rotini
111 Perrins's saucy partner
112 Complex elements (abbr.)
113 Deciding as a group who's responsible for a project's failure
117 Small herding dog
120 Gourmands
121 Sartre work
122 He played Strangelove
123 Sandra Bullock movie
124 Wild times
125 Antigone's sister

DOWN

1 Made a small sound
2 Imposes, as a tax
3 Solid as ___
4 St. Thomas, for one
5 Pt. of USNA
6 Treeless region
7 Singer Lenya
8 LAX posting
9 The agency in *The Agency*
10 Bulletin board item
11 Mural lead-in

12 Happened
13 Hamlet, for one
14 Trauma sites, for short
15 Stored for the future
16 Excitement
17 The third-longest river in the world
18 Highways and byways (abbr.)
19 Newman's Own competitor
24 Painter Watteau
27 "Now I get it!"
31 Bicolored killer
32 Mountain guides
33 Campus military group
34 Sock end
36 Computer game with a sequel called Riven
37 Half a Chinese symbol
41 Hefty baby, for example
43 XLIII x XIII
44 Tread the boards
45 Literary collection
48 Camera support
49 Straight
50 The main dish
51 Frank holders
52 Electronic science magazine
53 Request of mother?
54 Character who like this talks, mmm?
59 Some musical compositions
60 Esoteric
61 Ogle
63 Greek consonants
64 Three-country European union
65 Alternative to ASCAP
66 Hydrocarbon suffix
68 Mozart's ___ *fan tutte*
69 Second in command, slangily
70 "Father of the Oratory" Philip
71 ___ II razor
72 Mourning one in an O'Neill title
78 Engrave on glass
79 Try to hit

80 ___ *Idylls of the King*
81 Word that often has an apostrophe
82 Do some lawn work
84 They may be picked
85 Gray area? (abbr.)
86 Beauty pageant accessory
87 All befuddled
88 Crunches help build them
89 Betrayer in Judges

90 Stir up
95 Missing links, perhaps
97 Opening number?
98 Rival of Sampras
99 List makeup, often
100 In one piece
101 Chuckleheads
104 Flip-flop part
106 Korbut and others
107 Oscar winner Berry

109 "Hey, over here!"
110 Asian river
113 Put on the line
114 Afore
115 British verb ending
116 Word before a maiden name
118 "___ So Fine"
119 State tree of Massachusetts

ANSWER, PAGE 239

OPERATION: OPERA

Never been to the opera? Here's a painless way to take part in the experience. The price of admission: one pencil and a few moments of your time. (It'll be over before you know it.) See if you can fit all 35 operas into the grid, crossword-style.

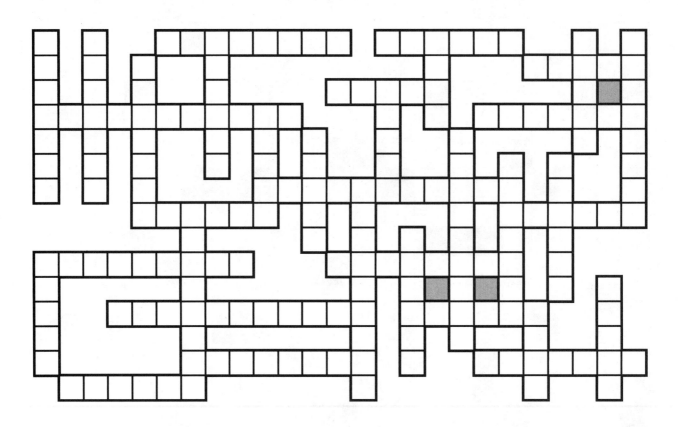

4-letter words
Aida
Goya

5-letter words
Lakmé
Manon
Norma
Orfeo
Thaïs
Tommy
Tosca
(La) Wally

6-letter words
Attila

Carmen
(The) Consul
Ernani
Jenufa
Martha
Mignon
Otello

7-letter words
Elektra
Fidelio
Macbeth
Nabucco
(Les) Troyens
Wozzeck

8-letter words
(La) Gioconda
Iolanthe
Parsifal
(La) Traviata
Turandot

9-letter words
Rigoletto
Tamerlano
(Il) Trovatore

11-letter words
(La) Cenerentola
Mefistofele
(Die) Zauberflöte

ANSWER, PAGE 244

A ROSE BY ANY OTHER...

Directions for solving are on page 13.

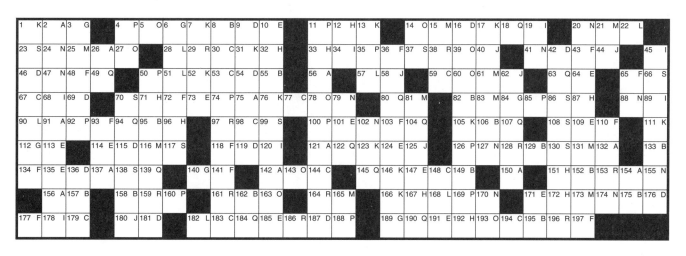

A. German-born U.S. political philosopher (2 wds.)

121 156 2 142 56 137 150 154 26 75 132 91

B. Site of golf's Masters Tournament (2 wds.)

133 162 195 129 82 157 106 149 152 175
8 55 95 158

C. Do-or-die time on the diamond (2 wds.)

183 53 59 144 98 194 148 30 77 67 179

D. English drama critic and *Oh! Calcutta!* producer (2 wds.)

176 16 187 54 9 46 115 136 69 181 42 119

E. Twice-filmed Ira Levin chiller (with *The*) (2 wds.)

191 185 109 171 113 135 124 10 114 147 73 101 64

F. CBS public affairs program since 1954 (3 wds.)

141 36 43 103 197 65 48 72 93 110 177 118 134

G. Hurt one's feelings

140 189 112 3 6 84

H. Jazz trumpeter and bandleader of "Worried Mind" (2 wds.)

172 96 87 33 167 192 151 71 12 32

I. March Madness event, for example

34 45 89 68 178 120 19

J. Period of greatest success

44 62 125 40 180 58

K. Actor who debuted in *Primal Fear*, 1996 (2 wds.)

146 13 105 166 31 7 17 1 52 76 111 123

L. Driving a sled dog team

57 51 90 28 182 22 168

M. Paulette Jiles's Civil War novel set in the Ozarks (2 wds.)

21 165 116 25 83 15 173 61 131 81

N. 1960s sitcom set aboard a P.T. boat (2 wds.)

20 127 47 88 102 41 170 79 24 174 155

O. Passé; obsolete (hyph.)

78 5 163 143 193 27 60 14 39

P. U2's 1988 rockumentary (3 wds.)

92 126 188 35 160 74 11 85 50 4 169 100

Q. "Compelling" novel of 2000 about a seductress

190 49 139 104 107 63 184 18 80 145 94 122

R. Author of Word Q (2 wds.)

29 97 196 164 153 161 159 186 128 38

S. The process of growing old

108 66 117 86 130 70 99 23 37 138

ANSWER, PAGE 227

WHAT AM I?

The grid not only holds the answers to the 15 riddles below—its shape is the answer to one of then (hint, hint). Work back and forth between the riddles and the grid, circling words and phrases as you go. Once you've found all the answers, the leftover letters will reveal one more riddle. (If you need help solving the riddles, the answers are listed on the answer page.)

```
        Y  L  F  R  E  T  T  U  B  I  A
     M  A  D  E  C  K  O  F  C  A  R  D  S
     W  P  O  S  T  A  G  E  S  T  A  M  P
        O  R  D  O  T  S  F  L  E  U  T
           G  L  O  V  E  T  E  R  R
              S  T  H  Y  R  D  R
                 E  E  E  A  M
                 D  F  D
                 T  O  W
                    R
                 O  I  R
                 A  A  N
              D  I  P  A  F
           E  N  W  E  R  N  T
        H  B  E  D  U  O  L  C  R
        Y  O  U  R  B  R  E  A  T  H  E
     W  W  I  O  S  S  A  L  G  R  U  O  H
     L  C  A  N  D  L  E  L  B  E  F  E  R
        D  I  C  T  I  O  N  A  R  Y  W
```

1. Just two hairs upon her head, but she wears a gown. And dances in the flower bed, the prettiest creature in town.

   __ __ __ __ __ __ __ __ __

2. My life is measured in hours; I serve by being devoured. Thin, I am quick...Thick, I am slow...A gust of wind is my greatest foe.

   __ __ __ __ __ __

3. When I am filled I can point the way. When I am empty, nothing moves me. I have two skins—one without and one within.

   __ __ __ __ __

4. I appear once in a minute, twice in a moment, but never in a thousand years.

   THE __ __ __ __ __ __ __

5. I am placed on the table, then cut, then passed around to everyone present, but I am never eaten.

   __ __ __ __   __ __   __ __ __ __

6. We are identical twins who see everything in front of us, but never each other.

   __ __ __ __ __   __ __ __   __ __ __ __

7. I am the only place where you will find yesterday after today.

   __ __ __ __ __ __ __ __ __

8. To use me you must throw me away, but you will retrieve me when I am no longer needed.

   __ __ __ __ __ __

9. I can circle the globe while never leaving a corner.

   __ __ __ __ __ __   __ __ __ __ __

10. I am lighter than the lightest feather, but no matter how much strength you have, you couldn't hold me for more than a few minutes.

   __ __ __ __   __ __ __ __ __ __

11. Without wings I fly, without eyes I cry.

   __ __ __ __ __

12. I am only a head; I have nothing within. I've got no mouth; I speak with my skin.

   __ __ __ __

13. Red and blue, violet and green, no one can touch me, not even a queen.

   __ __ __ __ __ __ __

14. I go up and down the hill, yet I'm always standing still.

   __ __ __ __

15. Two bodies have I, though both joined as one. The stiller I stand, the faster I run.

   __ __ __ __ __ __ __ __ __

ANSWER, PAGE 245

* * * * *

JUST MY TYPE

The next time you sit down at your computer, figure this one out: Which hand does more of the typing: the left hand or the right hand?

ANSWER, PAGE 236

ROSEANNE SEZ...

We ran a page of Roseanne's quotes last time, so we figured that was that. But she said she'd beat us up if we didn't run another one, so here goes. The letter substitution changes from one cryptogram to the next; if you need more directions or solving hints, see page 7.

1. PGU FGYB PYIW TGMMGF MOYU HQPGU TGVYZWG

   QUXN PGU VYU ZUBGFWMYUB MOG VQUVGIM QR

   YU KUVO GAZYXXKUE Y OZUBFGB PKXGW.

2. ZYJHI RYJAKPBI PEYNM AFHJHIDMFNPK DSIVFYJH,

   ENM B MUBIO YW BM PD MUH YIKS MBJH YW

   MUH JYIMU B RPI EH JSDHKW.

3. K MCAYO VBY JPGVBKUN CVGEY JPYEA KT CBY

   BMO MULVBKUN VG SMAY SY PGGA VBKUUYE,

   MUO CBY CMKO, "BGI MZGRV M IYYA KU

   *ZMUNPMOY-CB?"

4. VP AXYD GM CAQC HQPM NGTT WD BIUUGUH

   CAD NXBTL, WDZQIMD CADU CADBD NXITL WD

   UX NQB. RIMC Q HBDQCDB DVYAQMGM XU

   VGTGCQBP QYYQBDT.

5. NGXNJZL LUI IWB LPWBVK QNCNJ PSZ IWBJ

   FPSVKJNQ SQ UQENJ. MPNQ SL U EWWK ZSDN?

   MPNQ IWB'JN RNNVSQE RNLZSCN?

ANSWER, PAGE 245

MR. MOONLIGHT

The Moon is our nearest neighbor and how much do we know about him? We never even went over and introduced ourselves when he moved in. Let's get out the old telescope and train it on the guy next door—it's all in the interest of science. Fill in the blanks with the correct numbers.

1. It takes ___ seconds for moonlight to reach the Earth.

2. If you weigh 120 pounds on Earth, you would weigh ___ pounds on the Moon.

3. The Moon is moving away from the Earth at the rate of about ___ inch a year.

4. The average temperature of the Moon can be as low as ___ degrees Fahrenheit.

5. The Moon is ___ miles in diameter (about 1/4 the diameter of the Earth).

6. It takes a bit over ___ days for the Moon to go through all of its phases.

7. A three-foot jump on the Earth would carry you ___ feet on the Moon.

8. The Moon reflects only ___ percent of the light it receives from the Sun.

9. Astronauts have brought over ___ pounds of Moon samples back to Earth.

10. If the Earth were the size of a fist, the Moon would be the size of a postage stamp placed ___ feet away.

-283	1 1/4	10	20	843
1/8	7	18	29	2,160

ANSWER, PAGE 245

* * * * *

HEY! UH...NICK!

Why are alternate names called nicknames?

a. Because Nick is short for Nicholas. When the term was coined, "Nicholas" was an extremely common name—the equivalent of "John" today.

b. It comes from the Middle English *an ekename*, meaning "an additional name."

c. It comes from the Irish folktale of Nick Shay, a drunkard who never paid for his drinks. In the story, he repeatedly fools a bartender into advancing him credit by using a variety of aliases.

ANSWER, PAGE 243

TAWK UH DA TOWN

What town? New Yawk, of cawse.

ACROSS

1 Not pass the bar?
7 Cobwebby area
12 Phone no. add-on
15 Univ. course
20 "___ Safari" (Beach Boys hit)
21 Moonshine
22 Society page word
23 Author Welty
24 Phrase popularized by New York deejay Murray the K in the 1960s
27 Chinese zodiac sign
28 Final (abbr.)
29 Maître d's offering
30 Yuletide spirit?
31 Meaning "buddy," it's from a pocket style worn in New York c.1900
33 Profs.' aides
34 Purity personified in Arthurian legend
35 Sandwich named for the New York deli where it was invented
38 Part of CBS (abbr.)
39 Song and dance, e.g.
40 Broadway turkey
41 Scottish lake
43 Opening words
48 Fruit-ful venue
51 Long, in Lahaina
52 Greek salad cheese
53 Hilo hiyas
54 Phrase that first meant beyond the reach of Babe Ruth in Yankee Stadium
59 Kind of music named after a New York magazine of the 1970s
61 Poetic monogram
62 Lowdown
63 Kill with humor
64 *The World of Suzie* ___

65 Neighborhood
66 "___ be a cold day in..."
68 Letters on old Europe maps
70 Feed the fire
72 Droll DeLuise
74 Posting at JFK
75 Frasier's brother
77 Harbinger
79 Blazing
81 Comical Charlotte
83 It may come from the Lower East Side pronunciation of "decalcomania"
86 Shopping site that's from the New York-Dutch word "vlie," short for "valley"
90 *2001* computer
91 HRH's reward
93 Takeout order
94 Nasty talk
96 Amt. for Julia Child
99 Skater Babilonia
101 Blackbeard's real name
103 Workers' rights gp.
105 June 6, 1944
106 Public util.
108 Bump on a bone
110 Places for pedicures
112 Olympics sword
114 Social ending
115 It first described gridlock on New York streets in 1890
117 Phrase derived from the fact that Sing Sing is north of New York along the Hudson
120 Hang on to
121 NYC rentals
123 Rock producer Brian
124 Thoughts of Paris?
125 For ___ (cheap)

126 What you can become overnight on Broadway
127 Moravian city
128 Mad., Park, Lex., etc.
130 ___ *Pinafore*
132 Name given a cattle rustler in New York in the 1800s
134 Baldwin of Hollywood
135 Dict. fillers
138 The first appeared in a 1777 edition of the *New York Gazette*
143 Albanian moolah
144 Santa ___, California
145 Make tracks
146 Drilling site at sea
147 It was first applied to New Yorker John Jacob Astor
152 Men's undies
153 One (prefix)
154 "Keep dreaming!"
155 Executed flawlessly
156 Swamp plant
157 Emilio, to Martin
158 Hoodlums
159 Birch relatives

DOWN

1 "...life ___ a dream"
2 Mosque leader (var.)
3 Everybody else's kids
4 Uncertain things
5 Final moment
6 Baby, to Bardot
7 "Get ___ of yourself!"
8 Heavy volume
9 Rugrat
10 German pronoun
11 Chubby little angel
12 Like some cookware
13 Crosses (out)
14 Asian holidays
15 Luxurious fabric
16 Mt. Rushmore's state

17 Quotable Berra
18 Swamp snapper
19 Chunk of hair
23 Whirlpool
25 Baseball stats
26 Pour house?
32 "Sorta" suffix
35 Sight from Santa's sleigh
36 Cybermessages
37 "As if!"
39 Bird (prefix)
40 Lunch order
42 Head of the "family"?
44 Author Ephron
45 Actress Birch
46 Stock car driver
47 Liam's role in *Schindler's List*
48 Was admitted to
49 *Hee Haw* type
50 Verdi opera
52 Depart in V-formation
53 Cat show entrant
55 Article in *La Prensa*
56 English Derby town
57 French mathematician
58 "...I could ___ horse!"
60 Cologne conjunction
64 We Five hit "You ___ My Mind"
67 Poland's Walesa
69 Descendant of Shem
71 Bagpiper's skirt
73 Sportscaster Albert
76 32-card game
78 Nick at ___
80 Aerie baby
82 Squeezed (out)
84 12-step program support group
85 Makes jubilant
87 Transmogrify
88 Salad green
89 Perfectly
92 Nobel category, for short

95 Mike of *Cat in the Hat*
96 ___ cotta
97 Makes a sharp turn
98 Green pasta sauce
100 Gambler's note
102 Straight, so to speak
104 Quilter's gathering
107 Gumshoe Charlie
109 "Doggone it!"
111 Cheerful
113 Waterway to the Hudson
116 What Paris Hilton leads
117 Enter casually

118 Cutesy-___
119 Bouncers check them
122 Ms. ___-Man
126 Tax form info.
127 Blues legend
128 Kyrgyzstan range
129 *Two Gentlemen of ___*
131 Russian fighters
133 Soaked
134 Sheedy and Walker
135 Even though
136 More desperate
137 Chicken feed

138 Goblin starters
139 Dublin's land
140 "Put ___ on it!"
141 Bottom of the barrel
142 Outback birds
144 The Kennedys, e.g.
148 Number one in Rome
149 Word from a herd
150 *Sands of ___ Jima*
151 Financial help

ANSWER, PAGE 245

UNCLE JOHN'S JOHN

Our uncle isn't the neatest of guys. Look, he's left these 39 items strewn all over the bathroom—including his own Bathroom Reader. Do you mind straightening up for him? See if you can put them all in their proper places in the grid, crossword-style.

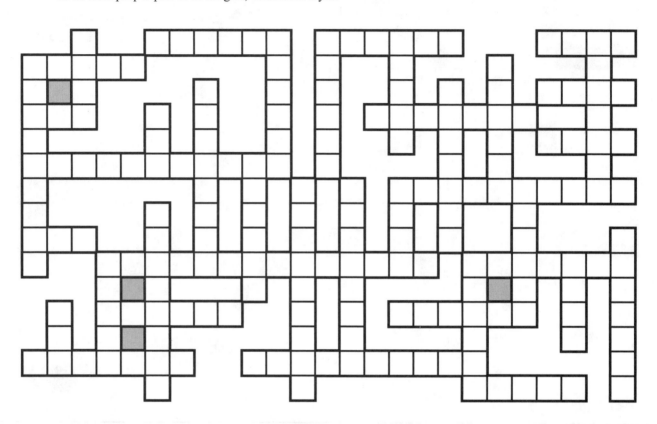

3-letter words
Cup
Fan
Gel
Tub

4-letter words
Bath
Comb
Plug
Robe
Soap
Tile

5-letter words
Basin
Floss
Razor
Scale

6-letter words
Faucet
Loofah
Lotion
Mirror
Mousse
Pomade
Shaver
Shower
Throne
Towels

7-letter words
Alcohol
Bath mat
Body oil
Cologne
Plunger
Shampoo

8-letter words
Cleanser
Hot water
Laxative

9-letter words
Facecloth
Hair dryer

10-letter words
Creme rinse
Toothpaste

11-letter word
Cotton balls

14-letter word
Bathroom Reader

ANSWER, PAGE 246

SPECIAL CROSSWORD SECTION

It all started in a brainstorming session at Uncle Al's place. He posed the question: What if we asked our contributors to tell us what their favorite all-time crossword puzzles were? Well, we like to keep Uncle Al happy, so we asked, and from that list we selected three Sunday puzzles from the *New York Times*, one of which goes as far back as 1969.

Before you have a go at them, allow us bring you up to date on crosswords and how the *Times* first entered the crossword business.

It started in New York, but not at the *Times*: The very first crossword puzzle appeared in the *New York World* newspaper on December 21, 1913, written by Arthur Wynne, a writer for the newspaper's game page. The puzzle was a big success and became a weekly feature.

That was that until 1924, when young Richard L. Simon came up with the idea of publishing a book of crosswords with the help of his college chum, M. Lincoln Schuster. Thus the publishing house of Simon & Schuster was born—and so also began the crossword craze of the 1920s.

The craze fizzled out in the 1930s, but the crossword still had its die-hard fans, one of whom was Arthur Hays Sulzburger, then publisher of the *New York Times*. But the *Times* didn't yet run its own crossword, so even Sulzburger had to buy copies of the rival *New York Herald Tribune* to feed his habit.

It wasn't until the early 1940s, at the suggestion of one of its editors, that the *Times* started running a regular crossword. The paper enticed Margaret Petherbridge Farrar away from Simon & Schuster to be the *Times*' first crossword editor. Over the years worn-out clues like "Stinging insect" for BEE and "Bird's home" for NEST were rephrased as "Nectar inspector" and "Nutcracker's suite."

At Farrar's death in 1969, the editorial reins were handed over to Will Weng, then City Desk Editor at the *Times*. And not only did Weng keep to the same clever style, he managed to improve on it.

The puzzle on the next page, "Thanksgiving Fare," was constructed by Will Weng himself. It was one of the first puzzles that not only included the style of clues that the *Times* had become known for; it also had a theme that was actually funny. To say it changed some people's lives is not an exaggeration. Merl Reagle, who wrote our Entry Puzzle on page 198, says that "Thanksgiving Fare" inspired him to make crossword puzzles his life's work; it suddenly occurred to him that he might be able to make a living writing puzzles and have fun at the same time.

A special thanks to current *New York Times* editor, Will Shortz, for helping us obtain permission to reprint the following puzzles, our constructors' favorites.

THANKSGIVING FARE

This is Will Weng's groundbreaking puzzle. It first appeared in the *The New York Times* on December 31, 1969, and puzzle fans still talk about it. If it seems a little outdated, hey, 1969 was a long time ago, and we didn't want to change a word.

ACROSS
1 Designation (abbr.)
5 Between *sum* and *fui*
9 Tricks
14 Lion
19 Whimpers
21 ___ a million
22 Creators of jams
23 Shape in a way
24 Holiday dining decor
27 Plant fiber
28 Columbus campus
29 Get the air
30 Of a body fiber (prefix)
31 Begins to work
32 Limousines
34 Ventured
36 Girl's name
38 Controversial
40 Mom's baking standby
44 Words of disavowal
48 Officer of ___
50 Keen qualities of sense
51 Supporting bar
52 Coty
53 Of a volcano
54 Frolics
55 Young one
58 Airstrips (abbr.)
61 Day times (abbr.)
62 Sandwich filler
63 Football platoon
65 Atelier items
68 C.P.A. job
69 U.S. composer
70 Yearly pay for a few
72 Foulard items
75 Derisive sound
76 Table decor
80 Roman hall
82 Western smokes
84 Social bore
85 Fawn
86 Moslem prayer
87 Dark rock
89 Late-flowering tulip
91 Soup seeds
94 Man's nickname
95 Bone (prefix)
97 Caesar's but
98 City in Picardy
99 Cubes and spheres
102 Hindu deity
104 Behaves well
105 Road menaces
107 Parallel
110 Novelist's problem
111 Sleigh for today's grandma
113 Shooting in a way
116 Bare the head, old style
118 It's ___ thing
120 Scourge
121 Scott hero
124 Some dogs
128 Certain Italian, to French
130 Peer Gynt's mother
131 Alert
132 Repast topper
135 Noncomformist
136 Skin (prefix)
137 Ten (Latin)
138 Obtain repairs
139 ___ work
140 Tree secretion
141 Biblical tower
142 Scout groups

DOWN
1 Place in proximity
2 Heartbeat control device
3 Strong approval
4 Your (French)
5 Inward (anat.)
6 Ocean research unit
7 One source of salt
8 Kind of serviceman (abbr.)
9 Prestige
10 Standout (slang)
11 Doer (suffix)
12 Subway workers
13 Silence!
14 Hit a high fly
15 Holiday menu item
16 1969 champs
17 Famed island
18 Arabian Sea gulf
20 Frugal one
21 Scot's alas
25 Privileged people
26 Well-done part of a roast
31 Red or White
33 Residue
35 Verb suffix
37 Possessive
39 Vegetable for mom's table
41 Mayan month
42 News pieces
43 Spanish relatives
45 State (abbr.)
46 Slue
47 ___ deal
49 Evergreen
51 Drool
54 Musical ending
55 Sea birds
56 In progress
57 Crux of a holiday meal
59 Kennel sound
60 Ad subject
62 Home-cooked item
63 Metric units (abbr.)
64 Tennis scores, in a way
66 Medit. island
67 Eagles
68 Galatea's beloved
71 Kiln
73 Craft
74 Agreed with
77 Khan
78 Well-known Italian
79 Small violins
81 Scottish county

83 Misfortunes
87 City of Brazil
88 Of an acid
90 Like a moonlit night
91 Bedside item
92 Ludwig
93 Spanish lad
94 Name in movies
96 Refrain syllable
99 Like a freshly-cleaned suit
100 Lower
101 Indian titles of respect

103 One who transfers property
105 Scottish precipitation
106 Slipped over
108 Girl with a headset (abbr.)
109 Veld animal
111 Short of
112 Third of a famous nine
114 Stick one's ___
115 Welcomes
117 Songs
119 Eastern V.I.P.

121 ___ avis
122 Was beholden to
123 Cake
125 Comparative suffixes
126 Prefix for god or john
127 Oxygen prefix
129 Navy V.I.P. (abbr.)
132 New Deal man
133 "Crusade" man
134 G-man (slang)

ANSWER, PAGE 246

GOOD NEIGHBORS

This extra-special puzzle was written by Trip Payne, whose work appears in nearly every section of *Uncle John's Bathroom Reader Puzzle Book #2*. Before you get started here's a gentle warning: You might want to keep an eraser handy until you figure out the theme.

ACROSS

1 Chemical used in perfumes
7 Like bananas Foster
13 Façade part
20 1954 title role for Audrey Hepburn
21 Pleasure trip vessels
22 Clinton, once
23 Fleshly
24 Socratic conclusions?
25 Money in reserve
26 Insect repellent ingredient
27 April 25, Down Under
29 "Swingin' the Blues" songwriter
30 Passage with a moral
32 Early afternoon time
34 Pulitzer Prize category
38 Bothers
41 Shipwreck cause, sometimes
42 Exiled Cambodian leader
43 Christmas decorations
47 Featured vocalists' selections
48 Caduceus creatures
50 Due follower
51 Grenoble's department
52 At ___ (befuddled)
54 Draft picks
55 Dainty gem
56 Oscar nominee Zellweger
57 "When I was a ___ ..." (storyteller's start)
59 Hardly try
60 Took on again, as a problem
62 Archipelago makeup (abbr.)

63 Humiliates
64 Cartoonist Addams
65 Hardy English sheep
67 The Hardy Boys' sidekick
68 Unrushed pedestrian
71 Speck
72 Play ball
76 Bazookas, basically
77 "I've had it!" inspiration
80 Flavorful
81 Command post (abbr.)
82 They may click with writers
83 Journalist Alexander
84 Place for a professeur
85 It could be to the left of center
86 *Gunsmoke* star
88 Give an ___ effort
89 *American Beauty* hero
90 Bitty bite
92 Pupil's place
93 Must
95 Group of gods led by Odin
96 Medium setting
98 Chef Emeril
103 Designer's concern
105 Dentists may take them
108 Rob of *The West Wing*
109 Sweet Italian wine
112 Upstairs window
113 In the center
115 Mopey one
116 Put on a pedestal
117 Break down
118 Léotard and Silhouette, e.g.
119 Peewee
120 Egypt's Lake ___

DOWN

1 Rights org.
2 Occult science
3 Diamond flaw?
4 Skin disease
5 Collected sayings
6 Sung syllables
7 Abbr. on a soda bottle
8 City founded by Pizarro
9 Storyteller
10 *Will & Grace* actress Mullally
11 Upset donkeys, often
12 Winding path
13 Cinematic barbarian
14 They've split
15 Barn dance moves
16 Lewinsky was one
17 Tell it like it isn't
18 Not be up-to-date
19 Geom. measure
28 Store total
29 Low-fat meat providers
31 Petitions
33 In a defensible manner
35 Preventing stoppages
36 Down in the dumps
37 Unalaska residents
39 Unwavering
40 Heaps
42 ___ *Girls*
43 Transportation to N.Y.C.
44 "Amazing Grace" ending
45 Site of an 1814 treaty
46 Sweet toppings
49 Cryptographer's need
53 Dieter's desire
55 Regatta
58 Suffix with telegraph

59 Edible holiday gift
61 Bright, to Brecht
63 Word with chop or swap
65 Arm of the Antarctic Ocean
66 Giants legend
67 Yellow
68 Parthenon honoree
69 Rich chocolate dessert
70 Entree covered with sauce
71 Zig or zag, e.g.
72 Slalom craft
73 Deaf as___
74 Parquet alternative
75 German river

77 Sportscaster Berman
78 Marvel superhero group
79 Ben Affleck, in *Pearl Harbor*
82 Possessed leader?
86 "So soon?"
87 Costa Rica's capital
91 Tries to buy
94 17th-century explorer
96 Goes hang-gliding
97 Café handout
99 Actors Robert and Antony
100 Besmirches
101 *Camel News Caravan* host, 1949-56

102 Sushi bar supplier
104 Red Skelton character
106 Roger of *Cheers*
107 Black Knights of college football
109 U.K. honor
110 Cercle et Carré artist
111 Outback jumper
112 N.Y.P.D. employee
114 Character in *Bambi*

ANSWER, PAGE 246

FAIRWAY FANTASY

One of our favorite contributors, Alan Arbesfeld, brought this David Kahn puzzle to our attention. We think it's a PGA tour de force.

ACROSS

1 Places to see waves
8 Counterpart to omega
11 Overcharge and then some
16 Jettisons
21 Feature of Cher or Madonna
22 Listen here
23 Like some stock
24 Style pioneered by Josef Albers
25 Space out
26 Good bit of competition
29 Sub
30 Unpaid loan result, sometimes
32 Has chits out
33 All excited
34 Madrid's ___ Sofia Museum
36 Cause of a revival? (abbr.)
38 Do over, as computer photos
40 Suffixes with glycer- and phen-
41 Do part of a driving test
45 Rock of comedy
47 Special people
48 With 28-Down, a 1996 western
49 Fencing move
52 Bud
55 1669 blast site
56 Staple of NBC's 1960s-70s Sunday night schedule
58 First to be called up
59 Dissects, in a way
62 E Street Band leader, informally
64 Getting bigger quickly
66 Short court session?
67 Babbler?
69 Give out
70 Ancient writing system
71 Where some 119-Across go
74 Settee site
77 Clever prank
80 Pen tip
81 "... and ___ grow on"
82 Golf score, or a description of the 18 hidden 65-Down in this puzzle
84 *Per Ardua ad* ___ (Royal Air Force motto)
86 Fleur-de-___

87 1960s pop trio Dino, ___ & Billy
88 Cantillate
89 Attic item
90 Reveals
94 Come down with
95 Carry away
97 *Sesame Street* creator Joan Ganz ___
98 Hepburn/Tracy comedy
103 Put out
107 Restaurant in *Vertigo*
108 Law firm employee, for short
109 Blue
111 In person
112 Vt. summer hrs.
113 Director Stanley
114 Henry VIII's sixth
115 Start of an aside, for short
116 Leave ___ (permanently damage)
119 See 71-Across
122 Org. for Mahmoud Abbas
125 Broke up
128 Giant teammate of Mize
129 Burdened
130 In-flight calling aid
132 Picture of health?
134 Regarding (abbr.)
135 Excoriate
139 Puncher
143 Like owls
145 Charity, often
146 ___ hand
147 Robert Morse Tony-winning role
148 Period in human development
149 Adlai's running mate in 1956
150 Mammoth things
151 Bewitch
152 Extends a visit

DOWN

1 Fit for a king
2 Part of a pot
3 End
4 Long-haired lagomorph
5 The U.N.'s Hammarskjöld

6 Food Network star
7 Collected
8 Hardly Mr. Personality
9 Mer contents
10 South end?
11 White coat
12 Fruit implement
13 Strike ___
14 Computer system acronym
15 Moralistic
16 Anno ___
17 Aware of
18 Sorbet flavor
19 Breck rival
20 Eye problems
27 Choice location?
28 See 48-Across
31 Dark coverings
35 Two-time U.S. Open winner
36 Patio furniture maker
37 Victimized
39 Skinny one
41 Meter reader?
42 Literary collection (abbr.)
43 1968 Peace Nobelist Cassin
44 Bridge, in Bretagne
46 Toot
49 Pool worker's aid
50 Groove-billed bird
51 TV pooch with a temper
53 *Private Benjamin* actor
54 Rakes, maybe
56 Brit. military award
57 Wood lice and similar creatures
59 Luau fare
60 Cape ___, Mass.
61 "___ Mater" (hymn)
63 About
65 See 82-Across
68 *High Noon* marshal
70 Singing nymph
71 Oversee
72 Hungry person's question
73 Counter

75 Legal thing
76 French pronoun
77 Richard Gere title role
78 Stock market event (abbr.)
79 Ålborg native
83 Warehouse
84 Stage opening
85 Breed from the British Isles
91 Santa follower?
92 Mr. ___ (old detective game)
93 Cobb and others
94 Crimebuster, informally
96 SHO alternative
98 To the left, at sea
99 Dapper one
100 It may follow you

101 Dennis Miller book ___, *Therefore I Am*
102 Yawner
104 Flag
105 Continuously
106 Retreats
110 "___ Remember"
113 Be afraid to
115 Dupin's creator
117 Seeds
118 "Pretty please?"
119 Yankee great Waite ___
120 Praying figure
121 Rural conveyance
122 ___ chat (ballet jump)
123 Tummy jobs

124 Praying figure
126 Shows
127 Wet one's whistle
131 Complimentary
133 *Iliad* warrior
134 Key point
136 Literary olios
137 ___ Park, N.Y.
138 Ideal place
140 Bearded grazer
141 Utmost
142 Afore
144 Mauna ___

CONTEST RULES:

1. Complete the puzzle on the facing page or print out a copy of it from our website: http://bathroomreader.com.

2. Send the completed puzzle and a self-addressed stamped business size envelope to:

   UNCLE JOHN'S CROSSWORD CONTEST
   5880 Oberlin Drive
   San Diego, CA 92121-4794

   postmarked no later than July 1, 2004. Make sure that your entry is **legible**: if we can't read it, we won't know what a fabulous puzzle solver you are.

3. In return mail, you'll receive the answer to the Entry Puzzle and, if your entry was correct, a copy of *The World's Hardest Crossword Puzzle*. Then all you have to do is correctly complete *The World's Hardest Crossword Puzzle* and send it back to us at the same address, postmarked no later than September 1, 2004.

4. All entrants who correctly complete *The World's Hardest Crossword Puzzle* will receive an Uncle John's T-shirt and will be eligible for the **Grand Prize drawing of $5,000**.

ENTRY PUZZLE

FOR THE WORLD'S HARDEST CROSSWORD PUZZLE CONTEST

ACROSS

1 Starbuckian drink
11 Park bench part
15 Scathing denunciation
16 A lo-o-o-ong time
17 "Why now?!"
18 St. Louis landmark
19 Qtys.
20 It's about the eligibility and powers of the President
22 It's knot-worthy
23 Tourist mecca in India
25 Lead role in *They Died With Their Boots On* (1941)
26 Still green
28 Ball elevator
29 Wrecking ball alternative
30 Word in the 23rd Psalm
33 Downs a sub
34 It's a matter of opinion
37 Home away from home, perhaps
40 Advice maven
44 Koufax's was 2.76
45 "How stupid of me!"
47 Fabulous
48 Some ball goers
50 Some ball throwers
52 Football's ___-Ten
53 Grist for the gossip mill
55 Mah-jongg piece
56 It might be filed
57 Went tit for tat
60 Common sports injury site
61 Interim
62 British chaps
63 Westheimer and Kinsey, e.g.

DOWN

1 Stephen who actually said, "*Our* country, right or wrong"
2 Take a long, hard look
3 Hubs
4 Stops stalling
5 Happiest happy hour day (abbr.)
6 Navigator's abbr.
7 Engaged in a battle
8 Princess topper
9 "Hop ___!"
10 Flirt with
11 Elite Navy group
12 Name heard in "Get Back," by the Beatles
13 Like some history
14 Prizes we're awarding for solving The World's Hardest Crossword Puzzle
21 Whisper the next line to
23 "...two peas in ___"
24 Former Spice Girl Halliwell
27 Tidbit for the tabloids
28 By way of, for short
31 Carve into glass
32 Word before "little" or "late"
33 Word on a mtn. sign
35 May race, familiarly
36 Closeout caveat
37 Reveals as a myth
38 Spaghetti sauce ingredient
39 Came from behind
41 One of those drugs that you're supposed to "ask your doctor about"
42 Ready to mobilize
43 Ebbs
45 German mag, ___ *Spiegel*
46 Seizes illegally
49 Lovett and Sparky
50 Modern wrinkle remover
51 Speechify
54 Simple
55 Film alternative
58 Post-Johnny Tarzan
59 Babysitter's handful

ANSWERS

TRUE CONFESSIONS

HOW TO WRITE A PERSONALS AD

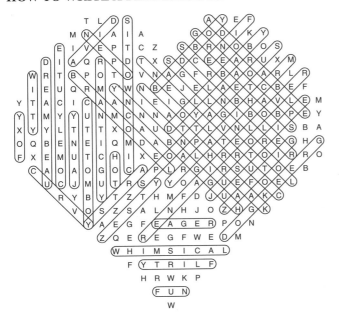

WONTON? NOT NOW!
1. He did, eh?
2. Too hot to hoot.
3. Never odd or even.
4. Sun at noon, tan us.
5. Todd erases a red dot.
6. God saw I was dog.
7. Too bad—I hid a boot.
8. No trace; not one carton.
9. Boston ode: Do not sob.
10. We panic in a pew.
11. Panic in a *Titanic*? I nap.
12. Was it Eliot's toilet I saw?
13. Amy, must I jujitsu my ma?
14. Eva, can I stab bats in a cave?
15. Campus motto: Bottoms up, Mac.
16. Live not on evil, madam, live not on evil.
17. No sir! Away! A papaya war is on.
18. Some men interpret nine memos.
19. No lava on Avalon; no lava, no Avalon.
20. Straw? No, too stupid a fad; I put soot on warts.
21. Anne, I vote more cars race Rome to Vienna.
22. Gateman sees name, garageman sees name tag.

TAKING DEBATE
e. It was the bathroom tissue issue. As reported in an article called "Uncle John's Stall of Fame" in *Uncle John's All-Purpose Extra Strength Bathroom Reader*, Ms. Landers' own opinion was that the paper should come over the top. Why? "Fine quality toilet paper has designs that are right side up," she explained.

IT SLICES! IT DICES!
1 – g (GLH#9 (Hair-in-a-can): "You can use it on your dog!")
2 – e (Inside the Eggshell Scrambler: "You'll use it a lot and every time you do, you'll save washing a bowl and fork!")
3 – a (The Miracle Mop: "It lets you wring out the head without putting your hands into the dirty water!")
4 – c (The Pocket Fisherman: "Attaches to your belt, or fits in the glove compartment of your car!")
5 – d (The Ronco Bottle and Jar Cutter: "A hobby for Dad, craft for the kids, a great gift for Mom!")
6 – b (The Ronco Rhinestone and Stud Setter: "It changes everyday clothing into exciting fashions!")
7 – f (The Veg-O-Matic: "No one likes dicing onions...the only tears you'll shed will be tears of joy!")

PLAY D'OH

1. I'm not normally a religious man, but if you're up there, save me, Superman!
2. Son, you tried your best and you failed miserably. The lesson is, never try.
3. If you really want something in this life you have to work for it. Now quiet! They're about to announce the lottery numbers.

CANDY BARS YOU'LL NEVER EAT

The fake candy bars are Crumbly Mumblies, the Lotsa Matzo Bar, and the Mood Bar.

THE QUOTABLE JOHN

It's All in the Game

Company lore has it that a salesman came up with R-I-S-K. Divine inspiration? No: the first initials of the Parker Brothers president's four grandchildren.

That Other Babe

Babe Didrikson once entered an AAU track meet as the only person on her team: she won six events, broke four world records and won the meet by eight points.

What, Me Worry?

Three issues flopped. But back then, it took so long to get sales reports that a fourth issue was already in the works. By then, *Mad* had begun to sell.

YE OLDE CRIME AND PUNISHMENT

EVERY DAY IN ANYTOWN
Eight
Five
Dessert
A fine
Prostitutes
CRIMES AND MISDEMEANORS
Luxurious
The roof
Cut out
Fortune-teller
More than two colors
Late
Baptism
A lighted lantern
MAKING THE PUNISHMENT FIT THE CRIME?
Wheelbarrow
Throw garbage

HOW FAMOUS CAN YOU GET?

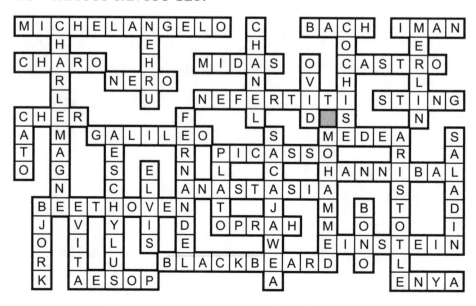

BRAZEN HUSSY!

R	A	P	T		C	H	A	P	S		D	I	G	S
E	S	A	I		R	E	S	E	T		A	C	R	E
E	T	A	L		A	N	E	R	A		L	E	A	N
F	O	R	E	I	G	N	A	F	F	A	I	R	S	
			N	S	A		E	F	T					
C	L	A	S	S		S	E	C		L	A	D	D	S
D	A	N	T	E	S		C	T	R		T	R	I	O
R	U	N	I	T	A	L	L	O	V	E	R	Y	O	U
O	R	A	L		D	O	A		S	N	E	E	R	S
M	A	L	L	S		N	T	H		T	E	R	S	E
			O	D	E		A	A	R					
	C	A	N	B	E	W	O	N	D	E	R	F	U	L
P	O	L	O		C	O	N	G	O		A	L	S	O
O	O	P	S		C	L	E	A	R		G	E	E	S
E	L	S	E		A	F	I	R	E		S	A	S	S

About 10 Down: Salvador Dali's painting, entitled Mae *West's Face Which Can Be Used as a Surrealist Apartment* (1934–35), is in the shape of her face; her hair, mouth and nose are where they belong, but the face is also the interior of an apartment, with wall and floorboards, and a crown sitting atop West's nose. Her eyes are inside picture frames on the wall.

If you're curious, you can see it at: http://www.nowsurrealgalleries.co.uk/view_pic.php3?pid=584&aid=44.

While you're there, check out Dali's "Debris of an Automobile Giving Birth to a Blind Horse Biting a Telephone." (We don't paint 'em, we just report the news.)

IF THEY MARRIED

1. Kitty Katz
2. Coco Pop
3. Demi Demme
4. Cat Dogg
5. Boog Alou
6. Juan Thieu Tree
7. G. Ghali G.
8. Jack Handy Capp Paar King
9. Julie London Bridges Fallon Down
10. Woody Wood Peck Hur
11. Kiri Durante Mull Berry Bush
12. "Dolly Parton Smothers Lucky Short Guy."

NO CAN(ADA) DO

Ottawa: Because of an anti-noise ordinance, it's illegal for **bees** to **buzz**.

Toronto: It's illegal to **drag** a dead **horse** along Yonge Street on a Sunday.

Nova Scotia: The law prohibits watering your **lawn** if it's **raining**.

Etobioke, Ontario: No more than 3.5 **inches** of water is allowed in a **bathtub**.

Montreal: It's a no-no to park your **car** so that it blocks your own **driveway**.

Halifax, Nova Scotia: It's illegal to walk a **tightrope** over the main streets.

Quebec: It's a crime to sell **antifreeze** to Indians.

Vancouver, British Columbia: It's illegal to ride a **tricycle** over 10 mph.

Burnaby, British Columbia: The town has a 10 p.m. **curfew** for **dogs**.

British Columbia: It's illegal to kill a **Sasquatch**.

Toronto: There's no riding a **streetcar** on Sunday if you've been eating **garlic**.

THE OBJECT OF MY REFLECTION

The acrostic: The rearview mirror

The quote: The first of these was introduced at the Indy Five Hundred in nineteen eleven. Up till then there were two people in each car: the driver and the mechanic, who also acted as lookout. What was it?

The clue answers:

A. THE FOURTH HAND
B. HOW THE WEST WAS WON
C. END OF THE LINE
D. RICHARD CONDON
E. ETCHASKETCH
F. APPETITE
G. RILED
H. VENETIAN
I. IVAN LENDL
J. ELVIN HAYES
K. WHEEL
L. MAUI
M. ICE SHEET
N. ROD STEWART
O. RECEDE
P. OUTFIT
Q. REPUTATION

A FEW OF MY FAVORITE THINGS

The toothbrush was the winner, followed closely by the automobile. The personal computer came in third, followed by the cell phone and the microwave.

PHRASEOLOGY 201

S	C	A	M		S	L	A	G		L	L	A	M	A
A	L	P	O		L	E	N	O		O	A	T	E	S
F	I	R	S	T	R	A	T	E		A	B	O	R	T
E	M	O	T	E		R	E	S	E	T		P	E	A
R	E	N		M	E	N		A	C	H	E			
			P	A	S	S	T	H	E	B	U	C	K	
D	I	F	F	E	R		C	I	O		O	N	E	L
A	D	L	E	R		R	O	T		S	L	I	D	E
F	E	A	T		L	E	O		T	O	A	T	E	E
T	A	K	E	B	Y	S	T	O	R	M				
			D	I	R	T		L	I	B		S	S	T
A	P	E		B	E	A	R	D		E	L	A	T	E
J	E	W	E	L		T	O	P	D	R	A	W	E	R
A	D	A	G	E		E	B	R	O		V	I	E	R
R	I	N	G	S		D	O	O	M		A	N	D	Y

FYI: Pass the buck (29 Across) originally referred to a buckhorn knife that was passed around the table and placed in front of the player whose turn it was to deal. Someone who "passed the buck" literally passed that responsibility to the person next to him.

LOST IN TRANSLATION
Dr. No

STUFF THAT FELL FROM THE SKY
The leftover letters spell: Has it ever rained cats and dogs? If so, there's no record of it.

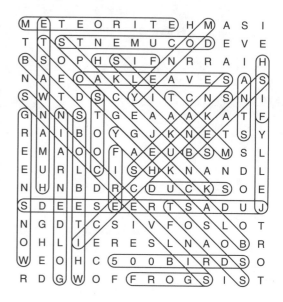

LITTLE THINGS MEAN A LOT
Band-Aid: TRUE.
Baseball Caps: TRUE.
Can Opener: FALSE. The first canned food was invented for the British Navy in 1815. The can opener wasn't invented until 50 years later. (While waiting, they used a chisel and a hammer.)
Flyswatter: TRUE.
Jockey Shorts: FALSE. A Midwestern underwear manufacturer copied the design of men's bathing suits that were popular in France at the time. Their patented design (the Y-front with overlapping fly) first appeared in Chicago in a Marshal Field and Company store window in the middle of the winter of 1935. Brrrr.
Matches: TRUE.
Paper Cup: TRUE.
Peanut Butter: TRUE. It never made it big as a medicinal remedy, but boy, did it catch on as an easy way to get kids to eat protein.
Running Shoes: TRUE.
Stethoscope: TRUE.
Vending Machine: FALSE. Vending machines have been around since the 17th century. The first one, in England, dispensed one pipeful of tobacco for a penny.
Wire Coat Hanger: TRUE.
Wristwatches: FALSE. The opposite is true: They were originally designed for women; men who wore them were considered sissies. But it did take more than a hundred years for men to start wearing them.
Yo-yo: TRUE.

PRIME-TIME PROVERBS
1 – c (Rev. Jim Ignatowski)
2 – g (Thomas Magnum)
3 – d (Herman Munster)
4 – b (Banacek)
5 – j (Artemus Gordon)
6 – e (Coach Ernie Pantusso)
7 – h (Michael Palin)
8 – m (Gomez Addams)
9 – i (Pappy Maverick)
10 – a (David Addison)
11 – k (Fonzie)
12 – l (Beaver Cleaver)
13 – f (Jed Clampett)

ASIAN CON-FUSION
c. Peking duck is the real thing. Chop suey, chow mein, and egg foo yung were Chinese-American creations, but the fortune cookie was the brainchild of Makoto Hagiwara, who first served them at his Japanese Tea Garden in San Francisco's Golden Gate Park.

THE 7 "OFFICIAL" ATTRIBUTES OF THE PILLSBURY DOUGHBOY

1. His skin must look like dough: "off-white, smooth, but not glossy"
2. Slightly luminous, but no sheen
3. No knees, elbows, wrists, fingers, ears, or ankles
4. Rear views do not include "buns"
5. Walks with a "swagger"
6. tomach is proportional to the rest of his body
7. He is not portly

THE TIME IT TAKES #1

Here are the answers in order:

1 second for a hummingbird's wings to beat 70 times

58 seconds for the elevator in Toronto's CN Tower to reach the top (1,518 feet)

4 hours for the *Titanic* to sink after it struck the iceberg

7 days for a newborn baby to wet or soil 80 diapers

30 days for a human hair to grow half an inch

12 weeks for a U.S. Marine to go through boot camp

1 year for Los Angeles to move two inches closer to San Francisco (due to the shifting of tectonic plates)

25 years equals the time the average American spends asleep in a lifetime

95 years for Easter to recur on the same date

500,000 years for plutonium-239 to become harmless

THE PRACTICAL YOLK

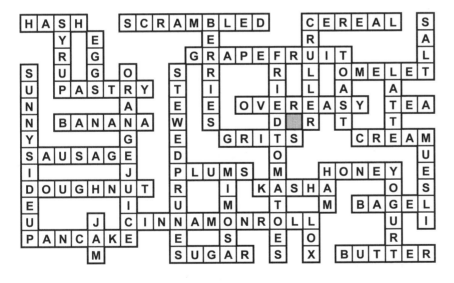

FILL IN THE LIMERICKS

1. Ball; entire; all
2. Dine; seven; nine
3. Nose; there; goes
4. Time; absurd; crime
5. Computer; across; neuter
6. Wise; ink; i's
7. Technique; bored; leak
8. Week; roar; squeak
9. Ball; foresee; hall
10. Worse; immense; purse

DROPPING BOMBECKS

1. When you look like your passport photo, it's time to go home.
2. A child develops individuality long before he develops taste.
3. If a man watches three football games in a row, he should be declared legally dead.

THE STUDIOUS ELVIS

e. *The Inner Elvis: A Psychological Biography of Elvis Aaron Presley*

WAS MURPHY RIGHT?

1 – b (Baruch's Observation: "If all you have is a hammer, everything looks like a nail.")

2 – e (The Golden Rule of Arts and Sciences: "Whoever has the gold makes the rules.")

3 – d (Green's Law of Debate: "Anything is possible if you don't know what you're talking about.")

4 – g (Hecht's Law: "There is no time like the present to procrastinate.")

5 – a (Lowe's Law: "Success always occurs in private, and failure in public view.")

6 – h (The Murphy Philosophy: "Smile. Tomorrow will be worse.")

7 – f (Thompson's Theorem: "When the going gets weird, the weird turn pro.")

8 – i (Todd's Law: "All things being equal, you lose.")

9 – j (Vac's Conundrum: "When you dial a wrong number, you never get a busy signal.")

10 – c (Zappa's Law: "There are two things on Earth that are universal: hydrogen and stupidity.")

I FOUND IT ON EBAY

Date with Brady: $6.19

Frog purse: $5.50

Butt picture: $1

Civil War dirt: $2.75

Wedding dress: $15.50

Francis D. Cornworth's virginity: $10 million

Ali's X-ray: $255.01

Set of eyeballs: $613

Elian's raft: $280 (minimum bid was not met)

Cadaver bag: $15

TV CATCHPHRASES

CLOSE ENCOUNTERS OF THE WAX KIND

The leftover letters spell: Each figure is two percent larger than the celeb's real size. (If you're wondering, it's because wax shrinks.)

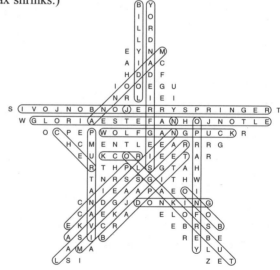

MIX-UP AT THE HONKY-TONK

1. "He's Been DRUNK Since His Wife's Gone PUNK"
2. "I Don't Know Whether to KILL Myself or Go BOWLING"
3. "If FINGERPRINTS Showed Up on SKIN, Wonder Whose I'd Find on You"
4. "I'll MARRY You Tomorrow but Let's HONEYMOON Tonite"
5. "I've Been FLUSHED from the BATHROOM of Your Heart"
6. "I've Got the HUNGRIES for Your Love and I'm Waiting in Your WELFARE Line"
7. "Mama Get the HAMMER (There's a FLY on Papa's Head)"
8. "TOUCH Me with More Than Your HANDS"
9. "She Made TOOTHPICKS Out of the TIMBER of My Heart"
10. "When We Get Back to the FARM (That's When We Really Go to TOWN)"

WHICH HUNT

1. **Democrats** tip better than Republicans.
2. **The world's largest stalagmite** (the one that grows up from the ground) is 105 feet, more than five times as long as the world's largest stalactite.
3. **The average cough** travels at 60 mph, compared to the average sneeze's 40 mph.
4. **Smokers** eat more sugar than nonsmokers.
5. **Hot water** weighs more than cold water.
6. **Red blood cells** last for 80 to 120 days; white blood cells last an average of only 13 days.
7. **Women** were given the right to vote in 1920. Native Americans had to wait until 1924.
8. **A cup of coffee** has roughly twice the caffeine of a cup of tea.
9. **Plastic flamingos** outnumber real ones in America.
10. **The oldest cat in history** was an English tabby that lived 37 years. The oldest spider in history was a tarantula that lived 28 years.
11. **The quarter**'s George Washington portrait is more accurate.
12. **Buying the can** costs the Coca-Cola company more money than making the cola.
13. **Americans who own pets** comprise 57% of the population.
14. **Whiskers** on the average cat outnumber claws (24 to 18).
15. **Being born with one blue eye and one brown eye** has about a 1 in 500 chance of happening. The odds of being born albino are 1 in 9,000.
16. **The amount of time between a whale's heartbeats** is 6.5 seconds. The memory span of a goldfish is 3 seconds.
17. **Coffee** is drunk more than beer—the average American will drink 77 gallons of coffee a year, and only 22 gallons of beer.
18. **The average speed of a golf ball in flight on the PGA tour** is 160 mph. The top speed of a champagne cork is 100 mph.
19. **Easter** prompts Americans to buy more candy than Halloween.
20. **The average American marriage**, you'll be happy to hear, has a lifespan of 9.4 years—edging out the average color TV set, which lasts only 8 years.
21. **Lard** has more calories than *any* food—902 for every 100 grams. Butter isn't too far behind, though, at 876 calories per 100 grams.
22. **Cracks travel through glass** at 3,000 mph. Pain travels through the human body at about 239 mph.
23. **"Brilliant but plain"** was preferred to "sexy but dumb" by 73% of women.
24. **The Dead Sea** has a salt content of 25%. The Great Salt Lake's salt content rarely gets above 15%.
25. **Hockey players** perform better on colder ice than figure skaters.
26. **The largest recorded litter of dogs** is 23, compared to 19 for the largest recorded litter of cats.
27. **Blondes** are preferred by mosquitoes to brunettes.
28. **The world's fastest mammal** (the cheetah) can travel 70 mph; the world's fastest fish (the sailfish) is slightly slower at 68 mph. (They're both no match for the world's fastest *bird*, though: The peregrine falcon can travel as fast as 225 mph.)
29. **Dog owners** include their pet in their wills 27% of the time; cat owners, only 21%. (Must be that "man's best friend" thing.)
30. **The largest pearl ever found** weighed 14 pounds, 1 ounce. The largest gallstone ever found weighed 13 pounds.
31. 41% of **people aged 18-24** wear seatbelts; only 18% of people aged 65 and over do. (Why, in their day they didn't even *have* seatbelts…)
32. **An English ton** weighs 2,240 pounds, compared to a U.S. ton's 2,000.
33. **The distance that the average person will walk in their entire life** is 65,000 miles. The average American car will drive about 9,500 miles in a year.
34. **Cro-Magnon man**'s life expectancy was 32 years, compared to Neanderthal man's 29 years.
35. **The South Pole** is colder than the North Pole.
36. **Non-Jews** buy about 76% of all kosher foods.
37. **The left hand** does 56% of the typing.
38. **Chinese chopsticks** are about 10 inches long. Japanese chopsticks are about 8 inches long—or 7 inches if they're women's chopsticks.
39. **All the other cookie types combined** account for about 2/3 of the cookies sold by Girl Scouts.
40. More people **participate** (70%) than refuse when confronted with a public-opinion poll.

EXCESSIVE LANGUAGE

The leftover letters spell: A few other redundant phrases are: foreign imports, ATM machine, passing fad, join together, future plans, invited guest, hollow tube, fellow colleagues, and sum total.

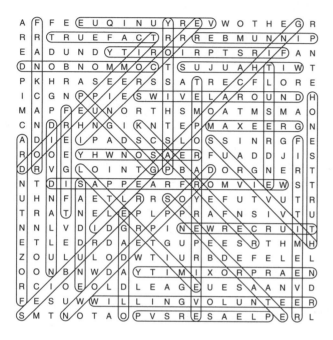

STATE YOUR NAME!

YOU'RE GETTING MARRIED IN THE MORNING

1. Good (Picking a date when the moon is waxing)
2. Bad (Picking a date when the tide is going out)
3. Good (Timing the wedding so that it ends in the second half of the hour—when the minute hand is rising; in fact, when everything—the moon, the tide, the hour—is rising)
4. Bad (Scheduling the wedding for early in the morning—in the old days the groom, and sometimes the bride, needed time to clean up after their farm chores. Now, it gives the groom a chance to recover from his bachelor party)
5. Good (Wearing a white wedding dress)
6. Bad (Wearing a black wedding dress—black symbolizes death)
7. Bad (Wearing a red wedding dress—red symbolizes the devil. If a bride wears red, she and her husband will fight before their first anniversary or her husband will "soon die")
8. Good (Wearing your grandmother's wedding veil)
9. Bad (Looking in the mirror after you've finishing dressing)
10. Bad (Being seen in your veil by any one but your family before the ceremony)
11. Good (Wearing earrings)
12. Bad (Wearing pearls—pearls symbolize tears: "For every pearl a bride wears, her husband will give her a reason to cry")
13. On the way to the wedding:
    a. Good (Seeing lambs, doves, wolves, spiders, or toads)
    b. Good (A bird flying over your car—it means you'll have lots of kids. Is that good?)
    c. Bad (A pig crossing your path)
14. Bad (A bat flying into the church)
15. Good (Crossing the threshold of the church right foot first)
16. Bad (Making your own wedding dress)
17. Bad (Making your own wedding cake)
18. Bad (Eating anything while getting dressed)
19. Good (Crying—tears symbolically wash away the bride's old problems, giving her a fresh start)

7 OF PRESIDENT GROVER CLEVELAND'S NICKNAMES

1. Big Beefhead
2. The Buffalo Hangman
3. The Dumb Prophet
4. The Stuffed Prophet
5. The Pretender
6. His Accidency
7. Uncle Jumbo

YOU'VE GOT JUNK MAIL!

The acrostic: Invented the microchip
The quote: Jack Kilby snagged a Nobel Prize in Physics for his pioneering work in electronics. When CNN asked him if he had any regrets about what his work hath wrought, he answered, "Just one...electronic greeting cards that deliver annoying messages."
The clue answers:
A. IN BAD SHAPE
B. NEW BRUNSWICK
C. VICHYSSOISE
D. EWAN MCGREGOR
E. NIGER
F. THE KING OF TORTS
G. EDWARD WESTON
H. DARYL HANNAH
I. TAKE THE A TRAIN
J. HELEN
K. EYELIDS
L. MOPED
M. INGRESS
N. CHUNNEL
O. REGGIE JACKSON
P. O IS FOR OUTLAW
Q. CRAZY EIGHTS
R. HIGH JINKS
S. INTO THE BREACH
T. PRINCE

ELVIS' GREATEST HITS

The steps are:
HOTEL
MOTEL
MOTES
MITES
MINES
MINDS

WELL, IT'S GOT TO BE *ONE* OF THEM...

1. The right lung is bigger on average.
2. The left nostril is more accurate when identifying smells.
3. Columbus sailed on the *Santa Maria*.
4. There were no Native Americans of blood type B before Columbus's arrival.
5. The right rear tire wears out the fastest.
6. Lake Michigan is the only one of the Great Lakes situated entirely within the United States.
7. The fingernail on the middle finger grows the fastest.
8. The sense of smell is the first to go as a person ages.
9. The big toe contains two bones.
10. People watch the most primetime TV on Thursday.

---

57 VARIETIES

The leftover letters spell: Heinz erected a forty-foot-long electrified pickle.

SIGNS O' THE TIMES

1. When this sign is under water, this road is impassable.
2. People are prohibited from picking flowers from any but their own graves.
3. Our motto has always been to give our customers the lowest possible prices and workmanship.

THE HOPE DIAMOND

An unknown thief
Sita
112-plus
Steely gray-blue
Torn apart by dogs
XIV
67
XV
Du Barry
Fell from favor and was executed
XVI
Marie Antoinette
Jeweler
Son
Henry Philip
Selling it to pay his debts
Poverty
Cartier
All of the above
All of the above
Smithsonian
American

HOW DARE YOU, SIR!

1 – c (An unfaithful spouse)
2 – k (One who works only when being watched; a slacker)
3 – d (Someone who believes that he or she is very small, or
that a part of his or her body has shrunk or is in danger   of
shrinking)
4 – e (A person who deals with things of no importance)
5 – b (One who is so miserly that he or she will not buy food)
6 – l (A thieving group of businessmen)
7 – a (A quivering coward)
8 – g (A person who sniffs out a meal and shows up uninvited)
9 – i (A person who whines or speaks through his or her nose)
10 – f (One who senselessly repeats words)
11 – h (One whose life is given over to luxury and sensual
pleasures)
12 – j (An inferior chess player)

LOGO A-GO-GO

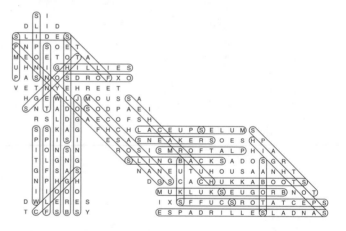

IT'S A SHOE-IN

The leftover letters spell: I did not have three thousand pairs of shoes. I had one thousand and sixty. (Imelda Marcos)

LOONEY LAWS

1 – a (go barefoot)
2 – c (fix it yourself)
3 – a (an ice cream cone)
4 – b (swimming on dry land)
5 – b (wear trousers)
6 – c (drinking milk)
7 – a (wiping their dishes dry)
8 – c (an ugly horse)
9 – b (carrying bees)
10 – a (other than candidates)

NO THANKS, I'M A VEGETARIAN

c. The name is an ethnic slur.

THE PRICE WAS RIGHT

The range of answers you can consider correct is given in parentheses.

1. $20 ($18–$22)
2. $100 ($90–$110)
3. 64¢ (58¢–70¢)
4. $19,700 ($17,730–$21,670)
5. 10¢ (9¢–11¢)
6. $1 (90¢–$1.10)
7. $25 ($22.50–$27.50)
8. $2 ($1.80–$2.20)
9. $175 ($157.50–$192.50)
10. $58 ($52.20–$63.80)
11. $3,300 ($2,970–$3,630)
12. 5¢ (4¢–6¢)
13. 38¢ (34¢–42¢)
14. $16.40 ($14.76–$18.04)
15. 97¢ (87¢–$1.07)
16. $300 ($270–$330)
17. $1.25 ($1.12–$1.38)
18. $200 ($180–$220)

THEIR NAMES LIVE ON

LIFESTYLES OF THE NOT-YET-RICH-AND-FAMOUS

1 – b (In his teens, Ozzy also worked as a car-horn tester.)

2 – a (The Scottish Connery has proudly worn many a kilt, though.)

3 – a

4 – a and b (Sorry, trick question: She held both jobs, and also once worked as a bank teller. And has a Ph.D. in Literature from NYU.)

5 – b (DeVito trained at the Wilfred Academy of Hair and Beauty in New York City.)

6 – a (DeGeneres also worked as a house painter.)

7 – a (Brimley had also been a farmer and rodeo rider.)

8 – a

9 – b

10 – b (Caan has had 11 shoulder operations, but at 63 (as of 2003) says he still enjoys saddling up.)

11 – a

12 – a (Irons also worked as a housecleaner and "busker" (a street entertainer, singing and playing guitar outside movie theaters).)

13 – b (An Episcopalian, Powell turned lights on and off so Jewish worshippers could observe the Sabbath ban on activity.)

14 – a (Other celebs who play hockey include Michael J. Fox, Michael Keaton, Chad Lowe, and Alan Thicke. But they weren't paid to play, as Leary was; he made as much as $1,000 a week on the ice.)

15 – b

16 – a (Lancaster also worked as a circus trapeze artist.)

17 – b (Stewart was also a paperboy, picture framer, and soccer player.)

18 – a (A chunker picks out the good middle slices of pineapple.)

19 – b (Harrelson says he was once fired from 17 jobs in one year because of his temper.)

20 – a (In a street fight when he was 17, Dutton fatally stabbed a man. In prison he joined a drama group, and has since won Tony, Emmy, and Golden Globe awards.)

21 – b (A knee injury ended his football career.)

22 – a

THE WORST-SELLER LIST
1 – h (*The Baron Kinvervankotsdorsprakingatchdern: A New Musical Comedy*)
2 – a (*Fish Who Answer the Telephone*)
3 – g (*Swine Judging for Beginners*)
4 – b (*The Gentle Art of Cooking Wives*)
5 – j (*Grow Your Own Hair*)
6 – c (*Harnessing the Earthworm*)
7 – d (*The History and Romance of Elastic Webbing Since the Dawn of Time*)
8 – e (*Manhole Covers of Los Angeles*)
9 – f (*Proceedings of the Second International Workshop on Nude Mice*)
10 – i (*A Toddler's Guide to the Rubber Industry*)

UNCLE OSCAR'S BIG NIGHT #1
1 – b (Diane Keaton, *Annie Hall*)
2 – d (Shirley MacLaine, *Terms of Endearment*)
3 – a (F. Murray Abraham, *Amadeus*)
4 – c (Jessica Tandy, *Driving Miss Daisy*)

TOMB IT MAY CONCERN
The leftover letters spell: A horseshoe is for protection against evil. Ivy is a symbol for undying friendship.

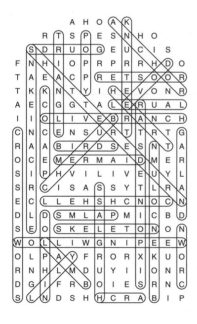

"SPECIAL" EVENTS FOR TOURISTS
The Haunting of Pettifog House is the phony event.

HOW TO AVOID GETTING HIRED
1. "My company made me a scapegoat, just like my three previous employers."
2. "Note: Please do not misconstrue my fourteen jobs as job-hopping. I have never, ever quit a job."
3. "Reason for leaving last job: Employees had to get to work by eight forty-five. Couldn't work under those conditions."

WOULD WE LIE TO YOU?
1 – b (The logo represents an airplane propeller.)
2 – a (Oreo is Greek for *hill*.)
3 – b (The founder was nicknamed Kinko because of his kinky red hair.)
4 – a (Sanka is a contraction of *sans caffeine*.)
5 – c (The inventor used a defective pill-making machine to make his first candies.)

BUMPER STICKERS SEEN AROUND THE UNIVERSE
1. Interstellar matter is a gas
2. Gravity—it's the law
3. Stop continental drift
4. Molecular biologists wear designer genes
5. Friction can be a drag
6. Black holes really suck
7. Quasars are far out
8. Neutrinos have bad breadth
9. Gravity brings me down
10. Molecular biologists are small

SO YOU THINK YOU'RE A TOUGH GUY?
b. Dustin Hoffman is the only one who wasn't considered for the role.

A CAPONE BY ANY OTHER NAME
a. Vince Capone was a cop.

BRAND X

Carnation. In 1901, while walking down a street in Seattle, the head of the Pacific Coast Condensed Milk Company noticed a box of Carnation Brand cigars in a store window. He decided it was a good name for his milk, too. With a picture of a flower on the label, it would be recognizable even to children.

Hamilton-Beach. L.H. Hamilton and Chester A. Beach perfected a high-speed, lightweight universal electronic motor and used it in the first commercial drink mixer in 1912. They went on to build small appliances for home use.

Zippo lighters. They were introduced as revolutionary windproof lighters in 1932 and named after another revolutionary invention of the time—the zipper.

Saran Wrap. In 1933 Dow researchers discovered a plastic called monomeric vinylidene chloride. They called it VC Plastic. In 1940 a salesman suggested they rename it Saran (the name of a tree in India). Dow liked the new name because it had only five letters and had no negative connotations. During World War II, Saran was used in everything from belts to subway seats. In 1948, it was marketed to housewives as a plastic film called Saran Wrap.

D	O	T	E	R		F	A	S	T		A	H	E	M
E	M	O	T	E		A	G	E	E		N	E	R	O
P	A	T	E	S		C	A	R	N	A	T	I	O	N
T	H	E		A	S	T	I		S	W	I	G	S	
H	A	M	I	L	T	O	N	B	E	A	C	H		
		T	E	A		E	R	R		T	A	O		
A	B	B	A		M	A	C	E		E	V	E	N	T
C	E	L	L		P	L	A	T	H		A	N	T	I
E	L	I	O	T		A	L	S	O		U	S	E	S
Y	A	Z		I	S	M		A	W	L				
		Z	I	P	P	O	L	I	G	H	T	E	R	S
	B	A	S	I	E		E	N	Y	A		N	I	A
S	A	R	A	N	W	R	A	P		C	R	E	P	T
A	L	D	A		E	C	R	U		K	O	R	E	A
D	I	S	C		R	A	N	T		S	W	O	R	N

PERFECT 10 #1

It takes **3** minutes for a fresh mosquito bite to begin to itch.
The water in one inch of rain is the equivalent of **10** inches of snow.
Baby giraffes can grow as much as **1** inch every two hours.
It takes the average person **7** minutes to fall asleep.
Albert Einstein couldn't read until the age of **9**.
The average female mannequin is **8** feet tall.
Boys are **4** times more likely to stutter than girls are.
The average American home contains **6** pounds of pennies.
Captain Kangaroo won a total of **5** Emmy awards.
A cubic yard of air weighs **2** pounds.

TALK ABOUT YOUR LIBERAL MEDIA

The quote: Karl Marx once reported for the *New York Daily Tribune*.
The clue answers:
A. THEATER
B. REX REED
C. BRAIN
D. PROFOUNDLY
E. MOONWALK
F. TRICKERY

THE FUR SIDE

The leftover letters spell: The Tasmanian devil completely devours its prey—bones, fur, and all.

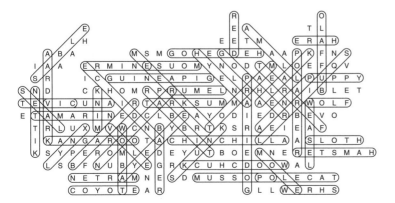

MR. & MS. QUIZ

1. **Men** are more likely to have larger brains—about 14% larger on average.
2. **Women** are more likely to have better hearing.
3. **Women** are about five times more likely to cry than men.
4. **Men** are more likely to make jokes.
5. **Women** are more likely to laugh at jokes.
6. **Women** are twice as likely to start a flirtation.
7. **Men** are more likely to be nervous on a first date.
8. **Men** are more likely to think that they're attractive to the opposite sex.
9. 61% of **women** believe that "the way to a partner's heart is through their stomach," but only 27% of men do.
10. Married **men** are more likely to sleep on the right side of the bed. Divorced men often switch to the left.
11. More **women** say that sex gets better after marriage, but it's a close call: 61% of women, 59% of men.
12. **Women** are more likely to blame themselves if sex goes badly.
13. **Men** are three times more likely to commit suicide after an unhappy love affair.
14. 9% of **women** and 4% of men blame their divorce on the kids.
15. **Men** spend more time in their cars on average—81 minutes per day, compared to the average female's 64 minutes.
16. **Men** are more likely to be involved in an auto accident—71% of all accident victims are male.
17. **Men** use more shampoo as teenagers.
18. **Women** use more deodorant as teenagers. (Do the last two answers seem counterintuitive, or is it just me?)
19. About 25% of **men** say they take naps on the job; only half that many women do.
20. **Women** are almost twice as likely to go on a diet.
21. **Men** tend to feel 5 degrees warmer at a given room temperature.
22. **Men** rid their bodies of caffeine quicker.
23. **Women** are *eight* times more likely to buy Father's Day cards.
24. **Women** are more likely to smile when delivering bad news.

TV OR NOT TV...

BASEBALL NAMES

The fakes are the San Francisco Giants (named in 1886 when their proud manager addressed them as "my big fellows, my giants" after a particularly stunning victory), the Cleveland Indians (when Luis Francis Sockalexis, the first American Indian to play pro baseball and a popular Cleveland player, died in 1913, the team was named in his honor), and the San Diego Padres (whose name was chosen in a name-our-team contest).

EVERYBODY'S A CRITIC!

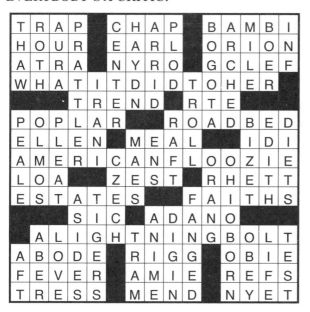

IT'S IN THE GARAGE SOMEWHERE…

The leftover letters spell: Sweep away the clutter of things that complicate our lives. (Henry David Thoreau)

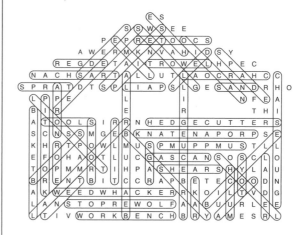

RAW MATERIALS

1 – g (Until 1850, golf balls were filled with feathers.)
2 – l (Some hummingbirds hold their nests together with spiderwebs.)
3 – i (Among other ingredients, dynamite contains peanuts.)
4 – f (At weddings during the Middle Ages, you were supposed to pelt the bride and groom with eggs.)
5 – a (The filaments for the first electric lamp were made out of bamboo.)
6 – c (George Washington used to whiten his teeth with chalk.)
7 – j (During World War II, the Oscar statues were made of plaster.)
8 – d (Sufferers of venereal disease in 16th-century France were advised to eat chocolate.)
9 – k (In old England, a common hangover cure was to rub one's hands and legs with urine.)
10 – h (Most types of lipstick contain fish scales.)
11 – e (Goodyear once made a tire entirely out of corn.)
12 – b (Ancient Romans dyed their hair with bird droppings.)

SOME DAY…
MONDAY and DYNAMO

STRANGE TOURIST ATTRACTIONS…
1. The Hall of Mosses (Washington)
2. Philip Morris Cigarette Tours (Virginia)
3. The Soap Tureen Museum (New Jersey)
4. The Testicle Festival (Montana)

MISFITS

1 – d (Scissors were never a weapon in the game of Clue.)
2 – c (Julia Roberts's lips are not insured…as far as we know.)
3 – a (P.T. Barnum did not try to buy the Grand Canyon.)
4 – b (J. Edgar Hoover didn't fire agents on the basis of shifty eyes.)
5 – b (Overproduction of blood is not a problem in zero-G. Actually, *under*production of blood is the problem.)
6 – c (The letter V *is* used to name hurricanes.)
7 – a (*Dracula* is not one of AFI's Top 100 American Films of the 20th Century.)
8 – b (June is not National Try a New Hairstyle Month. It is National Frozen Yogurt Month, though, for what that's worth.)
9 – d (France uses spades, hearts, diamonds, and clubs on their card decks. In fact, those four symbols originated in France.)
10 – c (Jane Fonda's daughter, Vanessa Vadim, attended her first protest (on Alcatraz Island) when she was one-and-a-half. Since then she's worked in the antinuclear and antiapartheid movements, and currently concentrates her activist efforts on gay liberation and needle exchange for AIDS prevention.)

JUKE JOINT
"Crazy" by Patsy Cline.

PHRASEOLOGY 202

HETERONYMS AND PROUD OF IT
1. Lead
2. Desert
3. Wound
4. Close
5. Number
6. Moped
7. Invalid
8. Sow
9. Sake
10. Refuse

THIS LITTLE PIGGIE & PALS
The leftover letters spell: The French say, "Cot-cot-cot-codet!"
In Arabic, it's "Kakakakakakakaka!"

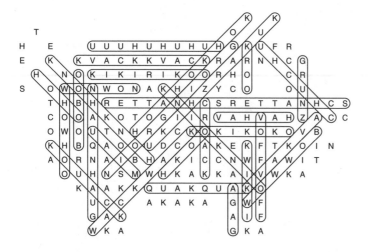

THE SIXTH ELEMENT
The 6 Nobel Prize Categories: Economics
The 6 Wives of Henry VIII: Anne of Cleves
The 6 Parts of the Circulatory System: Heart
The 6 Categories of Dog Breeds: Hounds
The 6 Layers of the Earth: Inner core
The 6 Branches of the US Armed Forces: National Guard
The 6 Elements in Buddhism: Wind
The 6 Hockey Positions: Center

THAT BITES!
The acrostic: He ate a lot of money, too.
The quote: Pac-Man got its name from
the word paku, which means "eat" in
Japanese. The video game was so popular
that Pac-Man was named *Time* magazine's
"man" of the year in nineteen eighty-two.
The clue answers:
A. HATCHED
B. EMPIRE STATE
C. AMAZEMENT
D. THE ROCK
E. ENCAMPS
F. APPIAN WAY
G. LUTHER
H. OMAHA
I. TWINS
J. OPENING NIGHT
K. FAJITAS
L. MADAME
M. OWENS
N. NEW WAVE
O. END GAME
P. YAMAHA
Q. TAPES
R. ONION RINGS
S. OUT OF TIME

YOU'RE (NOT) THE TOPS
1 – c (Mayonnaise)
2 – b (Crackers)
3 – a (Assault)
4 – d (Hillsdale)
5 – b (Community Chest)
6 – c (Seminole)
7 – d (Prunes)
8 – b (Pit bull terriers)
9 – c (Car trouble)
10 – a ("The Know-It-All")

EXPECT THE UNEXPECTED

WHAT'LL YOU HAVE?

Coffee is the winner—the average American drinks 77 gallons of coffee a year, and only 22 gallons of beer.

PARLEZ-VOUS EUPHEMISMS?

1. Jail
2. Love
3. Money
4. Censor
5. Cartel
6. Briefcase
7. Mistake
8. Fire someone
9. Acid rain
10. Calendar
11. Drop in test scores
12. Explosion
13. Undertaker
14. Physical education

IT'S IN THE BAG

The leftover letters spell: "Papa's Got a Brand New Bag" cemented James Brown's legacy as the Godfather of Soul.

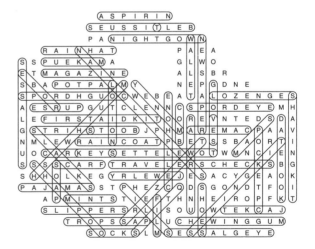

IT'S FOR YOU, MR. PRESIDENT

TALKING DIRTY

HE LOOKS MUCH TALLER IN PERSON

c.   56 steps, one for each year of Lincoln's life.

OUCH!

Two Eskimos sitting…in a kayak were chilly, but when they lit a fire in the craft, it sank, proving once and for all that you can't have your kayak and heat it, too.

This guy goes to a costume party…with a girl on his back. "What the heck are you?" asks the host. "I'm a snail," says the guy. "But, you have a girl on your back," replies the host. "Yeah," he says, "that's Michelle."

There's a nudist colony…for communists. Two old men are sitting on the front porch. One turns to the other and says, "I say, old boy, have you read Marx?" And the other says, "Yes…I believe it's these wicker chairs."

PLITZ-PLATZ, I WAS TAKING A BATH

1. AAH-CHOO!
2. SPLASH!
3. CHOO-CHOO!
4. UPSY-DAISY!
5. KITCHY-KITCHY-KOO!
6. UH-OH!
7. BEEP BEEP!
8. CHUGALUG!

By the way, "Plitz-platz" is Greek for splash.

TOM SWIFTIES

1 – f ("Hey, these pants are getting too small for me," Tom said fitfully.)
2 – h ("I never use that Parmesan cheese that comes in a can," Tom said gratingly.)
3 – b ("I took her picture when she wasn't looking," Tom said candidly.)
4 – c ("I've got a great anagram for 'Santa,'" Tom said devilishly.)
5 – a ("I've got to buy some new sunglasses," Tom said brightly.)
6 – d ("It's not nice to pull your sister's Barbie doll apart," Tom said disarmingly.)
7 – e ("Look! I filled in that big crack in the ground," Tom said faultlessly.)
8 – i ("My office is on this floor," Tom said levelly.)
9 – g ("She's got an apartment in London," Tom said flatly.)
10 – j ("Wow, honey, that's a really big cup you won," Tom said lovingly.)

I CAME, I SEWED, I CONQUERED

The quote: Napoleon designed Italy's national flag based on the French flag.

The clue answers:
A. FENDER
B. PALADIN
C. LEBANON
D. TOFFEE
E. NO-NOS
F. CITY LIGHTS
G. ANGELS
H. GALAHAD

AND IF YOU BELIEVE THAT ONE…

1 – c (The first potato chips were actually known as "Saratoga Crisps.")
2 – d (Oregon City really is in Oregon.)
3 – b (It certainly would have been quite a coincidence, though, wouldn't it?)
4 – c (The D in D-day actually stands for "day.")
5 – b (Yes, the Angora goat really is a goat. For the record: The koala bear is a marsupial, the firefly is a beetle, and the glass snake is a lizard.)
6 – a (Thomas Edison *did* tell reporters in 1920 that he was working on a machine that would talk to the dead, but he was merely kidding and revealed the joke a few days later.)
7 – c (Safety glass is made by sandwiching a layer of plastic or artificial resin between two panes of glass.)

I DON'T GET IT

1. **Q:** What is the difference between ignorance, apathy, and ambivalence?
   A: I don't know and I don't care one way or the other.

2. **Q:** What do the letters DNA stand for?
   A: National Dyslexics Association.

3. **Q:** Did you hear about the two antennas that got married?
   A: The wedding was terrible, but the reception was great.

4. **Q:** What's the difference between mashed potatoes and pea soup?
   A: Anyone can mash potatoes.

5. **Q:** How many narcissists does it take to change a light bulb?
   A: One. He holds the bulb while the world revolves around him.

6. **Q:** What did one cannibal say to another while they were eating a clown?
   A: "Does this taste funny to you?"

7. **Q:** Did you hear about the corduroy pillows?
   A: They're making headlines.

8. **Q:** Why couldn't the sesame seed leave the gambling casino?
   A: Because he was on a roll.

9. **Q:** What did the bird watcher exclaim when she saw a flock of geese flying south for the winter?
   A: "Migratious."

10. **Q:** What do you get if you don't pay your exorcist promptly?
    A: Repossessed.

MURPHY, JR.

1 – i (Harrison's Postulate: "For every action, there is an equal and opposite criticism.")

2 – c (Hutchin's Law: "You can't out-talk a man who knows what he's talking about.")

3 – e (Issawi's Law of Progress: "A shortcut is the longest distance between two points.")

4 – b (Johnson and Laird's Law: "A toothache tends to start on Saturday night.")

5 – a (Johnson's Law: "If you miss one issue of any magazine, it will be the issue that contained the article, story or installment you were most anxious to read.")

6 – h (Kirby's Comment on Committees: "A committee is the only life form with 12 stomachs and no brain.")

7 – j (Murphy's Paradox: "Doing it the hard way is always easier.")

8 – f (Perkins' Postulate: "The bigger they are, the harder they hit.")

9 – d (The Queue Principle: "The longer you wait in line, the greater the likelihood that you are standing in the wrong line.")

10 – g (The Salary Axiom: "A pay raise is just large enough to increase your taxes and just small enough to have no effect on your take-home pay.")

THE TIME IT TAKES #2

Here are the answers in order:

.05 second for a human muscle to respond to stimulus

4 seconds for 3,000,000 gallons of water to flow over Niagara Falls

1 minute for a newborn baby's brain to grow 1.5 mg

4 hours, 30 minutes to cook a 20-pound turkey at 325 degrees F

25 days for Handel to compose "The Messiah"

35 days for a mouse to reach sexual maturity

89 days, 1 hour for winter to come and go

4 years, 8 months to receive your FBI file after making the appropriate request

27 years was the length of Nolan Ryan's pitching career

1,800 years to complete the Great Wall of China

SUDDENLY IT ALL COMES CLEAR

The quote: Glass is not a solid; it's a fluid with extremely high viscosity

The clue answers:

A. ACIDITY
B. ELVIS
C. GIMLET
D. SHOUT
E. SHADOWS
F. TOILS
G. HISSY FIT
H. RELAXING

TOILET TECH

Please Rise and Flushed With Color are the dishonest johns.

YUPPIE PUPPIES

Dog's Best Friend and Doggy-Go-Round are the fakes.

STAMP OF APPROVAL

The leftover letters spell: Madame C.J. Walker became one of America's wealthiest women during the decade of the nineteen tens by developing and selling hair care products.

In case you didn't recognize all of the distinguished ladies on our list, here's the poop on some of the less famous among them.

Theda Bara (1885 or 1890–1955) The silent film star got her first big break in *A Fool There Was*, playing a ruthless femme fatale. The studio wanted her fans to believe that she was an exotic half-French, half-Egyptian, but she was really just a nice Jewish girl from Cincinnati. She was known as The Vamp, and one of her lines, "Kiss me, my fool!" became a popular phrase.

Pearl S. Buck (1892–1973) Born in America, Buck went to China with her missionary parents when she was three months old. When she returned after 40 years, she became active in the American civil rights and women's rights movements. Her novel, *The Good Earth*, was the first glimpse most Americans had seen of day-to-day life in China. It became the best-selling book of both 1931 and 1932, won the Pulitzer Prize in 1935, and was made into a film in 1937. In 1938, Buck won the Nobel Prize in literature, the first American woman to do so.

Mary Lyon (1797–1849) A girl or lady going about without wearing a bonnet was unheard of—as was higher education—when Mary Lyon founded Mount Holyoke College (then Mount Holyoke Female Seminary) in 1837. Lyon served as president of the school until her death. Mount Holyoke's most famous students were poet Emily Dickinson (who has a stamp of her own) and Lucy Stone (see below).

Edna St. Vincent Millay (1892–1950) You learned about her in school. She was the first woman to receive the Pulitzer Prize for poetry and as bohemian as they come. Her best-known poem is probably "First Fig," which she wrote in 1920. It goes like this: "My candle burns at both ends; /It will not last the night;/ But ah, my foes, and oh, my friends--/It gives a lovely light!" Her friends called her "Vincent."

Margaret Mitchell (1900–1949) The author of *Gone With the Wind* (her only major work) was shocked when critics compared her to Tolstoy and Dickens. The book, the Harry Potter of its day, won a Pulitzer Prize and was made into (as if you didn't know) a feature film. To the anguish of rabid fans who were waiting for a sequel, Mitchell was run down by a drunk driver on a street in Atlanta.

Alice Paul (1885–1977) A suffragist with attitude, Ms. Paul thought that most feminists of her time were a bunch of wusses; she thrived on civil disobedience. Trying to get the vote for women in 1917, she was part of a group who chained themselves to the White House fence. Her frequent jail time included force feedings and being assigned to the psychiatric ward where the inmates nearly drove her crazy. She wrote an equal rights amendment and introduced it in Congress in 1923. She was still lobbying for one well into her 60s.

Lily Pons (1898–1976) The French-Italian opera singer made her debut at the Met in New York City in 1931. Hollywood discovered her and she starred in three mediocre movies during the '30s. There's a town in Maryland that named itself "Lilypons" in her honor.

Ayn Rand (1905–1982) The author of *The Fountainhead* and *Atlas Shrugged*, Rand coined her own libertarianlike political philosophy called Objectivism. In 1947, she testified against the activities of "communist propagandists" in Hollywood before the House Un-American Activities Committee. In spite of her wish that her name never be used to promote Objectivism, the Ayn Rand Institute Center for the Advancement of Objectivism has since registered her name as a trademark.

Lucy Stone (1818–1893) An important lecturer on women's suffrage and the abolition of slavery, she founded the *Woman's Journal*, the chief publication of the 19th century women's movement. Stone created quite a controversy by retaining her maiden name after her marriage as a symbol of a woman's right to individuality. Her followers were known as Lucy Stoners.

Ida Tarbell (1857–1944) One of the top investigative journalists and muckrakers of all time, she made a special target of Standard Oil maven John D. Rockefeller because he'd put her father out of business when she was a girl. Tarbell spent two years putting together a series of articles on Standard Oil: the first installment was published in 1902; the entire 19-part series was collected into a book in 1904. The series was a smash hit, and it gave a new energy to the antitrust movement. As a result, the Supreme Court decided to break up Standard Oil and Congress passed a bill to guard against future monopolies.

WHERE'D YOU GET THOSE DUDS?

Tuxedo: TRUE. Heir to the tobacco fortune, Pierre Lorillard IV was a blueblood New Yorker who set the fashion world on its collective ear in 1886. His family commissioned and wore the first of the future prom rentals to the Autumn Ball at his exclusive country club in the village of Tuxedo Park.

Stetson: FALSE. A fellow named John Stetson worked in his family's Philadelphia hat business as a boy, and traveled out west in the 1860s to improve his health. When he returned to Philly, he started making hats that were suited to the needs of the Western cowboy. The hats soon became the most popular cowboy headgear in the west. Buffalo Bill, General George Custer, Annie Oakley, and Calamity Jane all wore 'em.

Pajamas: FALSE. From late in the 16th century both men and women wore nightgowns (true!). Two hundred years later, as women's nightgowns got filmier, men's got shorter, and turned into nightshirts. The loose pants called "pajamas" were worn on the bottom. The two didn't match, of course. But eventually they did, and—voila!—the pajamas that we know today.

Negligee: TRUE. Women of certain classes could always sit back and take it easy, but in the 18th century, as women's and men's nightwear started to diverge, a feminine, sometimes lacey, nightie became popular. It was just as good for relaxing at home as for sleeping, so it came to be named after what a woman did while wearing it—neglecting housework.

Shoes: FALSE. Egyptian sandals of woven papyrus were the first footwear, worn as early as 2000 BC. Greeks had fashioned fitted footwear from leather by 600 BC, followed by the Romans who added rights and lefts around 200 BC. But our word for shoe comes from the Anglo-Saxon *sceo*, pluralized to *schewis*, meaning "to cover."

PAGE ONE

M	I	R	A		D	A	Y	O		M	E	D	I	C
E	T	A	L		O	V	U	M		O	R	A	T	E
A	C	T	I		T	I	R	E		R	O	U	S	E
T	H	E	G	R	E	A	T	G	A	T	S	B	Y	
		N	I	L			A	M	A					
E	M	S		F	L	O	G		O	L	D	H	A	T
N	A	T	A	L		G	L	E	N		A	I	D	E
T	H	E	S	E	C	R	E	T	G	A	R	D	E	N
R	E	E	K		H	E	A	T		D	E	E	P	S
E	R	R	A	T	A		M	A	U	I		R	T	E
		A	R	C			M	E	D					
	T	H	E	C	O	L	O	R	P	U	R	P	L	E
T	R	I	C	K		A	L	A	I		A	L	U	M
N	A	C	H	O		M	E	I	R		C	A	L	M
T	Y	S	O	N		P	O	L	E		O	N	L	Y

FICTIONARY

The leftover letters spell: Reincarnation is the belief that after you're dead and gone, you'll come back as a lapel flower.

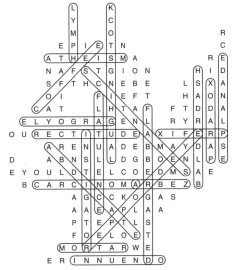

PROVERBIAL WISDOM

WHAT'S THE WORD?

HERE'S THE DEAL...

e. Lady in a Closet is the phony.

UNCLE OSCAR'S BIG NIGHT #2

1 – b (Jodie Foster, *The Silence of the Lambs*)
2 – c (Ray Milland, *The Lost Weekend*)
3 – d (Tom Hanks, *Forrest Gump*)
4 – a (Gwyneth Paltrow, *Shakespeare in Love*)

THE CLASSIFIEDS

1. Girl wanted to assist magician in cutting-off-head illusion. Blue Cross and salary.
2. Mixing bowl set designed to please a cook with round bottom for efficient beating.
3. Open house: Body shapers, toning salon. Free coffee and donuts.
4. Nordic Track: Three hundred dollars. Hardly used. Call Chubby.
5. Free puppies: Half cocker spaniel, half sneaky neighbor's dog.

THAT'S WHY THEY CALL IT TRIVIA

1 – b (Spaghetti was the only food his mother could keep down during the difficult pregnancy.)
2 – c (She married one while he was still in prison, the other when she was eight months pregnant with his child.)
3 – b
4 – a
5 – a
6 – b (It was Russell Crowe who bought the 129 cows.)
7 – c (Answer a is from comedian Steven Wright; b is from Woody Allen.)
8 – b (The award was for her performance as the lovestruck psychopath in *The Crush*.)
9 – They're all true.
10 – a
11 – b
12 – c
13 – c
14 – a (Answer b—"I like to cook. I'm really interested in killing things and eating them"—is from Tommy Lee Jones; answer c—"I wanted to be Barbie and I was as opposite to Barbie as you could get"—is from Lucy Liu.)
15 – c
16 – a

ROOM FOR RENT UPSTAIRS

```
B A Y . C R U S O E . C A R E
E L O . L E G A C Y . O N E A
T A U . A L L T H E L O O P S
S I N . R E Y E S . A N N O Y
. G R I N . . R R S . . . . .
O U T O F T H R E A D . A S S
S T U D Y . E A C H . A S T I
T I R E . E X P O S . S T E M
E L K O . V E I L . S T R A P
R E S . G A R D E N T O O L S
. M E N . . . . E A R L . . .
A T S E A . A T O L L . O L D
G O I N R E V E R S E . G A R
E G A D . P I A N O S . E N O
S A M S . A S S E N T . R E P
```

WOODSTOCK III

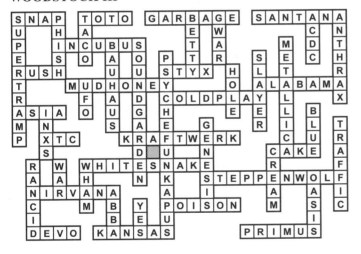

HOOPING IT UP

1 – i (big gun)
2 – p (get chest-to-chest)
3 – g (terrible shot)
4 – b (impossible comeback time)
5 – m (weak team's hometown)
6 – e (shoot very well)
7 – t (making shots look tougher)
8 – q (good shooter when unguarded)
9 – k (end of the game)
10 – f (aggressive fouler)
11 – l ("cool" player)
12 – c (high jumper)
13 – o (result of blocked shot)
14 – j (very high jumpers)
15 – s (do every move possible)
16 – d (get underneath a jumper)
17 – r (classic shot)
18 – a (dunk while spinning)
19 – h (move then pass)
20 – n ("eaten" blocked shot)

HELLO? DOLLY?

The quote: Dolly Parton once *lost* a Dolly Parton look-alike contest.
The clue answers:
A. COLOR
B. PLATOON
C. DONATELLO
D. STORE
E. NICKEL
F. TODAY
G. YOLKS
H. PLANT

LITTLE THINGS MEAN A LOT MORE

Ballpoint Pen: FALSE. It *was* invented by a Hungarian, but he manufactured them in a factory in *England* that was eventually taken over by a *French* company called Bic. As in "Flick your Bic."
Cellophane: TRUE.
Electric Blanket: FALSE. It was based on the electrically heated flying suits that US Air Force pilots wore during World War II.
Miniature Golf: TRUE.
Paper Towels: TRUE.
Scotch Tape: TRUE.
Shopping Carts: TRUE.
Vending Machine: FALSE. Vending machines have been around since the 17th century. The first one, in England, dispensed one pipeful of tobacco for a penny.
Wire Coat Hanger: TRUE.
Yo-yo: TRUE.

HOBO LINGO

The leftover letters spell: The caboose of a train was the "accommodation car."

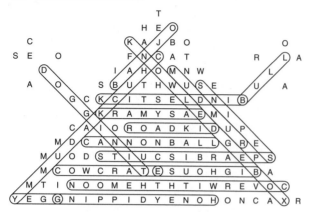

BIG SPENDERS

The acrostic: Now that's a capital idea

The quote: Ancient Sparta had a creative way of preventing wealth and capital from fleeing the realm during hard times. They made their coins so large and heavy that it was almost impossible to take them out of the country.

The clue answers:

A. NOAH WYLE
B. OUT OF SIGHT
C. WADED
D. TIMOTHY HUTTON
E. HART TO HART
F. AARON SORKIN
G. TAMPA
H. STACCATO
I. AFFECTED
J. CAUSE CELEB
K. AMHERST
L. PRAISED
M. IN THE RIGHT
N. THE IN-LAWS
O. AVENGERS
P. LITTLE EVA
Q. IMPROVEMENT
R. DREAD
S. ELAINE MAY
T. AMPLIFYING

PHRASEOLOGY 203

INSIDE HOLLYWOOD

1. *Fast Times at Ridgemont High* (Cage is hard to recognize, but he's there.)
2. *Rain Man*
3. *Blazing Saddles* (Black Bart, the new sheriff, was "whipping out" his speech.)
4. *Breakfast at Tiffany's*
5. *One Flew Over the Cuckoo's Nest*
6. *The Sting*
7. *Duck Soup*
8. *As Good As It Gets*
9. *The Treasure of the Sierra Madre*
10. *The Terminator*

Points:

Now add up your points.

0-10: Get me a grande half-caf latte at Starbucks after you send that memo and pick up my dry-cleaning.

11-20: All right, all right, give me the script and I'll read it over the weekend.

21-30: Baby! Let's do lunch! The sooner, the better!

DEEP THOUGHTS

1. I wish I had a kryptonite cross because then you could keep both Dracula and Superman away.
2. Consider the daffodil. And while you're doing that, I'll be over here, looking through your stuff.
3. Why do the caterpillar and the ant have to be enemies? One eats leaves and the other eats caterpillars... Oh, I see now.

BATTER UP!

The leftover letters spell: "I take a two-hour nap from one o'clock to four." "I'm as red as a sheet." "Steve McQueen looks good in this movie; he must have made it before he died."

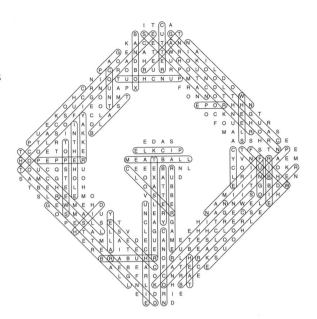

ALLEY: The section of the outfield between the outfielders. Also called a gap.

AROUND THE HORN: A double play going from third base to second to first.

BACKDOOR SLIDER: A pitch that appears to be out of the strike zone, but then breaks back over the plate.

BANDBOX: A small ballpark that favors hitters.

BATTERY: Term referring to the pitcher and catcher combination.

BLAST: A home run.

BUNT: Short hit that's executed by letting the ball hit the bat (not swinging). Used to surprise the fielders or to advance a runner

CAN OF CORN: An easy catch by a fielder.

CAUGHT LOOKING: When a batter is called out on strikes.

CELLAR: Last place. Also "basement."

CHEESE: A good fastball. Also called good cheese.

CHOKE-UP: Gripping the bat up on the handle away from the knob of the bat.

CIRCUS CATCH: An outstanding catch by a fielder.

CLOSER: A team's relief pitcher who finishes the game.

COUNT: The number of called balls and strikes on a hitter.

CUTTER: A cut fastball (one with a late break to it).

CYCLE: When a batter hits a single, double, triple, and home run in the same game.

DINGER: A home run.

DISH: Home plate.

FIREMAN: A team's closer or late-inning relief pitcher.

FUNGO: A ball hit to a fielder during practice. It's usually hit by a coach using a "fungo bat," which is longer and thinner than a GAP: See "alley." A ball hit here is a "gapper."

GOPHER BALL: A pitch hit for a home run, as in "go for."

HEAT: A good fastball. Also called a heater.

HOMER: A home run. Also blast, dinger, dong, four-bagger, four-base knock, moon shot, tape-measure blast, and tater.

HOT CORNER: Third base.

IN THE HOLE: Said of a batter after the on-deck hitter.

MEATBALL: An easy pitch to hit, usually right down the middle of the plate.

NAIL DOWN: As in "nail down a victory." Refers to a relief pitcher finishing off the game.

ON THE SCREWS: When a batter hits the ball hard. Also "on the button."

PAINTING THE BLACK: When a pitcher throws the ball over the edge of the plate.

PEPPER: A pre-game exercise where one player bunts brisk grounders and line drives to a group of fielders who are standing about 20 feet away. The fielders try to throw the ball back as quickly as possible and the batter hits the return throw. (Some ballparks ban pepper games because wild pitches could land in the stands and injure spectators).

PICKLE: A situation where a runner is caught between two bases. Also called a rundown.

PUNCHOUT: A strikeout.

RHUBARB: A fight or scuffle.

RIBBIE: Another way of saying RBI. Also "ribeye."

ROPE: A hard line drive hit by a batter. Also "frozen rope."

RUBBER GAME: The deciding game of a series.

RUTHIAN: With great power.

SET-UP MAN: A relief pitcher who usually enters the game in the 7th or 8th inning.

SWEET SPOT: The part of the bat just a few inches from the barrel.

TABLE SETTER: Batter whose job is to get on base for other hitters to drive him in. Usually bats toward the top of the batting order.

TATER: A home run.

TEXAS LEAGUER: A hit that drops between an infielder and outfielder.

TOOLS OF IGNORANCE: Catcher's equipment.

TOUCH 'EM ALL: Hitting a home run (touching all the bases).

UNCLE CHARLIE: A curve ball.

WHEELHOUSE: A hitter's power zone. Usually a pitch waist-high and over the heart of the plate.

WHEELS: A ballplayer's legs.

WHIFF: A strikeout.

YAKKER: A curve ball.

ELVIS LIVES!
1. NO ADMITTANCE
2. BOTTOMS UP
3. ESKIMOS
4. AN OLD SHOE
5. LIFE ON MARS
6. THE PIANO BENCH
7. NORWEGIANS
8. ASTRONOMER
9. THE COUNTRYSIDE
10. A PSYCHIATRIST
11. THE ARCHEOLOGIST
12. THE RELIEF PITCHER

HEY, LADY!
1 – b (she was addicted to snuff)
2 – c (chocolate-covered garlic balls)
3 – a ("Your Majesty")
4 – b (watch *Gunsmoke* on TV)
5 – a (whistle through her teeth; they were five years old at the time)
6 – c (she was a terrible speller)
7 – a (spinning silk from White House silkworms)
8 – c (import sheep to graze)

NOW *THAT'S* SLOW
The quote: The average drop of Heinz ketchup travels at twenty-five miles *per year*.
The clue answers:
A. TICKED OFF
B. REVIVE
C. HEAVY METAL
D. TEETER
E. WASHINGTON
F. LAZARUS
G. PREPPY
H. ETHER

GORE LORE
1. There is no human problem which could not be solved if people would simply do as I advise.
2. Those who have not undergone minor disasters are being held in reserve for something major.
3. Half of the American people never read a newspaper. Half never voted for president. One hopes it is the same half.

GOOD SPORTS

```
C  D O U B L E F A U L T      N        T I E B R E A K   G   B S
A  R               N          N        E           M     A T P
N  O  P O A C H   F O O T F A U L T     S E R V E   L     S   I
O  S               R          M        O U T         L     S   N
F  H   D A V I S C U P        U         R A N K I N G  E    L
B  O   E           S          R         N       E   N
A  L   U           E          N         I       T   E
L E    E   P A C E  E   O V E R H E A D S M A S H      S H O T
S      E            E   R     R   C   E              L     D
   C H I P          S   R     O   O   N              L     R
P A R T N E R S     R A C Q U E T   D R I L L        O     A
   I       E   E         C     R            C   O          A
G R O U N D S T R O K E          T E N N I S E L B O W
```

DON'T KEEP YOUR DAY JOB!

```
C L A S S   S P A S   C H A N
B E T T E   T A C H   L A C E
S T O L I   I N D O   E S T A
      P U Z Z L E C R E A T O R
      K E A T S   T U N E R S
R A T E D G   A I R S
U S O   A L A S   O U T D O
M I N I S T E R T O S P A I N
P A S S E   A P O P   L O U
    A V I D   A O L E R S
A D O B E S   P A R K A
G O V E R N M E N T S P Y
O R A L   T U R N   A D A P T
G I L L   O N M E   N O L I E
O S S A   K I S S   A G E N T
```

THE FACE IS FAMILIAR...
1 – g (Shaggy's actual first name was Norville)
2 – i (Jimmy Hoffa's middle name was Riddle)
3 – e (Howdy Doody's sister was Heidi Doody)
4 – h (Barney Fife's middle name was Oliver)
5 – d (Donald Duck's middle name is Fauntleroy)
6 – c (The first hurricane given a male name was Hurricane Bob)
7 – b (Little Red Riding Hood's first name is Blanchette)
8 – j (Gilligan's first name was Willy)
9 – a (The name of the monster in the novel *Frankenstein* is Adam)
10 – f (Dr. McCoy's daughter was Joanna) And if you knew that already, live long and prosper.

GREETINGS FROM EARTH

The leftover letters spell: "We are happy here and you be happy there."

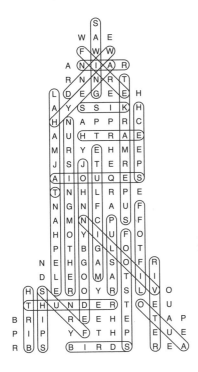

A ROSE BY ANY OTHER...

The acrostic: Hanks for the Memories

The quote: One hundred and twenty men named Henry attacked each other during a "My Name Is Henry" convention in Sydney, Australia. The melee was set off when one Henry accused another of not being a Henry at all but an Angus, provoking an instant fistfight.

The clue answers:
A. HANNAH ARENDT
B. AUGUSTA GEORGIA
C. NINTH INNING
D. KENNETH TYNAN
E. STEPFORD WIVES
F. FACE THE NATION
G. OFFEND
H. RAY ANTHONY
I. TOURNEY
J. HEYDAY
K. EDWARD NORTON
L. MUSHING
M. ENEMY WOMEN
N. MCHALES NAVY
O. OUT-OF-DATE
P. RATTLE AND HUM
Q. IRRESISTIBLE
R. ETHAN BLACK
S. SENESCENCE

SUCH A NASTY PLACE!

```
B U G S B O T T O M   S H O O T U P H I L L   B
U   I                 H                         U
R   G R E A T B U L G I N G   B A M P T O N     N
P   G       S         R       I                 N
H A L T W H I S T L E   E G G B O R O U G H     Y
A   E       A         W       S
M   S L A C K B O T T O M   N E M P N E T T     N
    W       S         L       R                 O
  P I L L   B A T A N D B A L L   U P P E R U P
P   C   C             O       U E T           L
I   K   Y O R N D E R B O G N I E   D         A
D   R   U             I       D D             C
D O R K I N G   L     N E T H E R W A L L O P E
L   E   L             G   A       E
E   P I T Y M E       L I M P L E Y S T O K E
```

YO!

dolls
come back
King George IV of England
being hauled to the guillotine
the Eskimo Pie
O-Boy Yo-Yo Top
Bing Crosby
40 million
all of the above
80 percent
edible
120
256
bounces back up

PERFECT 10 #2

The average beard grows **5** inches a year.

In her Oscar-winning "Midnight Cowboy" role, Sylvia Miles was onscreen for **6** minutes.

The average American worker has held **8** different jobs by age 40.

The most yolks ever found in one egg is **9**.

There is **1** time zone in China.

The average skywritten letter is **2** miles high.

The speed of a roller coaster increases an average of **10** mph when it's raining.

It costs **3** cents to make a dollar bill.

It takes **4** hours to hard-boil an ostrich egg.

There are **7** spikes in the Statue of Liberty's crown.

AND A JIFFY AND A TRICE?

The quote: Technically, a moment lasts about ninety seconds.

The clue answers:
A. CONNECT
B. LAUNCHED
C. STANLEY
D. BEATTY
E. MALTS
F. OMISSION

ALL THAT JIVE

A	N	D	I	E			S	A	M		C	R	A	B
S	E	I	S	M		T	A	L	E		L	I	T	E
T	H	R	O	B		O	F	F	T	H	E	C	O	B
A	R	K		R	I	F	E		E	U	R	O	P	E
B	U	S	T	Y	O	U	R	C	O	N	K			
			R	O	W		O	R	T		A	P	T	
C	A	S	A		A	W	O	L		S	A	B	L	E
A	L	T	I		N	Y	L	O	N		H	E	E	L
L	A	Y	L	A		A	E	R	O		E	L	A	L
M	I	X		D	S	T			T	E	A			
			M	I	T	T	P	O	U	N	D	I	N	G
G	R	A	D	E	A		R	A	P	T		L	O	O
R	U	G	C	U	T	T	E	R		I	D	I	O	M
A	L	E	C		U	K	E	S		C	E	A	S	E
D	E	S	I		S	O	N		E	L	D	E	R	

TOM SWIFTIES: A VARIATION

1 – j ("Eat my dust!" Tom said winningly.)
2 – i ("En garde!" Tom said pointedly.)
3 – e ("Hey, baby, I'm your handyman," Tom said fixedly.)
4 – b ("I vant to sock your blahd," Tom said bitingly.)
5 – d ("I'll see you on the dark side of the moon," Tom said delightedly.)
6 – f ("It's beginning to look a lot like Christmas," Tom said frostily.)
7 – h ("Maxwell House. Good to the last drop," Tom said perkily.)
8 – g ("Pants pressed while you wait," Tom said ironically.)
9 – c ("To get to the other side," Tom said crossly.)
10 – a ("What a long, strange trip it's been," Tom said acidly.)

WOULD WE LIE TO YOU, SPORT?

1 – c (It's a distortion of the French word *oeuf*, meaning egg.)
2 – b (It's a variation on the word *cadet*.)
3 – b (It was "thrown up as a prayer.")
4 – a (Puck is a variation of the word *poke*.)
5 – c (It refers to a second bowstring carried by archers.)

ODD JOBS

The fakes are: Scum Sucker, Peephole Plugger, and Ho Counter.

TALKIN' TRASH

The leftover letters spell: Sign on an electrician's truck: Let us fix your shorts.

Business slogan match-up:

1 – f (AUTO BODY shop: May we have the next dents?)
2 – n (BAKERY: While you sleep, we loaf.)
3 – a (BUTCHER: Let me meat your needs.)
4 – h (CHIMNEY SWEEP: We kick ash.)
5 – q (CONCRETE company: We dry harder.)
6 – m (DIAPER service: Let us lighten your load.)
7 – j (DRY CLEANER: Drop your pants here.)
8 – r (FUNERAL HOME: Drive carefully, we'll wait.)
9 – g (GARDEN shop: Our business is growing.)
10 – e (MASSAGE STUDIO: It's great to be kneaded.)
11 – i (MUFFLER shop: No appointment necessary. We'll hear you coming.)
12 – d (PASTRY shop: Get your buns in here.)
13 – s (PLUMBER: A good flush beats a full house.)
14 – k (PODIATRIST: Time wounds all heels.)
15 – l (RESTAURANT: Don't stand there and be hungry, come in and get fed up.)
16 – o (TAXIDERMIST: We really know our stuff.)
17 – b (TOWING company: We don't want an arm and a leg...just your tows!)
18 – p (TRASH service: Satisfaction guaranteed or double your trash back.)
19 – c (VACUUM CLEANERS: Business sucks.)

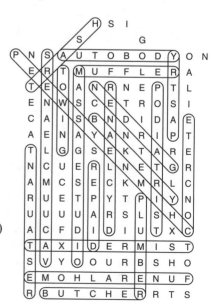

WORDS AT PLAY

S	P	A	S	■	D	E	A	R	E	■	S	A	L	T
O	R	S	O	■	A	D	M	I	X	■	C	H	O	O
N	O	T	H	I	N	G	A	F	T	E	R	A	L	L
S	W	O	O	S	I	E	■	T	E	N	A	B	L	E
■	■	R	E	S	T	■	R	I	P	■	■	■	■	■
S	Q	U	E	A	L	■	R	A	I	D	■	C	P	R
P	U	R	G	E	■	H	A	L	O	■	S	A	L	A
L	E	G	A	L	S	E	P	A	R	A	T	I	O	N
A	U	E	L	■	T	R	E	S	■	S	E	R	T	A
Y	E	S	■	C	H	E	Z	■	U	T	M	O	S	T
■	■	W	O	E	■	E	R	N	E	■	■	■	■	■
P	A	T	E	L	L	A	■	A	M	R	A	D	I	O
A	N	U	N	D	E	R	S	T	A	N	D	I	N	G
L	E	N	D	■	N	A	K	E	D	■	O	D	O	R
S	W	A	Y	■	A	B	I	D	E	■	T	I	N	E

THAT'S A LOT OF PEPPERONI

The quote: Every day, Americans eat an estimated eighteen acres of pizza.

The clue answers:

A. MERGE
B. AMAZE
C. DAYTONA
D. FAIRIES
E. INDIANA
F. CHEEVER
G. AZTECS
H. TYPESET

THAT SETTLES THAT

The quote: If you can't beat them, arrange to have them beaten. —George Carlin

The clue answers:

A. BRIGHTEN
B. ROUTER
C. TAMALE
D. CHENEY
E. MAGNET
F. GOETHE
G. CABANA
H. FAVORITE

HONK IF YOU LOVE REARRANGING THINGS

1. If you're happy and you know it, clank your chains.
2. Ask me about my vow of silence.
3. I drive way too fast to worry about cholesterol.
4. Red meat isn't bad for you. Fuzzy green meat is.
5. Never do card tricks for the people you play poker with.

WHAT? IT'S NOT?

The quote: "It is wonderful to be here in the great state of Chicago."—Dan Quayle.

The clue answers:

A. CHINA
B. ALBERT
C. CEILING
D. HOFFA
E. OATES
F. TUTORED
G. SEGA
H. EDEN
I. QUITE
J. WORTHY

YOU KNOW THE OLD SAYING

Blind as a bat: Bats aren't blind and most species of bats can see very well, thank you. But bats that hunt tiny insects at night don't rely on their vision. Instead, they rely on personal sonar, or "echolocation."

You can't teach an old dog new tricks: Oh, yes you can. Dogs can learn tricks at any age, if they're smart enough. Often it's breed, rather than age, that helps a dog learn. Border collies, poodles, German shepherds and golden retrievers are said to learn tricks the fastest.

Sweat like a pig: Pigs have no sweat glands and are unable to sweat. Instead, they wallow in mud to cool down. Their mucky appearance gives pigs a reputation for slovenliness. Actually, pigs are some of the cleanest animals around.

KURT REJOINDERS

1. Beer is actually a depressant. But poor people will never stop hoping otherwise.
2. Beware of the man who works hard to learn something, learns it, then finds himself no wiser than before.
3. Say what you will about the sweet miracle of unquestioning faith. I consider a capacity for it terrifying.

PARK IT!

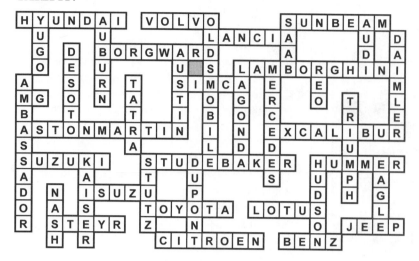

If you're not familiar with all the makes and models on our list, here's some info on the more obscure among them:

Auburn: An American car company started in Auburn, Indiana by the Eckhart Carriage Company in the early 1900s.

Borgward: Founded by German engineer Carl Borgward (1890–1963), and famous among aficionados for the Lloyd, the Hansa, and the Isabella.

Steyr: An Austrian company founded in 1920 that's today known as Steyr-Puch.

Tatra: A Czechoslovakian company that produced its first car in the late 1800s.

WORD GEOGRAPHY

The word list:

1. Ghetto
2. Babble
3. Coach
4. Blarney
5. Cologne
6. Tariff
7. Bayonet
8. Seltzer

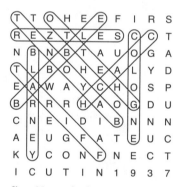

The leftover letters spell: The first *Naugahyde* was produced in Naugatuck, Connecticut, in 1937.

OF ALL THE LUCK!

1 – a (a note from his grandmother)
2 – c (Thursday the 12th)
3 – b (hand him a green pen)
4 – a ("Magic time!")
5 – b (holding his left hand over his head)
6 – a (only uses car names that begin with the letter C)
7 – c (belched)
8 – a (an apple)
9 – b (Ward Bond; the two actors made more than 20 films together)

SCAREDY-CATS

A	R	C	S		Z	O	L	A		P	R	I	O	R
P	O	O	H		I	R	O	N		R	O	N	D	O
E	M	M	E		L	O	U	D	N	O	I	S	E	S
R	E	P	E	A	L		T	R	I	X		E	L	I
		U	N	T	I	L		E	P	I	S	T	L	E
P	O	T	A	T	O	E	S		S	E	W			
I	K	E		U	N	A	P	T		S	A	L	A	D
L	A	R	D		S	C	I	O	N		Y	O	G	I
L	Y	S	O	L		H	E	R	O	D		N	E	O
		M	A	T		S	T	R	A	N	G	E	R	
P	I	N	E	N	U	T		S	T	R	E	W		
E	L	O		G	N	A	T		H	E	R	O	E	S
C	E	M	E	T	E	R	I	E	S		U	R	S	A
A	D	A	I	R		O	K	I	E		D	D	A	Y
N	E	R	D	Y		T	I	N	A		A	S	I	S

COLOR ME GULLIBLE

Pink: Studies show that people almost always believe "pastries from a pink box taste better than from any other color box."

Blue: Blue inhibits the desire to eat; in fact, researchers say, "people tend to eat less from blue plates."

Orange: Orange is a quick attention-getter, and when it's used on a product, it "loudly proclaims that the product is for everyone."

Green: Green is used to sell vegetables and chewing gum. But people avoid using it to sell meat, because it reminds consumers of mold.

AND HOW ABOUT A RUSTY NAIL?
The acrostic: New Meaning to Tool Time
The quote: American engineers working in the Middle East oil fields created the drink known as the screwdriver when they surreptitiously added vodka to small cans of orange juice. Why the name? They stirred the mixture with their screwdrivers.
The clue answers:
A. NECESSITY
B. EDDIE VAN HALEN
C. WITHERS
D. MICKEY ROURKE
E. ETHEL MERMAN
F. ANDREW WYETH
G. NIGHT CHILLS
H. INDEPENDENCE
I. NEXUS
J. GRIFTERS
K. TERRIER
L. OUT OF THIS WORLD
M. TITHE
N. OVERACHIEVERS
O. OTHERS
P. LUCKY JIM
Q. TATTERS
R. INDIRA GANDHI
S. MISTAKES
T. EDWARD WOODWARD

NAME DROPPINGS

THE TIME IT TAKES #3
Here are the answers in order:
.6 seconds for an adult to walk one step
10 seconds for 50 people to be born
45 minutes to reach an actual person when calling the IRS during tax time
96 hours to completely recover from jet lag
29 days, 12 hours, 44 minutes and three seconds from a new moon to a new moon
38 days for a slow boat to get to China (from New York)
91 days, 7 hours, 26 minutes, and 24 seconds for the Earth to fall into the Sun if it loses its orbit
6 years in a snail's life span
33 years was the life expectancy of a Neanderthal man
45.35 million years to reach the nearest star, Proxima Centauri, in a car going 65 mph

COMING CLEAN WITH THE STORY
The acrostic: Was *Cyrano de Bergerac*
The quote: Edmond Rostand didn't like to be interrupted while working. Rather than risk having to turn away any friends who might drop by to visit, he took refuge in his bathtub and wrote there all day. His biggest bathroom success?
The clue answers:
A. W. E. B. GRIFFIN
B. APTITUDE
C. SPIRIT
D. CHILDHOOD
E. YANKEE STADIUM
F. RISOTTO
G. ARKWRIGHT
H. NOTABLES
I. ORTHODONTIST
J. DONT KNOW WHY
K. EVENING STAR
L. BOBBLEHEADS
M. EVERYTHING
N. RIGHT-HANDER
O. GENE SHALIT
P. EMMY AWARD
Q. RUSH HOUR
R. ATTRIBUTED
S. CONKS

YOU'VE BEEN WARNED!

Word Lst:
1. BURNING
2. CATAPULT
3. DO NOT COVER
4. DRIVE
5. DRYING PETS
6. EAT TONER
7. FIRE
8. HIGHWAY
9. ICE CREAM
10. MICE
11. ORALLY
12. RECTALLY
13. REMAINING EYE
14. REMOVE INFANT
15. SLEEPING
16. TO FLY
17. WINDOWS

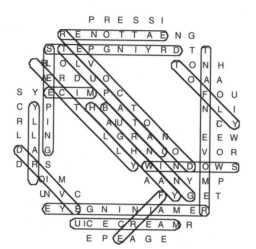

EH TWO, CANADA?
1. Belgium (medical marijuana)
2. Mongolia (coldest national capital: Ulaanbaatar)
3. Saudi Arabia (oil reserves)
4. Australia (immigrant population)
5. United States (gum chewed)
6. Russia (largest country)
7. Finland (water quality)
8. Great Britain (jet airplane)
9. Australia (red meat)
10. Japan (workaholic)

The leftover letters spell: Pressing too hard as you circle words may puncture page.

The complete answer list:
1. On a vacuum cleaner: "Do not use to pick up anything that is currently **burning**."
2. On a CD player: "Do not use the Ultradisc 2000 as a projectile in a **catapult**."
3. On a pair of shin pads: "Shin pads cannot protect any part of the body they **do not cover**."
4. On a cardboard sunshield for a car: "Do not **drive** with sunshield in place."
5. In a microwave oven manual: "Do not use for **drying pets**."
6. On a toner cartridge: "Do not **eat toner**."
7. On a Duraflame fireplace log: "Caution—Risk of **fire**."
8. On a plastic, 13-inch wheelbarrow wheel: "Not intended for **highway** use."
9. On a bottle of hair coloring: "Do not use as an **ice cream** topping."
10. On a box of rat poison: "Warning: Has been found to cause cancer in laboratory **mice**."
11. On a toilet bowl cleaning brush: "Do not use **orally**."
12. In the instructions for a digital thermometer: "Do not use orally after using **rectally**."
13. On a laser pointer: "Do not look into laser with **remaining eye**."
14. On a portable stroller: "**Remove infant** before folding for storage."
15. On a propane blowtorch: "Never use while **sleeping**."
16. On a Batman costume: "Warning: Cape does not enable user **to fly**."
17. On an air conditioner: "Avoid dropping air conditioners out of **windows**."

WOULD WE LIE TO YOU AGAIN?

1 – b (Spiders coat their legs with spittle to make them nonstick.)
2 – a (Coins were once saved in "pygg jars.")
3 – a (Cashews don't have shells.)
4 – c (June weddings were meant to honor Juno.)
5 – b (Birds find worms by feeling for their vibrations.)

MIND YOUR MANNERS, PART ONE

1. Don't affect a lisp or talk baby talk. Somebody will probably kill you sometime if you do.—*Compete!* (1935)
2. Never put your cold, clammy hands on a person, saying, "Did you ever know anyone to have such cold hands as mine?"—*Manners for Millions* (1932)
3. Sending out a letter with a crooked, mangled or upside-down stamp is akin to letting your lingerie straps show.—*Good Housekeeping's Book of Today's Etiquette* (1965)

SIMPLY MAUVELOUS!

A	B	Y	S	S	■	P	E	A	C	H	■	D	A	I	S	■	E	M	I	L
B	L	E	A	T	■	A	T	R	I	A	■	I	L	S	A	■	N	A	S	A
C	O	T	T	O	N	C	A	N	D	Y	■	V	I	O	L	E	T	R	E	D
S	C	I	E	N	C	E	S	■	■	R	H	E	A	■	E	X	I	T	E	D
■	■	■	E	O	S	■	M	A	I	A	■	■	T	S	A	R	■	■	■	■
O	B	S	E	S	S	■	W	I	L	D	W	A	T	E	R	M	E	L	O	N
T	O	I	L	■	■	S	Y	N	G	E	■	R	O	S	E	S	■	O	N	O
H	O	T	M	A	G	E	N	T	A	■	S	C	A	L	P	■	S	U	E	T
E	N	E	■	L	O	I	N	S	■	C	H	I	T	A	■	S	O	T	T	O
R	E	D	H	O	T	S	■	■	S	E	I	N	E	■	P	A	R	S	O	N
■	■	A	T	O	M	I	C	T	A	N	G	E	R	I	N	E	■	■	■	■
P	O	T	I	O	N	■	N	O	I	S	E	■	■	I	N	E	R	T	I	A
S	C	A	R	F	■	A	S	O	N	E	■	C	E	N	T	S	■	I	N	N
H	U	M	S	■	A	P	I	N	G	■	M	A	N	G	O	T	A	N	G	O
A	L	I	■	T	I	L	D	E	■	S	A	W	T	O	■	G	A	O	L	■
W	I	L	D	B	L	U	E	Y	O	N	D	E	R	■	C	H	A	S	T	E
■	■	R	O	M	S	■	■	S	R	U	E	D	■	D	O	E	■	■	■	■
A	R	S	E	N	E	■	H	E	R	B	■	■	B	A	L	L	G	I	R	L
G	O	L	D	E	N	R	O	D	■	B	A	N	A	N	A	M	A	N	I	A
O	N	E	G	■	T	O	M	E	■	E	B	B	E	D	■	E	L	T	O	N
D	A	D	E	■	S	T	E	N	■	D	E	C	R	Y	■	T	A	S	T	E

PERFECT 10 #3

The ashes of the average cremated person weigh **9** pounds.

The average American eats **4** pounds of "artificial flavorings, colorings and preservatives" each year.

The average yawn lasts **6** seconds.

A pelican's beak can hold **2** gallons.

The average Ph.D. candidate spends **7** years on his/her dissertation.

Babe Ruth's jersey number was **3**.

You dream an average of **5** times each night.

The average speed of traffic in New York City during the 1980s was **10** mph.

A coffee tree yields about **1** pound of coffee in a year.

The average grocery shopper stands in line **8** minutes.

HAVE YOU HERD?

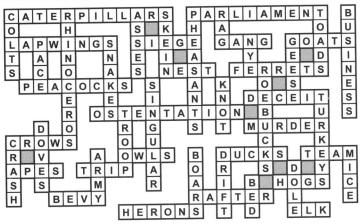

WHERE AM I?

1. Fort Dallas
2. Hot Springs
3. Fort Dearborn
4. Lancaster
5. Terminus
6. Cole's Harbor
7. Waterloo
8. Willingtown
9. Oyster Point
10. New Netherland
11. All Saints
12. Lake Crossing
13. New Connecticut
14. Rumford

HABLA ES-PUN-OL?

VENI, VIPI, VICI
COGITO EGGO SUM
RIGOR MORRIS
RESPONDEZ S'IL VOUS PLAID
QUE SERA SERF
LE ROI EST MORT. JIVE LE ROI
FELIX NAVIDAD
HASTE CUISINE
HARLEZ-VOUS FRANCAIS
VENI, VIDI, VICE
QUIP PRO QUO
ALOHA OY
VISA LA FRANCE
L'ETAT, C'EST MOO
ICH BIT EIN BERLINER
E PLURIBUS ANUM

WISE WOMEN

1. Rita Mae Brown: "If the world were a logical place, men would ride side-saddle."
2. Helen Keller: "The heresy of one age becomes the orthodoxy of the next."
3. Katherine Mansfield: "Regret is an appalling waste of energy; you can't build on it; it is only good for wallowing."
4. Anna Freud: "Creative minds have always been known to survive any kind of bad training."
5. Erica Jong: "If you don't risk any thing, you risk even more."

I DO SOLEMNLY SWEAR

```
P M S   R O P E R   D E C A L   T A X I
B A I T   A P O L O   A N O D E   V A I L
O L D E   G R O S S   L U M E N   D A V E
S O M E G U Y H I T M Y F E N D E R
S M A L L   S E R A   L L A M A S
Y A Y   A N G   A N I M A L   S M Y T H
S C O O T S   E T A L I A   A F T A
T H E O T H E R D A Y A N D I S A I D
N C A A   K Y O T O   H I K E D   I C E
E E K S   S O R   B O D E   S E A R
O N E T O   U N T O H I M B E   A R L E S
S A U D   I T S A   A M A   A A R P
O P T   S E N O R   L O W O N   B D A Y
F R U I T F U L A N D M U L T I P L Y
F E R N   S T A D I A   T S E T S E
T E N D S   S N E E R S   D A H   M O M
O N S E T S   I E O H   A W A R E
B U T N O T I N T H O S E W O R D S
T W I T   R I S E N   T A R O T   O D E A
R A C E   A L L E N   E R N I E   D I A S
I D I D   P E O N S   E A S T S   Y S L
```

...IT MEANS THE WORLD TO ME

The leftover letters spell: "Money speaks sense in a language all nations understand."

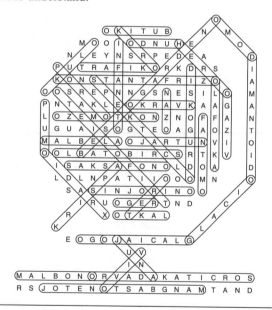

ESPERANTO...

1 – ii (AKVOFALO – waterfall)
2 – nn (BESTOGARDENO – zoo)
3 – ff (BUTIKO – shop)
4 – cc (DIAMANTOIDO – rhinestone)
5 – q (DISKOGURDO – jukebox)
6 – n (DOMO – house)
7 – k (FANTOMO – ghost)
8 – p (GLACIAJO – ice cream)
9 – o (GLACIO – ice)
10 – m (HEROO – hero)
11 – d (HUNDO – dog)
12 – a (INFANETO – baby)
13 – kk (JOGO – yoga)
14 – ll (JUNA – young)
15 – z (KONSTANTA FRIZO – permanent wave)
16 – l (KORO – heart)
17 – s (KRISPA – kinky)
18 – bb (KVARKO – quark)
19 – w (LAKTO – milk)
20 – hh (MALBELA – ugly)
21 – f (MALBONO – evil)
22 – b (MANGBASTONETOJ – chopsticks)
23 – x (NAZO – nose)
24 – v (NOKTOMEZO – midnight)
25 – j (NUTRAJO – food)
26 – g (OKULO – eye)
27 – i (PLUMO – feather)
28 – aa (PORKO – pig)
29 – r (REGO – king)
30 – dd (SAKSAFONO – saxophone)
31 – c (SCRIBOTABLO – desk)
32 – t (SINJORINO – lady)
33 – mm (SORCITA KADAVRO – zombie)
34 – y (SPEKTACLO – pageant)
35 – e (TERO – earth)
36 – gg (TRAFIKO – traffic)
37 – ee (TRIFOLIETO – shamrock)
38 – u (VIVO – life)
39 – h (VIZAGO – face)
40 – jj (X-RADIO – x-ray)

DOROTHY PARKER SEZ...

1. Not So Deep as a Well
   Oh, life is a glorious cycle of song,
   A medley of extemporanea;
   And love is a thing that can never go wrong;
   And I am Marie of Roumania.

2. I'm never going to be famous. My name will never be writ large on the roster of Those Who Do Things. I don't do anything. Not one single thing. I used to bite my nails, but I don't even do that anymore.

3. I misremember who first was cruel enough to nurture the cocktail party into life. But perhaps it would be not too much to say, in fact it would be not enough to say, that it was not worth the trouble.

UNCLE OSCAR'S BIG NIGHT #3

1 – c (Dustin Hoffman, *Kramer vs. Kramer*)
2 – d (Marlon Brando, *The Godfather*)
3 – a (Russell Crowe, *Gladiator*)
4 – b (Kevin Spacey, *American Beauty*)

HOW TO DRIVE PEOPLE NUTS

1. In the middle of the night, noisily bury a fully dressed mannequin in your backyard. Arrange lawn furniture on the fresh mound and sit down in it quickly when the police arrive.
2. Call the Q-Tips customer service number and say that one of the cotton swab parts just came off in your ear. When they reply, keep shouting, "What? What? What did you say?"
3. Rush yourself to the ER and explain to the night nurse that you were resting on your leg for a long time and now it feels like pins and needles. Ask if they'll have to amputate.
4. Go to the polar bear enclosure at the zoo and shout, "C'mon, Larry. Take off that costume and come back to the office."

MONOGRAMS

The leftover letters spell: "Vowel Woman" stands for Vanna White. "Muppet Porker" would have to be Miss Piggy.
Word List:

1. Asks Trivia - ALEX TREBEK
2. Aviatrix Extraordinaire - AMELIA EARHART
3. Aces Regularly - ANDY RODDICK
4. Awesome Putter - ARNOLD PALMER
5. Blasts Baseballs - BARRY BONDS
6. Classic Couturiere - COCO CHANEL
7. Eerily Authored Poems - EDGAR ALLAN POE
8. Highly Recognizable Congresswoman - HILLARY RODHAM CLINTON
9. Mrs. Schwarzenegger - MARIA SHRIVER
10. Married Bancroft - MEL BROOKS
11. Notable Astronaut - NEIL ARMSTRONG
12. Plays Bond - PIERCE BROSNAN
13. Riles Liberals - RUSH LIMBAUGH
14. Surrealist Dandy - SALVADOR DALI
15. Signifies Christmas - SANTA CLAUS
16. Television Titan - TED TURNER
17. Wrote Sonnets - WILLIAM SHAKESPEARE

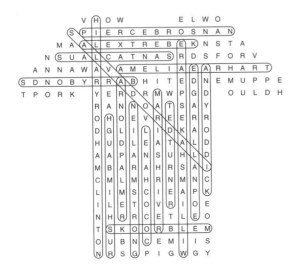

A TRULY GAUCHE PUZZLE

THAT MAN IN THE WHITE HOUSE

1 – a (the swivel chair)
2 – a (Harry Truman)
3 – b (to charity)
4 – a (The Three Blind Mice)
5 – b (attend his own inauguration)
6 – b (speeding…in a horse and buggy, no less)
7 – a (women)
8 – c (White House china)
9 – b (Maxwell House Coffee, when offered a cup of coffee at the Maxwell House hotel in Nashville)
10 – a (too religious)

SOMETHING'S BREWING

The leftover letters spell: "In London, love and scandal are considered the best sweeteners of tea."—John Osborne

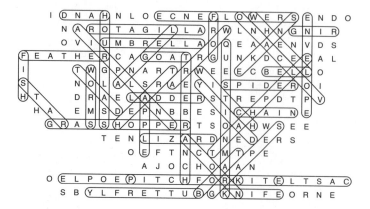

Word List:

ACORN: Good health, good luck

AIRPLANE:Unexpected journey; if wings are shattered, danger

ALLIGATOR: Strength and power

ANGEL: Good news, luck in love

APPLE: Long life, gain in business

ARROW: A letter; if bent, bad news

BELL: Good news, wedding

BOAT: Friendly visitor

BUTTERFLY: Frivolous pleasure

CASTLE: Marrying into money

CHAIN: Early marriage; if broken, an unhappy one

DAISY: A new love

ELEPHANT: Good luck, health, happiness

ENVELOPE: Good news; if blurred, bad news

FEATHER: Frivolity, lack of responsiblity

FENCE: Obstacles

FISH: Good news from far away

FLOWERS: Loyal friends, happy marriage, success

FROG: Beware excessive pride

GOAT: You're surrounded by enemies

GRAPES: Happiness

GRASSHOPPER: A friend will leave, perhaps never to return

HAND: Friendliness

HEART: A letter or lover is coming

HOURGLASS: Danger nearby

KITE: Trip that will lead to a valuable friendship

KNIFE: Danger

LADDER: Success, travel

LIZARD: Treacherous friends

PEOPLE: Good omen

PITCHFORK: Deceitful member of the opposite sex

QUESTION MARK: Beware all major decisions

RING: Marriage

SNAKE: Enemy, threat

SPIDER: Unexpected inheritance

STAR: Achievement and success

TOAD: Unknown enemy

TREE BRANCH: Better health

UMBRELLA: New opportunities

VOLCANO: Major upheaval

WHEEL: Unexpected gift or inheritance

WITCH: A strange occurrence

WORMS: Secret enemies

THE BAD BOOK

The acrostic: Called "the Wicked Bible"

The quote: Two London printers left one word out of an official edition of the Bible and the mistake nearly sent them to jail. The word was "not," and they left it out of the Seventh Commandment, which now told readers, "Thou shalt commit adultery."

The clue answers:

A. CHIEFS
B. ATTACHMENTS
C. LYNDON JOHNSON
D. LOOPHOLE
E. EARTHWORM
F. DAVID LETTERMAN
G. THE EIFFEL TOWER
H. HEAD OF STATE
I. EFFORTFUL
J. WOODWARD
K. INTUIT
L. CHOO-CHOO
M. KITTIES
N. ENTERTAINMENT
O. DULUTH
P. BITTY
Q. IN HARMS WAY
R. BOLTON
S. LITTLE WOMEN
T. EDMOND DANTES

KATE THE GREAT

1. I find men today less manly. But a woman my age is not in a position to know exactly how manly they are.
2. Life is to be lived. If you have to support yourself, you had bloody well better find some way that is going to be interesting.
3. Sometimes I wonder if men and women really do suit each other. Perhaps they should live next door and just visit now and then.

JUST MY TYPE

The left hand does 56 percent of the typing.

LOONEY LAWS REVISITED

1 – a (take a bath)
2 – b (remove his hat)
3 – a (margarine instead of real butter)
4 – c (peel an orange)
5 – a (coins)
6 – b (a picture of a man)
7 – b (fall asleep)
8 – a (sitting on the back of a giraffe)
9 – c (draw funny faces on)
10 – b (advertise on).

UNDER THE INFLUENCE

The acrostic: Butch Cassidy's origin
The quote: As a teen, Robert Parker idolized a criminal named Mike Cassidy, and eventually began using Cassidy's last name as an alias. He picked up the name "Butch" while working in a Rock Springs, Wyoming, butcher shop.
The clue answers:
A. BOGIES
B. UPPER CASE
C. THE SUNDANCE KID
D. CHESTER GOULD
E. HEBREW
F. CRAB APPLE
G. ALAMEDA
H. SCRIMSHAW
I. SALAMANDER
J. INNER MAN
K. DAILY DOUBLE
L. YAWLS
M. SCANNING
N. OH! SUSANNA
O. RIKKI-TIKKI-TAVI
P. ITEMIZE
Q. GHOST STORY
R. IMPINGE
S. NANCY

WOULD WE LIE TO YOU ONE MORE TIME?

1 – c (The phrase refers to horse manure.)
2 – a (The phrase refers to two stagecoaches having a near miss.)
3 – b (The phrase refers to a boxer unable to continue fighting.)
4 – b (The phrase refers to a flintlock musket that fails to fire.)
5 – a (The phrase refers to a cosmetic spoiled by dead flies.)

ON THE CAMPAIGN TRAIL

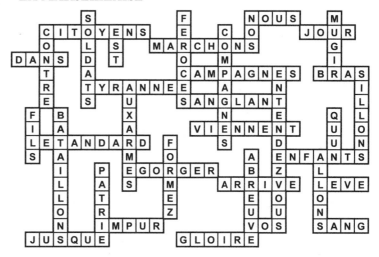

LA MARSEILLAISE

FYI: The rousing battle song was originally called "War Song of the Army of the Rhine," but it got its nickname "La Marseillaise" because the fierce soldiers from Marseilles were singing it when they entered Paris in 1792.

I'LL BUY THAT
All three are true.

THE 5 MOST-READ U.S. NEWSPAPERS

1. *The Wall Street Journal*
2. *USA Today*
3. *The Los Angeles Times*
4. *The New York Times*
5. *The Washington Post*

SHORT BUT SWEET

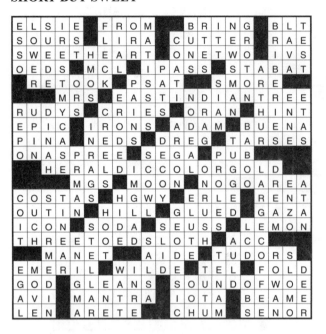

THE SAME, ONLY DIFFERENT

HONK IF YOU LOVE MORE ANAGRAMS

1. I want to make love in the worst possible way—standing up in a canoe.
2. Diplomacy: the art of letting someone else get your way.
3. Hukt on fonix reely wurkt for mee!

UNITED STATES

1. A razor (AR/AZ/OR)
2. I am dorky. (IA/MD/OR/KY)
3. Malarial (MA/LA/RI/AL)
4. Ganymede (GA/NY/ME/DE)
5. Cooking a meal (CO/OK/IN/GA/ME/AL)
6. Wade paid a kid. (WA/DE/PA/ID/AK/ID)
7. His diamond mine
   (HI/SD/IA/MO/ND/MI/NE)
8. Van cuts corks in Vail.
   (VA/NC/UT/SC/OR/KS/IN/VA/IL)
9. Wine can do harm to rinks.
   (WI/NE/CA/ND/OH/AR/MT/OR/IN/KS)
10. Macon car lane alarms many moms.
    (MA/CO/NC/AR/LA/NE/AL/AR/MS/
    MA/NY/MO/MS)

WORDS YOU DON'T SEE EVERY DAY
The leftover letters spell: "Gardyloo" is thought to be derived from the French "*garde a l'eau*" or "look out for the water." (*Garde a l'eau!* was a warning cry about "dirty" water thrown from windows to the street below.)

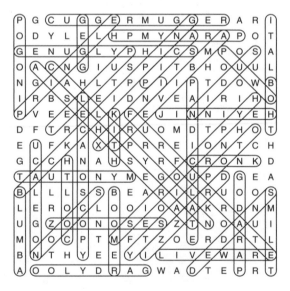

SHOOTING UP
The quote: Bamboo can grow as much as thirty-five inches a day.
The clue answers:
A. BECOMING
B. AUSTIN
C. HOOF
D. BAHAMAS
E. SCRATCHY
F. DRIVEWAY

LUCKY SEVENS

The leftover letters spell: NASA astronauts Scott Carpenter, Gordon Cooper, John Glenn, Gus Grissom, Wally Schirra, Alan Shepard, and Deke Slayton were the Mercury Seven.

Word List:

MR. HOWELL
MRS. HOWELL
PROFESSOR
SKIPPER

The Magnificent Seven **actors:**
Charles BRONSON
Yul BRYNNER
Horst BUCHHOLZ
James COBURN
Brad DEXTER
Steve MCQUEEN
Robert VAUGHN

The 7 Cardinal Virtues:
CHARITY
FAITH
FORTITUDE
HOPE
JUSTICE
PRUDENCE
TEMPERANCE

Gilligan's Island **castaways:**
GILLIGAN
GINGER
MARY ANN

GRAMMAR
LOGIC
MUSIC
RHETORIC

The 7 Deadly Sins:
AVARICE
ENVY
GLUTTONY
LUST
PRIDE
SLOTH
WRATH

The 7 Dwarfs:
BASHFUL
DOC
DOPEY
GRUMPY
HAPPY
SLEEPY
SNEEZY

The 7 Liberal Arts:
ARITHMETIC
ASTRONOMY
GEOMETRY

The 7 Sisters Colleges:
BARNARD
BRYN MAWR
MOUNT
HOLYOKE
RADCLIFFE
SMITH
VASSAR
WELLESLEY

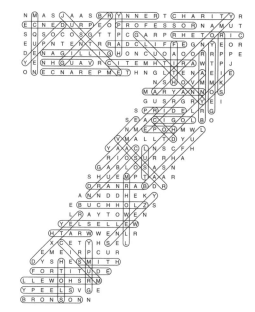

TECHNOSLANG

	P	L	A	I	N	S		L	A	C	T	I	C		D	E	L	A	Y	S
P	E	E	R	S	A	T		O	R	I	A	N	A		A	R	A	R	A	T
R	E	V	O	L	V	E		T	R	A	C	T	M	A	N	S	I	O	N	S
E	P	I	C			P	A	T			K	E	E	N	E		D	U	G	
G	E	E	K	O	S	P	H	E	R	E		R	A	T		M	I	S	T	Y
O	D	S		R	H	E	A		O	R	A		B	O	D	Y	N	A	Z	I
			A	C	E		A	T	O	R		O	I	L	S		L	E	N	
T	H	E	C	A	R	B	O	N	C	O	M	M	U	N	I	T	Y			
R	E	N	T		P	U	M	A			L	A	T	E	X		O	R	A	L
I	T	T		M	A	N	N		B	B	O	Y			A	D	O	R	E	
P	E	R	C	U	S	S	I	V	E	M	A	I	N	T	E	N	A	N	C	E
O	R	E	O	S			E	N	I	D		E	R	L	E		D	A	R	
D	O	E	S		E	S	T	E	E		I	R	A	E		M	O	N	A	
		I	N	T	H	E	P	L	A	S	T	I	C	C	L	O	S	E	T	
A	D	A		I	C	O	N		U	N	A	S			T	O	W			
B	E	G	A	T	H	O	N		X	A	S		O	A	R	S		T	E	A
S	L	I	P	S		T	Y	S		T	H	O	N	G	A	T	H	O	N	S
	I	T	E		P	A	S	T	A		L	E	A			A	P	T	S	
B	L	A	M	E	S	T	O	R	M	I	N	G		S	H	E	L	T	I	E
E	A	T	E	R	S		N	A	U	S	E	A		S	E	L	L	E	R	S
T	H	E	N	E	T		S	P	R	E	E	S		I	S	M	E	N	E	

SCREEN DEBUTS

	C	H	U	T	E		S	T	A	B	B	E	D		S	T	A	C	K
T	H	A	N	E	S		H	O	N	A	L	E	E		L	A	U	R	A	S
S	I	Z	Z	L	E	B	E	A	C	H	U	S	A		A	R	G	Y	L	E
E	M	A	I	L		A	P	S	E	S		R	H	Y	S		B	I	D	
T	E	R	P		B	R	A	T		O	R	S	O		I	N	A	N	E	
S	I	D		J	E	R	R	Y	M	A	G	U	I	R	E		C	B	E	R
E	N	S	N	A	R	E	D		C	O	R	E	R		G	R	A	Y		
		O	V	E	N		H	A	L	E		C	R	O	A	K	E	R		
P	E	T	C	A	T		K	O	N		I	S	S	U	E	S		I	S	O
O	S	H	A		S	E	A	R		E	S	C	O	R	T	S		L	S	U
S	T	E	L	E		A	N	N	I	E	H	A	L	L		I	N	L	E	T
T	A	D		Z	I	G	G	I	N	G		L	A	S	S		B	E	N	E
E	T	E		I	S	L	A	N	D		D	E	R		N	A	C	R	E	D
R	E	V	E	N	U	E		U	B	E	R		B	A	I	T				
		I	N	E	Z		O	R	C	A	S		A	A	R	D	V	A	R	K
A	B	L	Y		U	S	S	T	E	A	K	E	T	T	L	E		B	E	I
M	E	S	A	S		A	C	E	S		R	A	M	S		G	R	A	D	
O	R	R		T	U	T	U		T	R	A	L	A		C	R	E	D	O	
S	T	A	M	O	S		L	O	V	E	I	S	O	N	T	H	E	A	I	R
T	H	I	E	V	E		A	L	I	A	S	E	S		B	E	T	S	E	Y
	A	N	T	E	D		R	E	E	L	E	R	S		S	T	A	T	S	

SUBURBAN LEGENDS

1. **TRUE, BUT...**

   The concept is based on an experiment designed to see if randomly selected people from all walks of life would be able to find a particular "target" person using only their own network of friends.

   It worked like this: A psychologist randomly selected pairs of people and designated one as the "source" and one as the "target." The source's job was to reach the target in the fewest number of steps possible, by using only people he knew. The source sent a letter to the person he knew who was most likely to know the target. If, say, the target lived in Boca Raton, the source would send a letter to a friend who lived in or near there, who in turn might send a letter to a person that she knew would be most likely to know the target. The number of intermediate links ranged from 2 to 10. The most common number wasn't six, it was five.

   For more on the phenomenon, see "Six Degrees of Kevin Bacon" in *Uncle John's Bathroom Reader Plunges into Great Lives*, page 325.

2. **FALSE, BUT THE REAL STORY IS BETTER...**

   Actually, a large raptor was discovered two years *before* the release of *Jurassic Park*, but apparently the all-powerful and all-seeing Spielberg didn't know it. He just took the raptors that Michael Crichton had used in the book of the same name, and made them bigger and more menacing. The real raptor, which may not have been a pack hunter like the velociraptors in the film, was found in Utah, and is now officially called "Utahraptor."

3. **FALSE.**

   This is patently untrue, according to the "Birdwatcher's Digest." But this is one urban legend that's been taken to heart by most modern brides and grooms, so they've replaced rice with birdseed as the post-nuptial projectile of choice. Which has, in turn, spawned another urban legend, that of the bridegroom who went to his doctor with a severe pain in his ear. A brief examination came up with the cause: A piece of birdseed had lodged in the bridegroom's ear and had sprouted in that warm and moist environment.

   Bring back rice!

4. **TRUE.**

   Flea circuses are not an urban legend—they're absolutely real and they've been entertaining incredulous audiences for more than 300 years. Fleas have certain talents that set them apart from other insects. They're strong—they can pull objects that are 160,000 times their own weight, the equivalent of a human pulling 24 million pounds. They can jump 150 times their own height and what's more, they can do it 30,000 times without stopping.

   If you're itching to learn more about the tiniest show on earth, read "Circus Minimus" in *Uncle John's Bathroom Reader Plunges into the Universe*, page 234.

5. **FALSE.**

   You've heard the story: Some idiot decides to spend the night alone in a haunted house. The next day he or she is found—now a blithering idiot whose hair has turned completely white. As much as we'd like to believe the yummy horror of it all, the phenomenon is probably legend and nothing more. See, hair is dead tissue and therefore can't turn white until it grows out from the roots. The myth may have its own roots in a condition called "diffuse alopecia areata," which can cause substantial hair loss, but only to pigmented hair. When it occurs in people with a mix of dark and gray/white hair, the only hair left would be the nonpigmented hair, thus giving the impression that someone's hair has turned white overnight. What gives this theory more credence is that the condition is believed to be caused by emotional stress. And what's more stressful than staying alone overnight in a haunted house...?

6. **TRUE, BUT...**

   It isn't chocolate but a naturally occurring compound found in chocolate that's poisonous to dogs. Theobromine causes different reactions in different dogs. Size is a major factor: The smaller the dog, the more affected it'll be. It also depends on the kind of chocolate: Dark chocolate is 10 times more toxic to dogs than milk chocolate.

7. **TRUE.**

   Someone did a study on it. But they didn't throw the cats off balconies or roofs (which is another suburban legend). They based their findings on stories of cats that had already fallen. Anyway, the answer is yes: At low and intermediate heights a cat, while plummeting to earth, can turn and land on its feet. At intermediate heights, say, above two stories and under five, they'll most likely break some bones. From great heights—what some researchers have called "high-rise syndrome" or HRS—a cat will "parachute" instead, flattening its body and landing on its chest and abdomen rather than its legs. The most common injuries in cats with HRS were jaw fractures, lung collapse, and occasional pelvic fractures as well.

8. **TRUE.**

   Don't do it.

9. **TRUE, BUT…**

   Botanically, yes. Legally—at least in the United States—they're a vegetable. The question was officially decided in 1893 when a food importer sued to recover taxes he'd paid under the Tariff Act. The act called for payment on vegetables, but not fruit. The Supreme Court based its interpretation of the act on the ordinary meaning of the words "fruit" and "vegetable" as opposed to the botanical meaning. The importer lost his case.

   Still, technically, tomatoes are the fruit of a vine. That means that other "vegetables" that aren't sweet, but which are used (and thought of) as vegetables, fall into the same category: Cucumbers, squashes, avocados, peppers, peas, and even pumpkins are, botanically speaking, fruit.

10. **TRUE.**

    Some initial research has shown remarkable reductions in weed populations when tillage of fields was done at night—as great as 80 percent but generally 50 to 60 percent. Tilling at night delays or even prevents some weeds from emerging, leaving them buried so that they're less viable and more prone to attack by soil microbes. If fewer weeds appear, that means fewer tractor trips and reduced herbicide use, the latter a nice thing for us vegetable eaters. Of course, there are always the exceptions: Large-seeded weeds like velvet-leaf and cocklebur still sprout after night tilling, and annual grass species aren't affected at all.

11. **TRUE.**

    A fire in most open fireplaces creates just enough heat to cause a convection current that sucks the smoke from the fire up the chimney. Which is where the smoke should go. But at the same time, the current is sucking out the heat generated by the fire, and lots of nice warm air from the house. The cold air that leaks into the house to replace the warm air that's lost up the chimney cools the house down.

12. **TRUE, IF…**

    If the water receptacle doesn't have a lid, some of the water will evaporate. The water that's lost in evaporation may diminish the mass enough to compensate for the greater temperature range it has to cover to get to freezing. Also, evaporation carries off the hottest molecules, which lowers the average kinetic energy of the molecules that are left. This is why blowing on your soup cools it: It encourages evaporation by removing the water vapor above the soup.

And what about human beings using only 10 percent of their brains? It's FALSE. Even though only about five percent of the brain's neurons are active at any given time, researchers haven't found any unused areas of the brain. Because it weighs only three pounds, the human brain is too small, uses too many of the body's resources (like oxygen), and has too much to do for 90 percent of it to be inactive.

LAWYERS ON LAWYERS

1. I bring out the worst in my enemies, and that's how I get them to defeat themselves. (Roy Cohn)
2. I've never met a litigator who didn't think he was winning, right up until the moment the guillotine dropped. (William E. Baxter)
3. An incompetent lawyer can delay a trial for months or years. A competent lawyer can delay one even longer. (Evelle Younger)

HOW MOSQUITOES CHANGED HISTORY

Africa, 1,600,000 BC (10) Our ancestors take their first upright steps. Thanks to mosquitoes, they are already infected with malaria.

India, 500 BC (2) Brahmin priest Susruta deduces that mosquitoes are responsible for the spread of malaria. No one pays any attention for the next 2,400 years.

Babylon, 323 BC (11) The lowly mosquito fells its first world-famous victim: Alexander the Great dies of malaria at the age of 33. His dream of a united Greek empire collapses within a few years, and widespread malarial infection further contributes to the decline of Greek civilization.

Rome, 410 AD (6) Marauding Visigoths finish off the once-great empire, already undermined by a fifth column of malaria-spreading mosquitoes in the low-lying areas surrounding the capital. Shortly afterward, Alaric, leader of the vanquishers, is vanquished in his turn by a treacherous mosquito.

Africa, 1593 (14) Yellow fever and malaria spread via the slave trade, laying the basis for epidemics that will decimate both colonial and aboriginal populations.

England, 1658 (1) Bitten by a possibly Royalist mosquito, Oliver Cromwell dies of malaria, paving the way for the return of the monarchy.

Barbados, 1690 (12) The spread of yellow fever halts a British expedition en route to attack the French in Canada.

New Orleans, 1802 (9) Napoleon sends a force of 33,000 to reinforce France's claim to Louisiana and put down a slave rebellion in Haiti. A whopping 29,000 of the soldiers are killed by mosquito-borne yellow fever. Shortly thereafter, Louisiana is turned over to the U.S. and Haiti becomes an independent republic.

Stockholm, 1902 (3) British army surgeon Dr. Ronald Ross receives the Nobel Prize for establishing the link between mosquito bites and malaria.

Panama, 1905 (7) Mosquitoes almost succeed in halting construction of the canal, as panicked workers flee a yellow fever epidemic.

Colorado, 1939 (4) DDT is tested and found to control mosquitoes and other insects. Mosquitoes eventually develop resistance to the chemical; humans don't.

Dutch East Indies, 1942 (5) Japanese troops seize the islands that provide most of the world's quinine, the only reliable malaria therapy known at the time, hoping mosquitoes will become a weapon against Allied forces. Nearly half a million American troops in the East are hospitalized with malaria over the next four years.

Vietnam, 1965–1975 (8) Mosquitoes spread malaria to as many as 53 American soldiers in a thousand every day.

Geneva, 1995 (13) The World Health Organization (WHO) declares mosquito-borne dengue fever a "world epidemic," while deaths from malaria rise to nearly 3 million a year.

MIND YOUR MANNERS, PART TWO

1. It is not correct to put the fork so far into the mouth that bystanders are doubtful of its return to the light. (*The Correct Thing in Good Society*, 1902)
2. After blowing your nose, do not open your handkerchief and inspect it, as though pearls had fallen out of your skull. (*The Book of Manners*, 1958)
3. The gloves that a fashionable woman should wear are never so tight that her hands have the appearance of sausages. (*The New Etiquette*, 1940)

WHAT DID YOU CALL ME?

The leftover letters spell: Interestingly nicknamed baseball players have also included Mordecai "Three-Finger" Brown, "Shoeless Joe" Jackson, "Tom Terrific" Seaver, "Hammerin' Hank" Aaron, Stan "the Man" Musial, and Jim "Catfish" Hunter.

The lineup:
BEAST = JIMMIE FOXX
BIG DOG = TONY PEREZ
BIG SIX = CHRISTY MATHEWSON
BIG TRAIN = WALTER JOHNSON
CHAIRMAN OF THE BOARD = WHITEY FORD
CHARLIE HUSTLE = PETE ROSE
COMMERCE COMET = MICKEY MANTLE
CYCLONE = CY YOUNG
DONNIE BASEBALL = DON MATTINGLY
FLYING DUCHMAN = HONUS WAGNER
FORDHAM FLASH = FRANKIE FRISCH
GEORGIA PEACH = TY COBB
GREY EAGLE = TRIS SPEAKER
IRON HORSE = LOU GEHRIG
MR. OCTOBER = REGGIE JACKSON
SPLENDID SPLINTER = TED WILLIAMS
STRETCH = WILLIE McCOVEY
SULTAN OF SWAT = BABE RUTH
WIZARD OF OZ = OZZIE SMITH
YANKEE CLIPPER = JOE DIMAGGIO

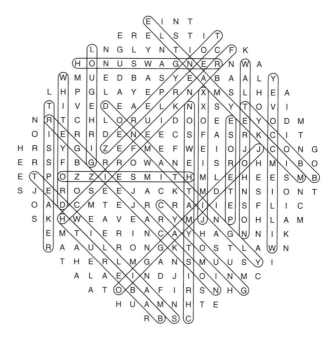

HELL ON WHEELS

The acrostic: Definitely not on a roll
The quote: The inventor of roller skates wanted to make a grand entrance at a party, playing his violin while wearing his new "wheeled feet," but he crashed into a full-length mirror and broke his violin, the mirror, and his new skates.

The clue answers:
A. DWEEB
B. ESMERALDA
C. FRIGHTEN
D. IN THE PINK
E. NUTHATCH
F. IRISH SETTER
G. THE WILD WILD WEST
H. ENGLISH HORN
I. LARVA
J. YEARNED
K. NIA VARDALOS
L. OWNERSHIP
M. THE CAT'S MEOW
N. OVERTAKE
O. NORTHERN
P. ANNIE OAKLEY
Q. RING OF FIRE
R. OUT ON A LIMB
S. LASTING
T. LAKER

FAMOUS LAST WORDS

HEY! UH...NICK!

b. It comes from the Middle English a*n ekename*.

MANGIA! MANGIA!

The Pastas:

Anelli: *rings*
Avemarie: *hail marys*
Ballerine: *ballerinas, little bells*
Cavatappi: *corkscrews*
Cubetti: *small cubes*
Eliche: *propeller, helix, screw*
Fettucce: *ribbons*
Fettuccine: *little ribbons*
Gemelli: *twins*
Gigli: *lilies*
Gnocchi: *little dumplings*
Lasagne: *sheets of pasta*
Linguine: *little tongues*
Maccheroni: *macaroni*
Manicotti: *pipes, small muffs*
Margherite: *daisies*
Nidi: *nests*
Ondine: *waves*
Orecchietti: *little ears*
Orsetti: *little bears*
Orzo: *barley or rice*
Pappardelle: *butterflies*
Penne: *quills*
Quadrucci: *squares*
Radiatori: *radiators*
Ravioli: *little turnips*
Rotelli: *small wheels*
Rotini: *spirals*

Ruote: *cart wheels*
Semi di melone: *melon seeds*
Spirali: *spirals*
Stelline: *little stars*
Strozzapreti: *strangle a priest* (because of their twisted shape—and who knows?—possibly a grudge held by the pasta maker)
Tagliatelle: *cut up*
Torchio: *torch*
Tortellini: *little fritters*
Ziti: *bridegrooms*

SCIENCE DICTION

1. In science the credit goes to the man who convinces the world, not to the man to whom the idea first occurred. (Sir William Osler, Canadian physician)
2. Art is made to disturb. Science reassures. There is only one valuable thing in art: the thing you cannot explain. (Georges Braque, French artist and cofounder of Cubism)
3. People think of the inventor as a screwball, but no one ever asks the inventor what he thinks of other people. (Charles F. Kettering, American inventor responsible for scads of inventions, the best known of which is the electric automobile starter)

OPERATION: OPERA

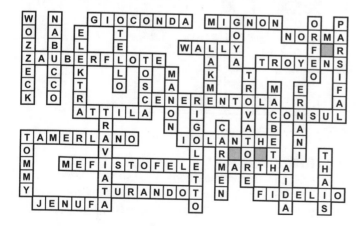

FYI: *La Wally* has nothing to do with Beaver Cleaver's older brother. Written by Alfredo Catalani, the opera is probably best known for its beautiful aria used in the very hip French movie *Diva*. But you knew that already.

ROSEANNE SEZ…

1. Men read maps better than women because only men can understand the concept of an inch equalling a hundred miles.
2. Women complain about premenstrual syndrome, but I think of it as the only time of the month I can be myself.
3. I asked the clothing store clerk if she had anything to make me look thinner, and she said, "How about a week in Bangladesh?"
4. My hope is that gays will be running the world, because then there would be no war. Just a greater emphasis on military apparel.
5. Experts say you should never hit your children in anger. When is a good time? When you're feeling festive?

THE AVENGERS

1. Patrick Macnee was an assistant producer on English TV when he was offered the lead role. He saw his future in production, not acting, so he asked for a ridiculously high salary to discourage the offer. To his shock, they accepted.
2. Honor Blackman played Steed's first sidekick, and TV's first "superwoman"—an anthropologist and judo expert. She quit to become a movie star when she was offered the role of Pussy Galore in *Goldfinger*.
3. The producers figured their only shot at selling the show in America was to offer something that Hollywood couldn't—England. So they purposely hammed it up with thick British accents, slang and scenery.

WHAT AM I?

The leftover letters spell: "I am a word of letters three. Add two, and fewer there will be." [The answer is] FEW.

Riddle answers:

1. BUTTERFLY
2. CANDLE
3. GLOVE
4. LETTER M
5. DECK OF CARDS
6. PAIR OF EYES
7. DICTIONARY
8. ANCHOR
9. POSTAGE STAMP
10. YOUR BREATH
11. CLOUD
12. DRUM
13. RAINBOW
14. ROAD
15. HOURGLASS

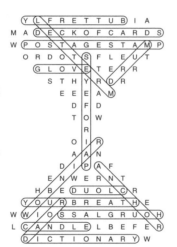

TAWK UH DA TOWN

```
I M B I B E   A T T I C   E X T     P S Y C H
S U R F I N   H O O C H   N E E   E U D O R A
B L A S T F R O M T H E P A S T   D R A G O N
U L T   T A B L E   R U M   S I D E K I C K
T A S   E N I D   R E U B E N   S Y S
  A R T S   B O M B   L O C H   I N T R O
G R O V E   L O A   F E T A   A L O H A S
O U T I N L E F T F I E L D   P U N K R O C K
T S E   D O P E   S L A Y   W O N G   A R E A
I T L L   S S R S   S T O K E   D O M   A R R
N I L E S   O M E N   A F I R E   R A E
  C O C K A M A M I E   F L E A M A R K E T
H A L   T I T L E   T O G O   V E N O M
T S P   T A I   T E A C H   N L R B   D D A Y
E L E C   N O D E   T O E S   E P E E   I T E
R U S H H O U R   S E N T U P T H E R I V E R
R E T A I N   A P T S   E N O   I D E E S
A S O N G   S T A R   B R N O   A V E S
  H M S   C O W B O Y   A L E C   W D S
H E A D L I N E   L E K   C L A R A   H I E
O I L R I G   M U L T I M I L L I O N A I R E
B R I E F S   U N I   N O W A Y   N A I L E D
S E D G E   S O N   G O O N S   A L D E R S
```

MR. MOONLIGHT

1. It takes **1 1/4** seconds for moonlight to reach the Earth.
2. If you weigh 120 pounds on Earth, you would weigh **20** pounds on the Moon.
3. The Moon is moving away from the Earth at the rate of about **1/8** inch a year.
4. The average temperature of the Moon can be as low as **-283** degrees Fahrenheit.
5. The Moon is **2,160** miles in diameter (about 1/4 the diameter of the Earth).
6. It takes a bit over **29** days for the Moon to go through all of its phases.
7. A three-foot jump on the Earth would carry you **18** feet on the Moon.
8. The Moon reflects only **7** percent of the light it receives from the Sun.
9. Astronauts have brought over **843** pounds of Moon samples back to Earth.
10. If the Earth were the size of a fist, the Moon would be the size of a postage stamp placed **10** feet away.

THANKSGIVING FARE

GOOD NEIGHBORS

UNCLE JOHN'S JOHN

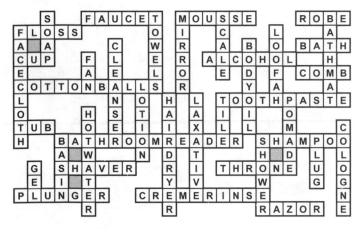

FAIRWAY FANTASY

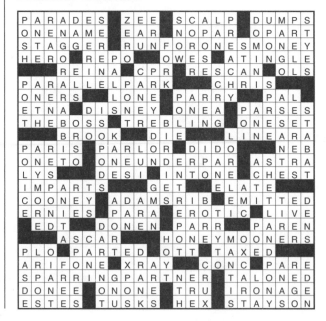

IT'S A DOG'S LIFE

1. Women and cats will do as they please, and men and dogs should relax and get used to the idea. (Robert A. Heinlein)

2. To a man the greatest blessing is individual liberty; to a dog it is the last word in despair. (William Lyon Phelps)

3. I've seen a look in dogs' eyes, a quickly vanishing look of (amazed) contempt, and (I) am convinced that (basically) dogs think humans are nuts. (John Steinbeck)